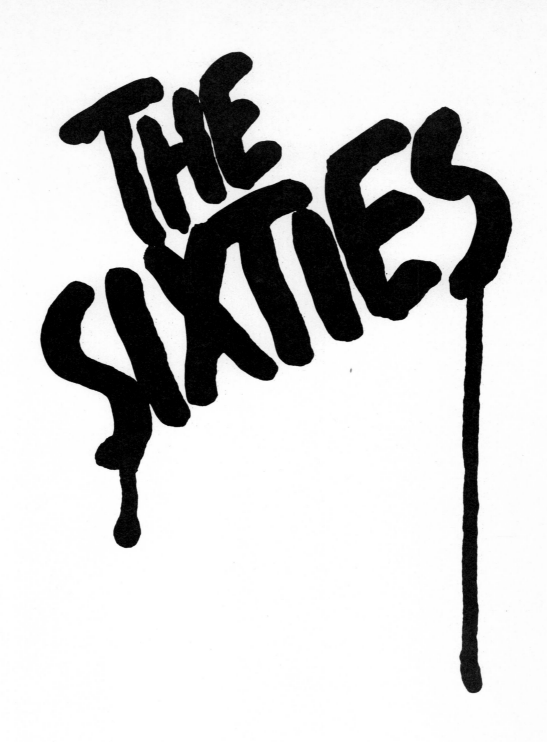

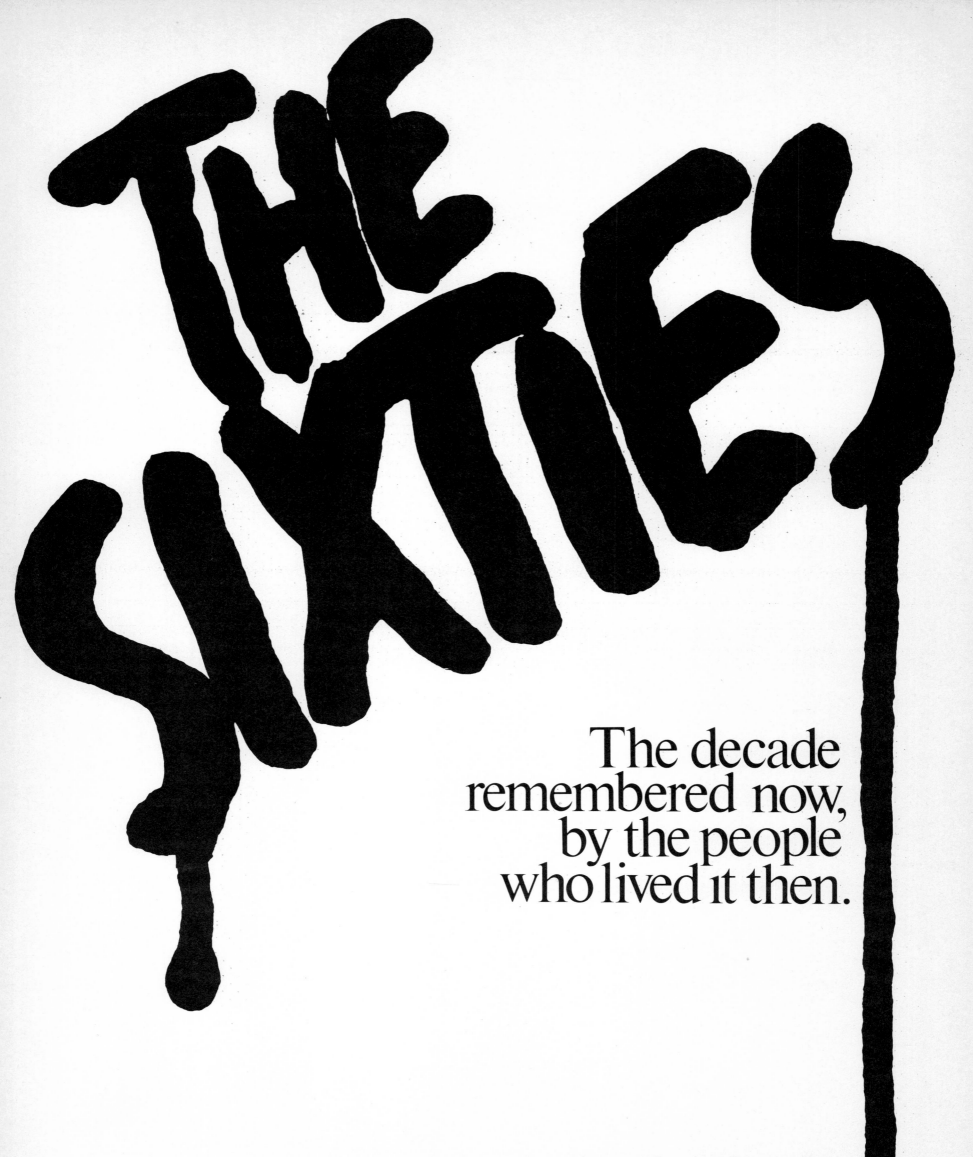

THE SIXTIES

The decade
remembered now,
by the people
who lived it then.

Edited by Lynda Rosen Obst
Designed by Robert Kingsbury

 ROLLING STONE

A Random House/Rolling Stone Press Book/New York

Library of Congress Cataloging in Publication Data:
Main entry under title:
The Sixties.
1. United States—History—1961–1963—Miscellanea.
2. United States—History—1963–1969—Miscellanea.
I. Obst, Lynda.   II. Rolling stone.
EH39.3.S58   973.92   76–53451
ISBN 0-394-40687-1
ISBN 0-394-73239-1 pbk.

Manufactured in the United States of America
2 4 6 8 9 7 5 3
First Edition

Rolling Stone Press gratefully acknowledges permission to reprint the following: Adapted sections of *Rock, Roll and Remember* by Dick Clark. Copyright © 1976 by Dick Clark. Used by permission of Thomas Y. Crowell Company, publisher. The material appears in "Dick Clark: How the Twist Discovered Bandstand." • Adapted sections of *More Power Than We Know* by David Dellinger. Copyright © 1975 by Trust for Non-Violent Revolution. Reprinted by permission of Doubleday and Company, Inc. The material appears in "David Dellinger: The Gagging of Bobby Seale." • "The Readers of Rolling Stone: Where We Were" taken from "Where Were You the Day They Shot the President," which appeared in *Rolling Stone,* December 6, 1973. Copyright © 1973 by Straight Arrow Publishers, Inc. Reprinted by permission. • "Peter Townshend: Talkin' 'Bout My Generation" adapted from "The Rolling Stone Interview: Peter Townshend" by Jann Wenner, which first appeared in *Rolling Stone,* September 14, 1968. Copyright © 1968 by Straight Arrow Publishers, Inc. Reprinted by permission. • "Ralph J. Gleason: Victims and Villains," which first appeared as "Perspectives: Like Zally We Are All Victims" by Ralph J. Gleason in *Rolling Stone,* November 23, 1967. Copyright © 1967 by Straight Arrow Publishers, Inc. Reprinted by permission. • "Lance Fairweather: Manson" reprinted by permission of Straight Arrow Publishers, Inc., from *Mindfuckers,* edited by David Felton. Copyright © 1972 by Straight Arrow Publishers, Inc. Originally printed in *Rolling Stone.* • "Muhammad Ali: The People's Champ" condensed by permission of Random House, Inc., from *The Greatest—My Own Story* by Muhammad Ali with Richard Durham. Copyright © 1975 by Muhammad Ali, Herbert Muhammad, Richard Durham. • The photograph on page 177 taken from *My Eyes Have Seen* by Bob Fitch. Copyright © 1971 by Glide Publications. Reprinted by permission. • The illustrations in "Stan Lee: Where Spider-Man Came From." Copyright © 1974 by Marvel Comics Group. Reprinted by permission of Simon and Schuster, a Division of Gulf and Western Corporation.

Rolling Stone Press

Editor: Lynda Rosen Obst
Managing Editor: Susan Brenneman
Consulting Editor: Abe Peck

Assistant Editors:
Linda Ross [Research],
Diana Kohn [Calendar],
Dallas Galvin, Leslie Strauss

Art Director: Robert Kingsbury
Picture Editor: Monica Suder

Project Director: Sarah Lazin

Production Manager: Jan Tigner, Random House
Copy Editor: Nancy Inglis, Random House

The Haight-Ashbury, 1968 (© Elaine Mayes).

VOTE NIXON

EXPERIENCED LEADER

RICHARD NIXON
FOR PRESIDENT

EXPERIENCED LEADER

RICHARD NIXON
FOR PRESIDENT

CHICAGO
Pick DICK

EXPERIENCE SPEAKS LOUDER THAN WORDS!
NIXON-LODGE
FOR PEACE AND SECURITY
VOTE STRAIGHT X REPUBLICAN
FOR PRESIDENT
NIXON

CONTENTS

*The astronauts of NASA's Mercury program
(Ralph Morse/Life Magazine, © Time, Inc.).*

ACKNOWLEDGMENTS

Thanks to my husband David Obst, to Jane and Jann Wenner, to my terrific agent Erica Spellman, and to editor Abe Peck. Thanks to Jim Silberman, Dick Snyder, Nora Ephron, and friends of Reporters News Service. The help of Dallas Galvin, assistant editor, was literally indispensable. Thank you also to Nord Haggerty, Ruby Jackson, Tim Oliver, Karen Payne, Sheila Kinney, Bill Eggleston, and Langdon Clay. Special thanks for the first-rate detective work of Bonnie Goldstein; to Michael Gross and Nancy Weinstock. Thanks to William Schurk, Jacqueline Jille, and to my brother Michael Rosen for his excellent sports research. Thanks to the fine historian of this era, Charles Perry, and to critics Jonathan Cott and Greil Marcus, for their suggestions; to the all-important support team at *Rolling Stone,* especially Susan Brenneman, Linda Ross, Diana Kohn, Monica Suder, Sarah Lazin, and Robert Kingsbury; and to Random House editor Susan Bolotin. Special thanks to Taylor Branch and the preface committee. These are my friends, and I thank them all for putting up with me while I learned to make this book. Especially David.

—Lynda Rosen Obst

I would like to thank the following people and organizations for their kind cooperation, their invaluable suggestions and their patience; especially the contributors to *The Sixties,* and the innumerable photographers who researched their files for the project: City Lights Publishing, Michael McClure, Bill Wilson, Ted Rogers, Dick Clark, Georgianna McGuire, Walter Hopps and Neil Printz of the Smithsonian Institution, James Rosenquist, the Sidney Janis Gallery, Jim Bouton, the New York Yankees, Al Haber, the Actors Studio, Nora Ephron, David Halberstam, Tim Page, James H. Karales, Bruce Morrow, Tom Rush, Dick Waterman, Byron Lenardos, Sid Bernstein, Barbara Garson, Stewart Brand, Tony Schwartz, Fred Hughes of The Factory, Viva, Jean Gleason, Bill Graham, Lou Adler, Ron and Pat Kovic, Julie Nixon Eisenhower, Gloria Steinem, Lynette Fromme, Don Snyder, George Gardner, Charles Gatewood, Jerry Hopkins, Mary Ellen Mark, Caterine Milinaire, Andrew Sacks, Stephen Shames, Peter Simon, George Ballis, Gordon Clark, Tom Copi, Larry Keenan, Jr., William J. Warren, John A. Kouns, Jeffrey Blankfort, Bob Adelman, Bob Fitch, Dennis Hopper, the ASMP in San Francisco, Annie Leibovitz, *16* magazine, the *San Francisco Chronicle,* Glide Publications and Nancy Weinstock.

Special thanks go also to the various photo agencies and libraries for their tireless efforts: Magnum Photos, Black Star, Globe Photos, Photo Trends, Time-Life, Liaison, AP and UPI, as well as the Dwight D. Eisenhower Library, the John F. Kennedy Library, NASA and the U.S. Navy.

—Monica Suder

Refugees flee Saigon, spring 1968
(© Philip Jones Griffiths/Magnum).

PREFACE

To many Americans, the drama of the Sixties is the most they have in common. As in the Second World War, they were seized by an extended American drama that irrevocably affected all who lived through it. At certain moments, the emotions were so great that we could tangibly feel what the Germans call *Zeitgeist*, the spirit of the times. Slowly, we who lived through that time, especially those of us who were coming of age, came to see how rare that moment was. And when it finally seemed all over, when all the shooting had died down, when the war was ending and we were speaking with our parents again, there was a lot to sort out on every side. In fact, "sides" seemed suddenly a hopeless word.

With that realization, I began to want to learn what it had been like on the inside of all the explosions whose shock waves reached my house. I started to talk to people who had participated in the major events of the decade.

Those dialogues began this "history" of the Sixties. I talked to 150 people who either had made a personal contribution to the historical events of the Sixties or had a unique perception of the time. I watched these people evoke moments they now recognize as central to their lives. I asked them to relive the experience while recalling the details of those memories. I was soon working on a different kind of history: not a textbook account or a definitive study, but an impressionistic oral history.

This book was not written in the usual sense. Even the writers here appear as participants rather than reporters. My intent was to present one person's experience, to keep the recollections as historically correct as individual perceptions will allow, and in every case to preserve the spontaneous quality of the conversations. These running monologues were then organized into a roughly chronological account of each event. There are exceptions: one piece is a previously unpublished excerpt from a private diary. Thirteen were written for this book; six were previously published. Taylor Branch interviewed Manuel Artime, Stanley Crouch interviewed Rashied Ali, Jann Wenner conducted the Peter Townshend interview in 1968 and David Felton interviewed Lance Fairweather. All pieces obtained from interviews are indicated by a star at the end of the last line of the contributor's biography.

Tackling the Sixties was difficult. Some people felt they no longer wanted to dwell on the past. Others were wary for political or philosophical reasons. Wavy Gravy, when approached with this project, reacted with a bemused grin. "The history of the Sixties?" he asked. "Why not write the history of Thursday?" And since the beginning of this project, I've personally had to grapple with the questions of what makes history and what qualifies an event as historical. Some occurrences—assassinations, political movements, wars—are clearly important as history. But when compiling a cultural history, one realizes that some events and people are only found historically significant in retrospect, and then only to some observers and not to others. Many events have yet to be recognized as pivotal and become a part of our history only as our perspective lengthens.

I tried to create one microcosm of the Sixties when there are millions. It was a decade of personal stories. This book is dedicated to all those accounts and those who can now tell them.

—Lynda Rosen Obst
June 1977

Coretta King and her children, leaving the plane that brought Martin Luther King's body home to Atlanta (Harry Benson).

1960

CALENDAR

January: 1 *The first community for senior citizens, Sun City, opens in Arizona;* **4** *Albert Camus dies in auto crash in France;* **5** *United Steelworkers win 41¢ raise plus fringe benefits after six-month strike;* **24** *"Running Bear" tops pop chart.*

February: 1 *Greensboro, N.C., black students stage first lunch-counter sit-in in segregated Woolworth's;* **11** *Jack Paar walks off his NBC-TV show, protesting censorship;* **13** *France becomes fourth nation to explode atomic bomb;* **16** *Lunch-counter sit-ins spread to fifteen cities in five Southern states;* **18** *First live televised Olympic Games open in Squaw Valley;* **26** *Xerox 914 copier enters the business world;* **28** *"Theme from a Summer Place" replaces "Teen Angel" as pop chart leader.*

March: 5 *Elvis Presley receives his Army discharge;* **15** *Police arrest more than 350 students during Orangeburg, S.C., lunch-counter protests;* **20** *Paul Anka reaches the Top Ten with "Puppy Love";* **30** *Publication of* Clea *completes Lawrence Durrell's Alexandria Quartet.*

April: 4 *Ben Hur captures a record eleven Oscars;* **14** *Bye Bye Birdie, loosely based on Elvis' Army induction, opens on Broadway;* **17** *Eddie Cochran dies in car crash;* **22** *During Cuban TV speech Castro accuses U.S. of plotting to overthrow him;* **29** *Dick Clark testifies before Senate in massive probe of radio payola.*

May: 1 *Soviets shoot down Francis Gary Powers in U.S. U-2 spy plane;* **2** *Caryl Chessman executed in spite of widespread pleas for clemency;* **4** *Lucille Ball divorces Desi Arnaz;* **9** *FDA approves first public sale of birth-control pills;* **10** *U.S. nuclear sub completes first underwater round-the-world voyage;* **13** *San Francisco police battle student protesters outside HUAC hearings;* **16** *Soviet premier Khrushchev uses U-2 incident to cancel summit conference with U.S.;* **29** *Everly Brothers top pop chart with "Cathy's Clown."*

June: 12 *Roy Orbison's "Only the Lonely" enters the Top 100;* **15** *Film release of* The Apartment; **16** *Alfred Hitchcock's Psycho debuts;* **20** *Emmys honor Rod Serling for his writing of* Twilight Zone *and Robert Stack in*

Top to bottom: Khrushchev speaks at the UN (Wide World Photos); black students sit-in with white support (UPI) and without it (UPI); Jack Paar leaves NBC with his daughter after walking off his show (UPI). Opposite page: Castro and Khrushchev meet in New York during the UN's 25th anniversary session (UPI).

The Untouchables *as best actor;* **30** *Belgium's grant of independence to the Congo leads to power struggle among black factions.*

July: 6 *President Eisenhower limits Cuban sugar imports in retaliation for Castro's seizure of U.S. oil refineries in Cuba;* **7** *Hughes Aircraft researchers announce achievement of first laser action;* **14** *UN votes to intervene in Congo strife;* **17** *"Alley Oop" leads singles chart.*

August: 1 *Born Free heads non-fiction list;* **14** *"Itsy Bitsy Teenie Weenie Yellow Polkadot Bikini" captures the pop chart lead;* **19** *Russia sentences U-2 pilot Powers to ten years for espionage;* **24** *U.S. okays use of oral polio vaccine.*

September: 3 *U.S. sprinter Wilma Rudolph wins unprecedented third Olympic gold medal;* **13** *American Ballet Theatre's opening night in Moscow marks the first performance of an American ballet troupe in Russia;* **18** *Sam Cooke enters Top Ten with "Chain Gang";* **26** *First of four Kennedy-Nixon debates;* **30** *The Flintstones debut.*

October: 12 *The UN 25th anniversary session is adjourned in pandemonium after Khrushchev pounds his shoe on the table;* **13** *Pittsburgh Pirates beat the Yankees to capture their first World Series since 1925;* **17** *Four national chain stores announce integration of lunch counters in 112 Southern cities;* **23** *"Save the Last Dance for Me" leads pop chart;* **26** *Kennedy phone call helps secure Martin Luther King's jail release following Atlanta sit-in arrest.*

November: 4 *Premiere of G.I. Blues starring Elvis;* **8** *Kennedy and Johnson edge out Nixon and Lodge in the closest presidential election since 1884;* **14** *American release of Bergman's The Virgin Spring;* **16** *Clark Gable dies;* **25** *Last seven radio soap operas go off the air;* **28** *The Rise and Fall of the Third Reich is best seller;* **29** *"Stay" rides chart lead.*

December: 2 *Pope John XXIII meets the Archbishop of Canterbury for first time since Catholic/Anglican split in 1534;* **3** *Broadway premiere of Camelot;* **15** *Exodus opens;* **16** *Midair plane collision over Staten Island kills 134 in America's worst aviation disaster;* **18** *Miracles' "Shop Around" enters charts.*

DAVID EISENHOWER
Grandfather Leaves the White House

Many, perhaps most, people my age look back on 1960 and the Kennedy promise as the beginning of something very exciting. That year marked a passage for many of us—the first real awareness of a political campaign; of being able to take sides. This awareness coincided with a mood: in Kennedy's words, the passing of the torch to a new generation.

I suppose my experience was very atypical. For my family the new beginning was a bittersweet and poignant ending to the eight years we had spent in and around the White House.

My family began the transition in 1959, moving from our home in Alexandria to a house on the corner of the Eisenhower farm in Gettysburg. We made a number of trips to Washington from Gettysburg, staying for weeks at a time at the White House. But our ability to drop by was curtailed and we children were continually reminded to begin thinking of Washington as a place we soon would not be able to enjoy.

For a child, the White House was and is a paradise. What's now the press room used to be a heated indoor pool equipped with shower and workout facilities. The East Wing housed a movie theater that ran top Hollywood selections at the virtual request of the White House. I fashioned a basketball court during the winter out of the wide third-floor corridor leading to the storage and laundry rooms, and in the spring I practiced infield by bouncing tennis balls off the even-surfaced walls. The South Lawn was the backyard of any child's dreams. I raced electric carts along the sloping driveway, and the trees provided perfect "cover" for grade school cowboys and Indians. The open expanse of grass was a perfect place to learn golf.

As the election approached, preparations for a new administration and First Family encroached. A new coat of paint on the third-floor wall ended infield practice. Shrubbery work ended our reenactments of Antietam, Shiloh, Gettysburg, Hastings and Thermopylae.

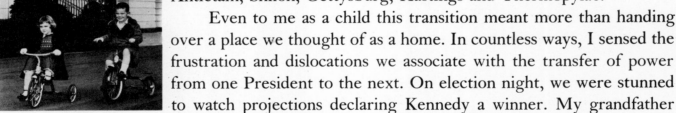

White House kids—David and his sister Barbara Anne tricycling at Grandfather's (courtesy Eisenhower Library).

Even to me as a child this transition meant more than handing over a place we thought of as a home. In countless ways, I sensed the frustration and dislocations we associate with the transfer of power from one President to the next. On election night, we were stunned to watch projections declaring Kennedy a winner. My grandfather went to bed early in disgust. As later returns chipped away at the projected "landslide," converting that election into one of the closest in our history, the mood became one of despair and self-doubt. There was no real sense that anything could be gained by demanding a recount. I don't remember feeling swindled or thinking that the election had been taken away. "What-ifs" haunted our few remaining visits to Washington. Our regrets, contrasting with the nation's sense of anticipation, gave me an inkling of our new isolation from mainstream thoughts and concerns.

Just before Christmas the family spent a farewell weekend at Camp David. The winter's first snow blanketed the Catoctins. I remember wishing the snow would sock us in for a long time. The camp bore my name, and I felt I had a proprietary stake in it. The thing that I regretted, and again this is through the eyes of a twelve-year-old, was that the camp would be renamed when we left. The boats named for my sisters had already been retired or renamed—the *Barbara Anne* had become the *Honey Fitz*.

Our last meal in the White House occurred shortly after the new year in the "family dining room" located off the State Dining Room on the first floor. It was a small, predominantly red room with a painting of Tyler in it. Several decorating magazines rated the room as among the leading one hundred rooms in America. Though perhaps too young to understand the significance of my grandfather's job, I had no trouble grasping what "top one hundred" meant. I usually took visiting friends to see that room first.

The discussion that night was somber. I recall distinctly the low and muffled tones near Granddad's end of the table, and the topic of discussion. He had recently briefed Kennedy on the deteriorating situation in Laos. He seemed intent and concerned.

Grandfather regretted passing problems down, and he disliked turning the White House over to a Democrat. But he viewed the Presidency as a call to duty, and his duty was done. In that sense, he had no need to come to terms with a personal loss, because the Presidency had not been a personal gain. His ideas were tempered by the crowning experience of his life, his leadership in World War II—and I think he always felt that nothing would ever match accepting the German surrender at the Reims cathedral. Our family would never, at least not officially, confuse personal gain and aggrandizement with the trappings of the Presidency.

Still, perhaps he was also wrestling with his often-stated declaration that he had long since had his fill of politics and high-level activity. The attitude had never been tested. Saying it was one thing; being confronted with the reality of a different pace and the end of one's truly useful activity was another. He had been sincerely reluctant to enter politics. Giving it up was a bit different, though any reluctance he may have felt did not persist. He became an elder statesman and settled beautifully into a well-deserved retirement.

*D*wight D. Eisenhower II in 1960 (courtesy Eisenhower Library).

Grandfather was a man for his time. Politicians have a need to define themselves as liberal, conservative or radical, but he defined himself as a nonpolitician. Much of the country defined itself the same way. The people revered him as a leader for fifteen years, and he responded by promising and delivering a fundamentally nonpartisan approach to problems. Though his administration has been classified as "conservative," Eisenhower's words and leadership sounded some of the most radical and far-reaching themes to come from a President since the war. Two decisions were made that permanently affected the fabric of our domestic life: the unconstitutionality of segregation and the importance of maintaining a large peacetime military establishment. Eisenhower's leadership promoted patience and understanding. His Presidency was an instrument of consolidation. By 1960 the presidential candidates appealed to an amorphous, inarticulate mood that the time for consolidation had ended. Kennedy charged over and over that it was "time to get this country moving again."

Richard Nixon's 1960 campaign rhetoric, though obscured today by Kennedy's hairbreadth victory, bore a resemblance to JFK's. Both candidates appeared to agree that the country was impatient for new initiatives, both viewed the reach of American power globally, and both shared a martial tone.

On Inauguration Day, I sat in the Secret Service station wagon parked outside our Gettysburg home to listen to the festivities on radio. The radio accounts of the parade described a both familiar and alien event. I vividly remembered Grandfather's inauguration in 1956. This one honored a man I did not know. I remember especially floats reenacting the PT-109 episode in JFK's life.

The Secret Service station wagon and the agents assigned to us left promptly at midnight, severing our most tangible link to the Presidency. The next night we packed and drove several miles to the Gettysburg town square, where the community was holding a celebration to welcome my grandparents home. The heavy snows might have forced us to stay in one of the old downtown hotels overnight. It was a beautiful night, dark and chilly. Floodlights blazed over a crowd of 2,000 or more people. My sisters and I joined a bunch of friends across the square from the podium to look on as part of the crowd. Our school band played "The Battle Hymn of the Republic." I knew everyone in the band—the strangest sensation of the day was watching friends serenade my grandparents. It was the first time I had seen them together with my grandparents. They were taking time out to welcome a new neighbor, and it gave me a glimpse of my grandparents through the eyes of others. I had never appreciated how people outside the family felt about them.

The floodlights highlighted tufts of Grandfather's white hair as he sat on the podium waiting to be introduced. He exuded pleasure and warmth. With the introduction, he stood up and waved, grinning and thanking everyone seated nearby. He gave a beautiful talk. I was never so proud of him.

*D*avid Eisenhower is the grandson of the thirty-fourth President, Dwight D. Eisenhower. He graduated from Amherst College and the National Law Center at George Washington University. He is currently working on a biography of his grandfather.★

*O*verleaf: the President, the First Lady, two First Grandchildren and their mom in the White House library (Wide World Photos).

ABBIE HOFFMAN
The First Time I Saw Berkeley

The University of California let you know it was there. It was a sprawling, impersonal megalopolis of the mind—a "multiversity," as President Clark Kerr was later to call it. They taught twenty-six foreign languages, but on registration day you stood in line for hours to receive IBM cards for each class. In 1964 an anonymous student was to scrawl a legendary slogan across one of those very cards: I AM A STUDENT—DO NOT FOLD, SPINDLE OR MUTILATE.

Even at the beginning of the Sixties there were strange rumblings all around Berkeley. In the fall of '59, Nikita Khrushchev got a rousing reception from thousands as he arrived at his hotel in San Francisco. A U.S. Air Force colonel's son went on a hunger strike protesting compulsory ROTC. His Pentagon papa showed up to talk him out of it. In time, I started dropping into discussions sponsored by a group called SLATE, the self-styled political conscience of the campus, and in early spring students staged nationwide demonstrations boycotting Woolworth stores for racist policies at lunch counters.

Caryl Chessman (Photo Trends).

On May 1st, a group of us caravaned out to San Rafael to stand vigil outside the tawny walls of San Quentin State Prison. Inside, a man in a cage was eating his last dinner. He was a thin, dark-haired fellow with a rather large nose, bearing a resemblance to Danny Thomas. He had been accused and found guilty of being "the red-light bandit" in a 1948 trial. Seems he, or someone, equipped with an automobile and a red spotlight, approached couples in parked cars, took their money, and on two occasions forced the women into his car and demanded blow jobs. For this, the man in the cage was sentenced to die in the gas chamber.

Caryl Chessman was the poor bloke's name. Since the trial he had fought a twelve-year battle with Death's Stinking Seat. He had written several popular novels and managed to stay the executioner's hand eight times. He had become a symbol for the battle against capital punishment, but tonight was his eleventh hour.

The only person who could spare his life—Governor Edmund G. "Pat" Brown—sat in his mansion while pickets marched and telegrams poured in, and repeated the statement he'd made earlier: "Under California's constitution, I am now constrained against my profound personal beliefs to take no further action in this case."

He said, "My hands are tied."

It was a cold night. The newspaper and radio stations blasted late-breaking reports of last-minute maneuvers designed to prevent the execution. Over a hundred people stood at vigil, some with signs saying things like "Thou Shalt Not Kill." I remember seeing Marlon Brando in the crowd.

We were still there the next morning waiting outside the prison gate. The news came first from a car radio, and then over a megaphone: "This meeting of the Citizens for Chessman is over . . . " At 10:12 A.M. Caryl Chessman had succumbed peacefully as per the laws of the state of California. Everyone had done all they could to save his life. May God rest his soul. Amen.

Around me people were in tears. You could hear hissing. Someone moaned, "No! No!" as if he had been wounded. No one made a loud comment. No one threw a rock.

Dazed, we piled into cars and headed back to Berkeley in silence. "How does that work?" someone asked of no one in particular. "In a democracy, I mean, no one wants to see him die and the state kills him?" There was silence.

A little more than a week later some of us were given an answer. The House Un-American Activities Committee opened hearings into alleged subversive activity in the Bay Area. The hearings at City Hall in downtown San Francisco were open to the public—only "the public" turned out to be friends of the committee. Admission was by a white card distributed to groups like the American Legion and the D.A.R. Stacked galleries for public pillorying. It was one of the great anticommie road shows designed to beef up the Cold War, get some teachers fired, and warn the nation about the ever-present *Red Menace*. People like J. Edgar Hoover wanted to keep their jobs. And his boys had nothing better to do, crime in America having been solved, I mean.

The papers were filled with notices advising HUAC to stay out of town. Not knowing of the secret pass system, students waited from dawn for the hearing doors to open. When they did open to admit only a selected few, the crowd surged forward, chanting, "Down with HUAC!" and "Let us in!"

Now, San Francisco is a jewel of a city. It is customary when traveling abroad to say, "San Francisco is the best city in the United States." I've heard people say that who've never even been to San Francisco. They should have been there on Black Friday, the second day of the hearings. There were police there that the students called the Goon Force. Each one was dressed in solid black except for a white crash helmet with a plexiglass visor. They carried clubs and manned water hoses.

The force of the water drove people smashing into walls. Students were clubbed to the ground, pulled downstairs and kicked in the face. I saw a pregnant woman tossed down a flight of stairs. All around there was panic. Things like this had happened in Japan when riot policemen attacked protesters, but those were just news images. Now it was real and it was terrifying.

Two blocks away, midday business went on as usual, but in the plaza a generation had cast its spirit into the crucible of resistance.

Abbie Hoffman received an M.A. in psychology from the University of California at Berkeley in 1960. One of the more visible activists in the antiwar movement, he and Jerry Rubin founded the Youth International Party (Yippie) in 1967, and he was one of the Chicago 8, tried on charges of conspiracy and inciting riots during the 1968 Chicago Democratic Convention. He was ultimately cleared. In 1974, Hoffman went underground in order to avoid imprisonment for allegedly selling cocaine. His latest book, coauthored with his wife, Anita, was published in 1976, To America with Love: Letters from the Underground.

Above, left: Demonstrators cross the Golden Gate Bridge on their way to the Chessman vigil; right: the central staircase at San Francisco City Hall, Black Friday, May 13th, 1960 (both reprinted by permission of the San Francisco Chronicle). (G. Mantegna/Photo Trends)

MICHAEL McCLURE
Nights in North Beach

This was still a time of cold, gray silence, but inside the coffeehouses of North Beach, poets and friends sensed the atmosphere of liberation. We were linked to the abstract expressionists, to the bardic tradition; we were restoring the body, with the voice as the extension of the body. We actually moved in front of the audience and they were free to shout "Great!" or "Don't read that one"—or "Go" like Jack Kerouac always yelled. It was an act of liberation to break down the old laws, the ones that said poets were little gray people smoking pipes and reading to other little gray people sitting on stools. Only when we started breaking the laws did we have the liberty to reestablish them.

Robert LaVigne in his studio (© Larry Keenan, Jr.).

We had readings at an Italian social hall, called Fugazi Hall, that held about three hundred people. It was on the corner of Green and Stockton, at North Beach, which had not been a beach for at least fifty years. It was a small section, bordered on one side by Chinatown, melting into the old Italian neighborhood on the other. Down the side ran the Barbary Coast, full of lights and girlie shows; housed throughout were old Italian families and the newer bohemians.

Bob LaVigne, a figurative painter that Allen Ginsberg met at Foster's Cafeteria by the Hotel Wentley, painted wonderful posters that announced the readings, and they were placed all over the city, or carried by poets and artists in parades. News of the readings spread quickly all over the city.

The audience was an enlightened group of proletarian anarchists: carpenters, college professors, old-lady schoolteachers, young people growing their first beards, buying their first pair of sandals, throwing their glasses away. Daring to write home and make peace with their parents, or daring not to write home for the first time.

After a reading at Fugazi we headed to The Place, a tiny bar in North Beach on upper Grant Avenue, a gathering spot for jazz musicians, artists, electronic composers, painters, sculptors and poets. It had a small bar, with a balcony overlooking it on three sides. The first time I went in there, there was a wonderful show of existential watercolors. I remember sitting down by one of the paintings, drinking a glass of wine and looking up, realizing that I couldn't see a show that beautiful if I were in a bar in Paris. I knew that San Francisco was it, happening right around me, that it was the place to be. Kenneth Rexroth said that San Francisco was the Barcelona of the thirties, a hothouse of anarchist movements.

The poets were in love and at war. We were engaged in more than a fight for space, we were fighting for expression of our own individuality. It was the conflict, the pressure against one another, that created what Leslie Fiedler called New Mutants in Poetry. We did mutate new parts of ourselves, and new thoughts into expression.

Gary Snyder, poet and visionary (Erik Weber).

One night at Fugazi Hall I told Allen I thought we were very cruel to each other—brutal. We pushed so hard in our beautiful territorial wars. Allen looked at me and laughed. He said, "I thought we were very sweet to each other." I realized instantly that we were both saying the same thing. We lived through the cruelty of criticism, we were solid in our camaraderie.

Allen was marvelous. He stood and moved his head back a little, looking down into the audience from the small podium, trying to speak to every single individual. He held "Kaddish" up in front of him, and paced the stage, reading with his full voice. Robert Creeley had a syncopated way of reading, related to the jazz he was listening to. It didn't sound like Miles Davis, but it was the poetic equivalent of Miles. His voice was

*San Francisco poets and survivors of the Beat
scene gathered in front of City Lights Bookstore in North
Beach in 1965. Front row, left to right: Robert LaVigne, Shig of City
Lights, poets Larry Fagin, Lew Welch, Peter Orlovsky, Leland
Meyerzove (lying down); second row, left to right: poets David Meltzer,
Michael McClure, Allen Ginsberg, Daniel Langton, a friend of
Ginsberg's, Richard Brautigan, Gary Goodrow of the
committee, and painter Nemi Frost; in back:
Stella Levy, Lawrence Ferlinghetti
(© Larry Keenan, Jr.).*

small and very intense, trembling, leaving me hanging for the next syllable. Phil Whalen read the way he felt that evening—I've seen Philip read in an incredibly uninteresting monotone or in an enlightened Buddhist way, depending solely on whether he was feeling grumpy—like Lenny Bruce or like Santa Claus. Philip Lamantia read in an oracular English style, with lovely intonation. Gary Snyder, always manly, read with heroic firmness and a smile. When I read, I tried to project into the mind of everyone in the audience with a monotone that would leave only the mystery of the language while I paced around, maintaining physical tension.

Allen never understood why I read almost in a monotone—he would not understand that I did it deliberately. When I got into a discussion with him, I'd get so locked into it that I couldn't read any other way to show him that I knew how. Our other problem was that Allen said my first poems were obscure

because they reflected no social cause—they were not concerned with the immediate political problems that troubled Allen. I felt that Allen lived in a sealed, limited universe, bound by the human, the city, the psychological extensions of the mind. We debated this all the time without my seeing that Allen was grasping beyond that dimension.

My concept of poetry was intensely alchemical, in part because of the times. It was like being on an elevator containing a lot of people with crew cuts and pin-striped suits. As I looked around them, I realized that I couldn't get off the elevator unless I discovered some alchemical or superhuman way of doing it. The way to escape was to create poems that were living creatures. My hope was that my poems might become alive, become living organisms through the energy that I threw into them. I wanted poems to grow their own eyes, ears, noses, legs and teeth.

My poetry was not the expression of the ideas that I'd been taught by the culture, but the expression of the fleshy facts of myself that I'd discovered in spite of the culture. And I think that's what all of us were doing—we were in the act of discovering ourselves, not what we had been instructed to discover by the culture.

Michael McClure is the author of several modern theater classics: The Beard, Gargoyle Cartoons *and* Gorf. *His most recent books of poetry are* September Blackberries *and* Jaguar Skies.★ *(© Paul Kagan)*

Above, left to right: Michael McClure, Philip Lamantia, John Wieners and David Meltzer (Gui de Angulo). Opposite page, clockwise from top left: Allen Ginsberg, circa 1960 (© Chester Kessler); *Kenneth Rexroth (Christa Fleischman); Philip Whalen, holding a drip-style portrait of himself by fellow poet Michael McClure (© Larry Keenan, Jr.); Robert Duncan, poet (Patricia Jordan); Lawrence Ferlinghetti, standing in his City Lights Bookstore (courtesy City Lights); center: Bob Kaufman, five years before the publication of his "Abomunist Manifesto," which spread the news of the beats (© Chester Kessler).*

BRUCE MORROW
Live from Coney Island

Even in the early days of rock 'n' roll radio, show biz was very, very evident. We were always running big contests and promotions, pulling crazy stunts. I was a disc jockey at WINS in the late Fifties, and after that at WABC. In those days we did a lot of "remotes," live radio shows broadcast on location, like the Palisades Park shows I used to do on Saturdays and Sundays. The crowds loved them. We gave away prizes and had live groups up on stage, lip-synching to their own songs while the kids danced. All the big name talents—Frankie Avalon, Tony Bennett, the Dave Clark Five, Freddie and the Dreamers—played these shows for free because we gave them so much good publicity; literally thousands of people would attend.

Dion, right, makes an appearance on location with Bruce Morrow (courtesy Bruce Morrow).

I remember beautiful afternoons at Palisades, with thousands of kids sitting in the audience, periodically jumping on stage to dance. Every week we'd offer some giveaway—a bag of groceries, boxes of Lux suds, a whole side of a cow—to the first five hundred people who came to the park to see the Cousin Brucie Show. I could probably name the first four or five rows of kids in the audience. I especially remember the kids from Philadelphia. When they came in, they really let you know. Philadelphia was the rock city, and Philly kids were very proud. They wore dressy clothes and sat in the audience combing and brushing their hair. They came to support the Philadelphia acts like Bobby Rydell and Fabian. Local kids asked for their autographs just because they were from Philadelphia.

Every group that performed at Palisades Park had a uniform: satiny touches of red or bright green, slicked-back hair, dressed to kill. I'd wanted something different—Cousin Brucie was different—in order to survive. I went to a tailor in the Bronx and explained that I wanted tuxedos made, that I wanted to see things that were really weird. He created a leopard-skin tuxedo and a multicolored tuxedo, with matching outfits for my miniature poodle Muffin. Muffin had become somewhat of a celebrity. He had a fan club of his own, and he marched out in front of me in a matching costume when I introduced the acts.

The strangest remote I ever did, though, was a special from Raven Hall Pool in Coney Island. It was late summertime, the hurricane season, and it had rained and rained for days before we got there. Now it had stopped. Out on Surf Avenue, thousands of people were lined up waiting impatiently for the gates to open.

It was still so wet that we couldn't get all our electrical lines in. We considered canceling the show. But we were already out there. It was nearly show time and this was a live broadcast. We couldn't switch back to the station, so we really had little choice. We decided to go on. The gates were opened, and each person donated his dollar to muscular dystrophy, my pet charity of the day.

On the bill that evening were Jan and Dean and a group called the Ivy Three, which had a record called, "Yogi"—a terrible record, but it was a biggie at the time. I was wearing one of my famous leopard-skin tuxedos, the kids were dancing, and everything seemed to be going just fine after all.

Now the Raven Hall stage was wooden and very old, a leftover from the 1800's when Alan Freed started out and Dick Clark was a kid. All of a sudden during the middle of the show I heard a cracking of wood. The kids, everyone, started screaming. I was over at the side of the stage. I looked around to the back where all our equipment was, and as I heard the creaking sound of wood snapping once more, the engineer went down. Down through the stage. It was about a ten-foot drop. I froze. We were on the air. We couldn't have dead air. I looked at the audience and then I glanced back: the program director, Rick Sklar, was standing on the engineer's shoulders, holding up the console and the electrical lines so the show could go on. His face was ashen, and the engineer was teetering. All I could think of was that we were going to be electrocuted.

Opposite page: the famous leopard-skin tuxedo and the famous Cousin Brucie (courtesy Bruce Morrow).

Wood was cracking and splitting like an earthquake everywhere. The audience was going wild. By now the engineer who was holding Sklar was waist-deep in water.

I was still on the side of the stage, or what was left of it, but the rift was getting closer and closer. I grabbed the microphones. More of the stage went. Now I was holding on to a piece of the stage, clutching my microphone and trying not to touch water. I had to think of something. But what? I did a commercial, a pimple commercial, while the rest of the stage was ripping apart. What a scene. Everybody loved it. The audience thought it was funny, a hoax, a new dance craze. Those were the good old days.

 *Bruce "Cousin Brucie" Morrow is currently working in New York for WNBC radio and television as a Top Forty deejay and an entertainment reporter on WNBC-TV's NewsCenter 4. He also heads a production company, Dapaimer Entertainment Ltd., which specializes in television variety shows. During the Sixties on WABC, Morrow perfected the quintessential AM radio personality and convinced more than one generation of adolescents that pimples were not a terminal disease.★ (courtesy Bruce Morrow)*

FRANCIS GARY POWERS
The Poison Pin Decision

From 1956 to 1960, the year the whole thing took place, I was working for the CIA, flying U-2s from Incirlik Air Force Base, near Adana, Turkey. It was the height of the cold war, and we were trying to keep our eyes not only on the Soviet Union, but on other countries as well. I flew over Israel, Egypt, Saudi Arabia and—unnamed friendly countries. But the most important photographic overflights were over the Soviet Union. It was completely isolated from the rest of the world, and was a tremendous threat because it had developed nuclear capabilities. This was why the U-2 program had been conceived, and I was proud to be a part of it.

I was flown to Peshawar, Pakistan, in late April. There were several flight cancellations, and then, on May 1st, I woke up at about two o'clock in the morning, after a very restless night's sleep. After a half-hour delay, I took off at 6:26 A.M. I'd asked them, "Why are you delaying the takeoff?" and they'd said, "We're waiting on a go or no-go from the White House."

Before takeoff they asked me if I wanted to take this little silver dollar with me. It wasn't an ordinary silver dollar; I knew it had some poison concealed in it. At an earlier briefing I'd asked, "If we go down, what should we do and what should we tell them?" The intelligence officer had said, "If you're captured, you may as well tell them everything because they'll get it out of you anyway. More than likely you'll be tortured. If you don't think you can withstand the torture, you might want to take your own life."

The silver dollar had a hole drilled in the edge, and a little straight pin which dropped into that. You'd unscrew a loop in the edge of the coin to take the straight pin out. It was just like one from your shirt or dress, except the pin part was actually a sheath covering a very fine needle. And the needle was covered with what I was told was curare.

I had never taken the silver dollar before, but this time, for some reason, I decided to take it with me.

 About thirty minutes after takeoff I got the go-ahead signal—one click of the microphone. Then there was radio silence. I crossed the border, and a couple of hours into the Soviet Union, I saw the condensation trail of a plane looking for me. I knew he had to be supersonic, but I could fly much higher than he could. That gave me

U-2 in flight (USAF/ SSgt. Theodore Kapes).

a sense of security and well-being: I thought, "Okay, they know I'm here, but they can't do a thing about it."

Until now, they had shot missiles at us and planes had tried to zoom up to us. The missiles apparently were uncontrollable at high altitude, and their planes would just stall out. But we also knew that they had spent four years trying to develop something to reach us, and that for the past year or so we had avoided certain areas that we thought might have antiaircraft missiles.

There were no indications on the maps of any antiaircraft missiles at Sverdlovsk, the city where I was hit. I was to go right over the city, but about thirty seconds after I rolled out of a turn, a tremendous explosion took place. The plane went out of control and broke up and fell down in hundreds of pieces. When the wings and the tail came off, the plane started whirling around, falling straight down. That caused so many G forces I couldn't use the ejection seat in the airplane.

After I'd fallen between six and ten miles, I made myself stop struggling and think. Then I released the seat belt, the canopy went, and the G forces threw me right over the nose.

Eventually, the parachute opened automatically. I knew that it had been set for 15,000 feet, and it took a good twenty or thirty minutes to come down. I was drifting, and the silence was deafening.

I had a map in my pocket which had headings to the nearest friendly countries: distance and how much time it would take. I thought, "This will incriminate all of those countries." So I tore that map into the smallest fragments I could and scattered them out into the air as I was coming down.

Powers, right, at the opening of his espionage trial in Moscow (Wide World Photos).

And then I thought of the silver dollar. I had my gloves off at this time, and I reached into the pocket and got it. Earlier, I'd been told that if I went down, maybe they'd think it was a good-luck charm and let me keep it. I looked at the silver dollar, and I said, "Now, that's the most idiotic thing I've ever heard." The first souvenir that any Russian in the heart of Siberia would want would be an American silver dollar. I said, "This won't work," and I opened the silver dollar and took the pin out and threw the coin away. I looked at the needle—and to this day I don't know why I didn't use it. I almost did. I was so afraid of the complete unknown, and I was thinking, "The worst things that can happen to a person are what they're going to do to me." I really, seriously considered it, and I don't know why I didn't use it. I guess it was just "Wait and see what happens."

Then I had another problem—what do you do with a straight-pin-looking gadget? Where do you conceal it? Well, I thought, pins are a common thing in clothing. So I dropped it into my pocket.

I landed on a collective farm. I don't know the name of the village it was near. It was May Day, a big holiday, and there were only two men working. One was driving a tractor, the other was helping him, and I

The Soviets display the wreckage of Powers' U-2 in Moscow (UPI).

hit within twenty to twenty-five feet of them.

When I looked up, one of the men was collapsing the chute and the other was trying to help me up. And by the time I got to my feet, there must have been seventy-five people out there. Just curious. I am sure they thought I was a Russian. They had no reason to think otherwise. They helped me get my helmet off and they kept asking questions and all I could do was shake my head. They became suspicious, naturally, but there was no rough stuff at all. Just a bunch of farmers.

They took me to the farm headquarters, where the local constable searched me. He took my cigarettes and cigarette lighter, and they stripped me down to my long underwear. But they didn't find the pin, and they returned the outer garment to put back on, with the pin still in it. Then we drove to a big stone government building in Sverdlovsk. That's where I told them that I was CIA, that I was civilian and not military, so they wouldn't consider my flight an act of military aggression and retaliate. They made a lot of phone calls, and it was there on the fourth search that they found the needle.

As long as I had that poison with me, I felt that I was in control of my destiny. It was very comforting to me to have that. Once they took it, I was really depressed. I wanted that thing back because I wasn't in charge any more. One man stuck it through the felt in the top of his briefcase, and then took me to Moscow. On the plane, a lot of things went through my mind—I even thought that if I could grab a pistol from one of the men in uniform, I could shoot one of the engines and crush the whole airplane.

In Moscow itself, the interrogations took place in a part of Lubianka Prison occupied by the KGB. After a while, the man with the briefcase started to leave. I called the interpreter and I said, "Could you tell that man to wait a minute?" He called to the man with the briefcase, and the man asked, "Why?" And I said,

"Well, just tell him to be careful with that pin." I've often wondered, if I had not said anything, if they would have ever found out. I don't know. But I didn't feel that I could take the chance. I didn't want anyone to get killed inadvertently. I was in enough trouble already.

In 1960, Francis Gary Powers was tried in Moscow and sentenced to ten years for spying on the Soviet Union. During the Kennedy administration, he was exchanged for Rudolf Abel, a Russian agent. He was killed in 1977 while working for NBC television in Los Angeles as a telecopter pilot. (Wide World Photos)

BILL WILSON
Backstage at the Kennedy-Nixon Debates

John Kennedy knew he needed a television man. He didn't know much about the medium, but he knew he needed an expert. I had been through Adlai Stevenson's campaign, and though that made me suspect in some ways, at least I had the experience. Some Stevenson people had introduced me to Kennedy in 1956. He was slighter than most remember him, with a great shock of hair on his head. When we met, I noticed that the girls around him were giggling and squealing, and found his enormous appeal fascinating.

After the conventions, both camps discussed the possibility of a presidential debate in the abstract. Kennedy tried the idea out on his closest advisers, people like Ted Sorensen and Pierre Salinger. I was the last in the Kennedy camp to know that he and Nixon were going to debate.

Nixon didn't have to do it. By taking on the debate when he had the advantage in the campaign, he said, in effect, that he was going to win. The Republicans were confident. Their attitude was "Thank God, Richard Nixon, a great mind and a great debater, is going to take John Kennedy and sling him over his shoulder."

The only agreement the candidates made about the mechanics of the debate was that there would be four reporters asking unrehearsed questions, and that each candidate would stand at a podium. None of the political advisers understood their ability to shape the events of the debate through its format. The head of Kennedy's media department, to whom I reported, felt that the decision to debate was enough; the rest was bullshit. None of the advisers had any sense of the connecting tissue that the media are made of, nor of how they function.

The networks knew what a breakthrough the debates would be for television. "The soapbox is back, and we've got it." But the networks also knew they were being watched by the press. They were careful to be as fair as possible so as not to appear partial to either candidate.

At the first session with the network heads, I met my counterpart on the Nixon side, Ted Rogers, the ex–NBC producer who did the Checkers speech. I liked the fact that he was organized, and saw that I could probably deal with him—I knew that not too far up the road, it would be the two of us against the world, we had the same problems to contend with. Countless times, we left meetings in order to discuss decisions the network officials had asked us to make. We'd go into another office, close the door, and say, "Whew!" and let our hair down. Then I'd bring out the obligatory coin and say, "Okay, Ted, it's my turn. I'll call it first this time."

Vice President Nixon, right; Senator Kennedy, left, during the first debate (Wide World Photos).

We both knew that positioning, lighting, and set design could affect the outcome of the debates. A very important issue, though we didn't know to what extent yet, was the question of reaction shots—the camera cutting to the debater not speaking.

I had suggested to Salinger and Sorensen that they rehearse Kennedy with very thorough questions. Sorensen, Dick Goodwin and Mike Feldman sat around Kennedy and shot negative questions at him. They did a wonderful job. The only problem I had with Kennedy was nerves. But they were the nerves of a high-strung race horse, not the nerves of someone who was worried about whether he was going to be good or not.

I made a point of creating a table-size mock set-up of the stage of the debates, down to lights, cameras, stairs and lectern. But all Kennedy wanted to know was if there were any problems. He'd learned to be his own man and to trust the work of the men on his team. He didn't understand the technical aspects, didn't want to participate in them. All I had to tell him was that he didn't have to be concerned, and that was fine. On the other hand, my impression was that Nixon's briefings made him want to know more. That, for a performer, is deadly. Being too conscious of the physical set-up can drain half the energy out of the performance.

Monday afternoon, I briefed Kennedy about procedure and chronology. He asked, "Is everything all right?"

I answered, "Everything is terrific." When I was with the Kennedys I used the word *terrific* a lot. They loved that word. But they looked at me doubtfully—motivation to go back and make sure that everything was fine.

All day Kennedy was completely involved with himself, while Nixon was involved with the performance and Kennedy. Kennedy seemed to be totally secure within the parameters of his own personality. The last trial question-and-answer sessions wound down. I kicked everyone out of the office, and they all complained. As Bobby Kennedy walked out he said, "Okay, Jack. Good luck. Kick 'em in the balls."

Then we were alone. Kennedy asked, "What am I supposed to do?"

I said that we had to get the makeup done. "I'll get the makeup done after Nixon gets his done."

I was nervous and had to run around the corner to see if Nixon was made up yet. I saw Ted Rogers looking around the corner and asked him if Nixon was coming out. "Not until Kennedy comes out."

I said, "This is stupid."

He said, "I know, but I can't do anything about it."

I went back and told Kennedy that Nixon wasn't emerging until he did. Kennedy replied, "I'm not coming out. It's that simple. Is the press out there?"

I answered yes, and he repeated his refusal. I said, "You've got to do something . . . "

He said, "Well, I don't care. I'm not going out no matter what you say."

I knew we had to put some makeup on, so I headed back to the makeup room to try to steal some stuff and take it back to Kennedy. The makeup man was standing and talking to an AP pool reporter. I knew I would blow it right there if I tried to sneak any makeup out, so I ran to a drugstore two blocks away and bought some Max Factor pancake. As I put it on him, he asked, "Is this going to work? Are you sure?"

I said yes, wondering what on earth a producer was doing putting on makeup. It was two minutes before air time. I wanted Kennedy at his podium so he could get the feel of the environment, get used to the visuals. But he had gone to the bathroom. I had to lead him away. He got onto the stage thirty seconds before air time. Nixon had gotten there too early; he was nervous and fidgeting. Kennedy's internal instincts were remarkable.

When I got to the control room, the first thing that struck me was how Richard Nixon looked. I knew he'd just been very ill, but I was shocked. He hadn't looked so bad on the set, but on television, the lights washed everything out. The lighting man had had too much time to light him.

The first debate in progress, above (Wide World Photos); right: a TV image (Philip Drell/Black Star).

Rogers and I were in the control room together. By now we were working in violent opposition. The camaraderie fell apart. We were flinging demands about the control booth, and Don Hewitt, the producer, was going bananas. We weren't even supposed to be in the control booth, and he was trying to concentrate on cutting a big show.

At this moment, I noticed the reaction shots on Nixon, while Kennedy spoke, were going to be beneficial to my man. Ted and I began to squabble, as he began to want fewer reaction shots of Nixon. I kept track of how many there had been on each candidate, shouting, "Now it's five; you owe us three!" Hewitt went crazy telling us to shut up. He wanted to kick us out altogether.

What was happening on the set was fascinating. While Nixon spoke, the camera would pick up Kennedy with a hint of exasperation. He had a natural disdain for everything going on at the other podium. He made notes; he could have been taking a bath. You definitely sensed that he felt what Nixon was saying just didn't count at all. Nixon would watch Kennedy very carefully when the reaction shot panned on him. He paid a lot of attention, the way an audience listens, and that only added credibility to what Kennedy was saying.

If you listened to the debate on radio, it was at least a stand-off, perhaps even a victory by Nixon. But on TV it was all Kennedy, and as soon as it was over I went to see him to tell him he'd been terrific. I was sure he'd won when I saw Mayor Daley beelining it through the police lines, past the security guards and the crowds, to be the first to congratulate him. Up to now, Daley had been lukewarm to Kennedy, but now he greeted him with the smile of a winner. I looked over to Ted Rogers and said, "I think we won."

*B*ill Wilson was John F. Kennedy's television producer during the 1960 presidential campaign, directing Kennedy's end of all four Nixon-Kennedy debates. He went on to work for the Robert Kennedy and Hubert Humphrey presidential campaigns and now works as an independent motion picture producer and political consultant. ★

*T*he contenders confer, top (Philip Drell/Black Star); above: an attentive Richard Nixon (Philip Drell/Black Star); left: Bill Wilson and Ted Rogers before the fourth debate (courtesy ABC).

1961

CALENDAR

January: 3 *U.S. breaks diplomatic relations with Cuba;* **20** *Kennedy's Inaugural speech: "Ask not what your country can do for you, ask what you can do for your country";* **31** *U.S. chimp Ham survives experimental space shot.*

February: 1 *Movie premiere of* The Misfits; **5** *The Shirelles have number one song "Will You Still Love Me Tomorrow";* **7** *U.S. release of Godard's* Breathless; **12** *Recently ousted Congo premier Patrice Lumumba is assassinated in continuing power struggle;* **15** *Air crash near Brussels kills 18 members of the U.S. skating team;* **19** *Lawrence Welk's "Calcutta" is number one single;* **23** *National Council of Churches approves artificial birth control in family planning.*

March: 1 *President Kennedy creates the Peace Corps by executive order; Mattel introduces a boyfriend named Ken for their Barbie doll;* **21** *U.S. sends military aid and advisers into Laos as buffer against Soviet-backed rebels;* **23** *JFK sets up a national program for physical fitness.*

April: 12 *Soviet cosmonaut Yuri Gagarin is first person to orbit in space;* **17** *CIA-trained Cuban exiles launch unsuccessful Bay of Pigs invasion against Castro's regime;* **30** *Del Shannon's "Runaway" replaces "Blue Moon" as number one pop single.*

May: 1 *To Kill a Mockingbird wins Pulitzer Prize for literature; first U.S. plane is hijacked to Cuba;* **4** *Freedom Riders leave Washington, D.C., to test desegregation in Southern bus station facilities;* **5** *Alan Shepard is first American in space; Kennedy signs bill raising minimum wage 25¢, to $1.25 an hour;* **8** *The Agony and the Ecstacy is fiction best seller;* **9** *FCC chairman Newton Minow declares TV programming a "vast wasteland";* **23** *"Mother-in-Law" tops pop chart;* **30** *CIA-financed assassins kill Dominican Republic dictator Trujillo.*

June: 3 *First meeting of Kennedy and Khrushchev takes place in Vienna;* **5** *Supreme Court orders Communist organizations to register;* **14** *Publication of Heinlein's* Stranger in a Strange Land; **16** *Russian dancer Rudolf Nureyev defects at the Paris airport;* **18** *Ben E. King's "Stand by Me" tops R&B chart;* **26** *JFK uses Taft-*

Top to bottom: Pablo Casals at the White House (JFK Library); the UN's Dag Hammarskjöld (Wide World Photos); astronaut Alan Shepard on the ground again at a reception with his wife, Louise (NASA); first hijacked plane's crew on their return to the U.S. (UPI). Opposite page: on the road with the Freedom Riders (© Bruce Davidson/Magnum).

Hartley Act to end maritime strike.

July: 2 *Ernest Hemingway commits suicide;* **16** *"Tossin' and Turnin' " rocks to top of pop chart, displacing "Quarter to Three";* **22** *Revised dating of human fossils found in Africa prove man is twice as old as scientists believed.*

August: 6 *Chris Kenner's "I Like It Like That" pushes into the number two slot on pop charts;* **10** *Justice Department drops its 27-year-old ban on importing the Paris edition of Henry Miller's* Tropic of Cancer; **13** *East Germany closes Berlin border and begins building wall;* **16** *Twenty American nations adopt Alliance for Progress charter.*

September: 1 *Russia resumes atmospheric nuclear testing, breaking a three-year moratorium;* **5** *U.S. outlaws air piracy following a rash of hijackings to Cuba;* **18** *UN Secretary General Dag Hammarskjöld dies in plane crash during Congo peace mission;* **21** *NBC's Saturday Night at the Movies brings movies to prime-time TV;* **24** *"Take Good Care of My Baby" leads pop chart; Rocky the Flying Squirrel stars in the TV debut of* The Bullwinkle Show; **25** *Theodore H. White tops nonfiction list with* The Making of the President 1960; **26** *Release of* The Hustler.

October: 1 *Roger Maris hits his record-setting 61st home run;* **2** Ben Casey *joins* Dr. Kildare *in the new TV season;* **5** *Publication of* Black Like Me; **6** *JFK pledges nuclear fallout protection for every American in view of Soviet A-bomb testing;* **23** *Sino/Soviet split surfaces when China's Chou En-lai walks out of communist world congress in Moscow;* **29** *Dion's "Runaround Sue" edges Ray Charles' "Hit the Road Jack" out of top chart spot.*

November: 13 *Pablo Casals ends boycott of U.S. to play for White House reception;* **16** *Speaker of the House Sam Rayburn dies;* **20** *Salinger's* Franny and Zooey *rules fiction list.*

December: 11 *Kennedy sends the first combat-level troops, 400 helicopter crewmen, to South Vietnam;* **17** *"Please Mr. Postman" by Marvelettes takes chart lead;* **20** *Reports show 2,000 U.S. military advisers and technicians" in South Vietnam;* **24** *"The Lion Sleeps Tonight" tops charts.*

MANUEL ARTIME
On Board at the Bay of Pigs

At the time of the invasion, I was civilian commander of the 2506 Brigade. On April 17th, my flagship, the *Blagar,* was leading 1,400 men through international waters. As we passed into Cuban waters, the order was given to lower the Panamanian flag our ship was flying and raise the Cuban flag. Everybody was standing at attention. I made a patriotic speech to the crew and the soldiers and the frogmen of my flagship. After that, everybody was silent.

When we arrived off Bahía de Cochinos, we sent a dozen frogmen in rafts to set out the landing lights. But the frogmen were surprised by the militia and the soldiers on the shore. From our ships, we could see the tracer bullets.

One of the frogmen made communication with us by radio. He said, "Please cover our operation because we are under very strong fire." I ordered the military commander of the flagship to shoot at the beach and protect our boys.

The captain of the *Blagar* was a Norwegian with a patch over one eye, like Moshe Dayan. He was beautiful-looking. He didn't know what was happening, but he was very impressed with all the fireworks and noise—until the artillery from the beach began to storm our ship. One shot hit near the captain and blew off a big piece of steel from the ship. The poor man came running. "Sir," he said, "they are shooting *bullets.*"

I said, "Of course. What do you expect them to shoot off? Chiclets?"

"But bullets can kill!"

"Of course. It is a war!"

Then the captain made the most surprising revelation that I ever heard in the middle of a war. There he was, the captain of the flagship, and he said, "I was not contracted to make a war, only for the carrying of troops for practice!"

Immediately I ordered him taken off to the ship's prison, and the first mate, who was a Cuban, became the captain.

I found it strange that the gentleman who was the captain of the ship did not know the operation we were going to carry out. He believed that it was practice—armies playing at war. I guess the CIA told him that. He never suspected that it was a real war.

We fought on the beach and in the surrounding area for three days, without rest, always waiting for the American support that never came. On the third day, with Cuban tanks in sight, we ordered a retreat. Most of those remaining headed into the swamps; a few swam away or found a boat and escaped. In the swamps many died, and the rest of us were captured.

I was in jail for twenty months. I was ransomed for $500,000 by President Kennedy. I was on the last prisoner-exchange flight out of Cuba. When I arrived from jail, one officer told me that somebody wanted me on the telephone. When I picked up the phone, I heard the voice of President Kennedy.

He said, "Hello, Manolo, I'm glad you're back." Then he said, "Will you please come and see me in Palm Beach?"

I went to Palm Beach and met President Kennedy. I asked him why he did not help us when we were in trouble at the Bahía de Cochinos. He told me he had been afraid that the Russians would attack Berlin if he openly attacked Cuba to help us. He said that now he believed the Russians had been bluffing. He said he'd learned a lot about the Russians.

I asked him to help us again against Castro. I said, "Mr. President, I understand your worry about blowing up the world. We Cubans would never ask you to blow up the world, even to regain our homeland. But I must ask you this. If you cannot give us the green light to attack Castro again, please don't give us the red light. All we ask is the blinking orange light."

He said, "See my brother Bobby."

I thought about that war again when the congressional investigators came to question me in Miami after some of my friends were in trouble for Watergate. They said, "If you lie to us, you will have to come to Congress and the committee of investigation. You will be questioned there by the senators in front of all the TV cameras and in front of U.S. public opinion. You will have to tell the truth under oath, and if you are not truthful, then you will have to go to jail."

They told me that they didn't understand why the Cubans who were openly accepted in the United States had conspired against the laws of the United States. I answered this way: "I would like to tell you first that I will be open. I accept what you say—that the Cubans really broke the law—and I'd like to confess to you that at one time, for a lot of years, I broke the law of the United States."

"Yes?"

"Yes. I will be so open that I will tell you the names of my co-conspirators."

They paid close attention, lifted their pencils and began to write.

"President Eisenhower. Vice-President Nixon, President Kennedy. Vice-President Lyndon Johnson. President Lyndon Johnson, Vice-President Hubert Humphrey. The State Department. The Pentagon. The CIA. The FBI. I remember three federal judges, three governors. The leaders of Congress. I remember at least fifteen sheriffs, the border patrols, and I remember the Coast Guard. The departments of Immigration and Customs. They were all my co-conspirators. I will tell you the name of the conspiracy: the Bay of Pigs invasion and commando operations against Cuba.

"I broke the law of neutrality against Cuba; I broke the laws of immigration; I broke the customs law. I passed weapons from one state to another state with the permission of all the organized police forces.

"I lied under oath because I received orders to say lies under oath. If you like, carry me to the trial and I will call all my co-conspirators, and I will begin to answer questions."

They looked at me like I was crazy. I told them, "The only thing I'd like to add is that we learned to conspire to break the law of the United States, following the indoctrination and teaching of the United States. And not only during one government, during a lot of governments. Every time somebody from a security agency comes to the Cubans, he says, 'I need your help for national security.' "

"National security" was the key word to break the law of the United States. They taught us that when the national security is in danger, you can break the law. Of course, national security is supposed to be the survival of the laws of the country—but you can break the law in order to defend the law.

I said, "I will go with you, sir, to the sacred judges of the Congress. I will be ready, sir. But I will give you some good advice. Never put the menace of jail in front of Cubans. Your beautiful jails here, with air conditioners and civil rights, are a dream to a lot of Cubans. So many Cubans now in the United States passed from Cuba through jail."

I told them that, after I was captured at the Bay of Pigs invasion, I appeared before some Cuban judges. The lawyer of defense began his speech by telling the judges, "I am sorry to defend this son of a bitch who has to be shot ten times. He is a traitor to his country. He is a killer. He is an assassin."

I said to the men questioning me in Miami, "Do you believe, after this, that I am afraid to go to Congress to answer some questions from some senators? I'd be very happy to go and talk to the senators. Maybe I can recognize some of my old co-conspirators. I'd be very happy to shake hands with them."

Opposite page: the President and the First Lady during the ceremony honoring the 2506 Brigade at the Orange Bowl, December 29th, 1962 (JFK Library). Above: Bay of Pigs survivors on their way to a Havana jail (UPI). Right: Artime at the time of his capture (UPI).

Manuel Artime came to the U.S. in 1959 after resigning from his post in the Cuban government in protest against Castro's move toward Communism. He became a leader in the CIA-backed Cuban counterrevolutionary movement based in Miami. After his imprisonment following the Bay of Pigs invasion, he returned to Florida, where he is now a practicing physician.★

DICK CLARK
How the Twist Discovered Bandstand

American Bandstand was broadcast five days a week, in glorious black and white. The ABC network carried it for an hour and a half, to millions of viewers. It was one of their highest-rated daytime shows.

The early regulars were there: Bob Clayton and Justine Carrelli, the blond "cutie pie" couple; Kenny Rossi and Arlene Sullivan, the most popular duo. These high school kids from Philadelphia were stars unto themselves. They danced to the Everly Brothers' big hit, "Cathy's Clown," and to their favorite slow number, "Theme from 'A Summer Place.'"

Chubby Checker teaches the twist to Dick Clark (UPI).

Then one day they began to Twist.

I was about to do the Record Revue when I saw a black couple doing a dance in which they revolved their hips in quick jerks so their pelvises heaved in time to the music. The white kids watched, fascinated. A few began to imitate the dance.

I called out to my producer, Tony Mammarella, "For God's sake, keep the camera off the couple near the Top Forty Board!" I was really scared that the dance would be shown on the air. It looked like a belly dancer's encore.

"Go into the Record Revue, then announce a Spotlight Dance," Tony said, hoping that the slow music would cool things down.

As soon as the kids were fox-trotting to "This Magic Moment," the Drifters' hit, I walked over to the couple. I asked them, "What is it that you're doing?"

They answered as if I were from outer space: "The Twist, man. Everybody knows it's the Twist."

Within days most of the kids were Twisting to songs that weren't even Twist songs. There was no way to stop it or ignore it. But it was a very scary dance. It looked lascivious, and I was sure it would be condemned.

I called some friends at Cameo Records, in Philadelphia, and described what was going on. They re-recorded a song that Hank Ballard had done a year or so before, using a relatively unknown singer who had once worked as a chicken plucker. His name was Ernest Evans, and he'd done a Christmas recording for my wife Bobbie and me the year before. Bobbie had told Bernie Lowe, the owner of Cameo, "He's cute. He looks like a little Fats Domino. Like a chubby checker." Later, Chubby Checker laughingly called Bobbie his godmother.

The Twist was the biggest dance in the history of popular music. Hank Ballard went on the charts with his version, then Chubby Checker made it to number one in 1960 and again in 1962. The Isley Brothers did "Twist and Shout." Sam Cooke recorded "Twistin' the Night Away." Gary "U.S." Bonds did "Dear Lady Twist." There was even something called "Twistin' Bells," a Christmas song by Santo and Johnny.

Jerry Lewis came down to the show and jumped around the studio while Joanne Campbell, who was a singer and choreographer, tried to "teach" the dance to him. *Time* and *Newsweek* did national feature stories. New York was fast becoming the Twist capital. One night in 1961, I was there with Joanne, Tony Orlando, Glen Campbell and a few other friends. We went to a joint on West 45th Street called the Peppermint Lounge, a stinky little sweathole that attracted the street people of the music business. The house band was Joey Dee and the Starliters, and when they recorded "Peppermint Twist," the place began attracting luminaries from all over the country. The street kids of the music business, people like Neil Sedaka and his writing buddy, Howard Greenfield, Wes Farrell of Chelsea Records, were squeezed out when Ahmet Ertegun of Atlantic Records

American Bandstand.

began to bring the international set. Soon Greta Garbo was seen Twisting there. So were Judy Garland and Norman Mailer. Even Jackie Kennedy was rumored to dance at the Peppermint Lounge.

The Twist just went on and on. Everybody could do it. It took absolutely no artistic skill. All you needed was stamina. It was done at bar mitzvahs, weddings and supermarket openings. Duane Eddy did a Twist album. So did Keely Smith. Everybody jumped on the bandwagon.

People ask me, "What's the most significant period in contemporary music?" And I give them a very bizarre answer. I say it was the day the Twist took over. It had social significance. When the Twist happened, adults could go into drinking establishments and ask for old favorites like "Blue Suede Shoes" and dance unashamedly. Overnight, it was all right to be older and say you liked rock and roll.

Dick *Clark began hosting a local Philadelphia television show called* Bandstand *in the summer of 1956. That show became* American Bandstand *on nationwide TV a year later, and 1977 marks its twenty-fifth anniversary. Clark, still* American Bandstand's *host, now heads a television and motion picture production company and is the author, with Richard Robinson, of* Rock, Roll and Remember.★ *(Frank Zinn/courtesy Dick Clark)*

Above: showing them how it's done at the Peppermint Lounge (Wide World Photos).

STAN LEE
Where Spider-Man Came From

In the late Fifties, the comic-book business was stagnating. Our Marvel Comics group, which was then called Atlas Comics, ground out one trendy monster story after another, and the work was tiresome. I got to thinking, why not try something different? Something I'd like to read? No more cardboard characters and predictable stories where the hero is 100 percent good and always wins, and the bad guy is 100 percent bad and doomed to lose.

I decided to start a series of fairy tales for grown-ups. I wanted the comics to be more lifelike. My formula became: Let's suspend disbelief for a moment and accept that a character can fly through the air, climb on walls or have the strength of fifty men. What would his life be like if he lived in today's world? Wouldn't he have to worry about halitosis, about making a living and so forth? Well, we worked on the idea, and in the fall of 1961, we came out with the Fantastic Four.

The Fantastic Four, issue number one (© Marvel Comics).

That series had several unique qualities for its time. Occasionally, the Four would lose—they'd stumble or the crook would get away. They had headquarters in an identifiable place, a building on the East Side, off Madison Avenue, in New York. That had never been done before. Heroes always lived in nonexistent places called Gotham City or Metropolis. Once our group was evicted for nonpayment of rent because Reed Richards, their leader, had lost all their money in bad stock investments. The rest of the team kept heckling him, saying, "Some superhero you are. You can't even hold on to our money."

The really unusual aspect of that series was the teenage member of the group, Johnny Storm, the Human Torch. Heretofore, teens had always been depicted as the hero's effervescent little sidekick. That bothered me. If I were a superhero—and don't for a minute assume that by saying that, I've conceded that I'm not—the last thing I would want would be to pal around with a fourteen- or fifteen-year-old kid. At the very least, people would talk. So we made Johnny Storm more realistic. He was a hero, but he was also a pest and an itch, a typical teenager. He was forever complaining, tagging along, and he always wanted more money, more glamour and prestige on the team.

The series was an immediate success. College kids read the Fantastic Four and considered it high satire. I even started to get the reputation of being a satirist, which proves how crazy the world is—if you try to show things the way they are, you're satirizing.

Then, in May 1962, I brought out the Hulk. He had thick green skin, and weighed about eight hundred pounds. I'd always loved Frankenstein stories, and I'd always thought the monster was the good guy. You know, he never wanted to hurt anybody, he just wandered around going "Ooo, boo," and those idiots with torches kept chasing him. I thought his pursuers were the bad guys, and that's what I did with the Hulk. He just wanted to be left alone, but everyone hounded him until he had to take action.

Later that same year—in August—Spider-Man, the ultimate anti-hero, was born. As a kid, I had read a pulp magazine called *The Spider, Master of Men,* and the idea of the spider hero had stayed with me. Spider-Man was the epitome of what I'd tried in the other books. He was endowed with "spider powers," but he was just a typical kid, kind of a nebbish. Steve Ditko's artwork gave him a pleasantly outward quality. He had allergy attacks and dandruff, and he lived with his widowed aunt. If it was raining, she wouldn't let him go outside unless he wore his galoshes and a scarf. There he was going to save the world from a terrible menace, but he had to bring his cough drops along. And of course girls wouldn't have anything to do with him in his real life as Peter Parker because he was too square.

A funny thing happened with the Spider-Man series though. When I first described the character to my publisher, Martin Goodman, he said, "Yech, who wants to read about spiders? I can't see that as a name for a hero or a series at all. People hate spiders."

The Hulk debuts (© Marvel Comics).

He didn't want to publish a Spider-Man comic book. But I knew about a series called *Amazing Adult Fantasy* which we were about to drop. The last issue was coming up. It had quite a cult following, but I guess the word "adult" turned a lot of kids off; sales were't too good. We had tried to tell stories with an O'Henry-esque twist, about five stories per issue, all of them drawn by Steve Ditko, and written by me. So I said to Martin, "How about if I put the opening issue of Spider-Man in the last issue of *Amazing Adult Fantasy?* There's nothing to lose. If the idea is rotten, we've dropping the series anyway, and this way I'll get to try it out." He agreed.

So Spider-Man was born in that last issue of *Amazing Fantasy.* We dropped the word "adult" from the title and promptly forgot about him until nine months later, when the sales reports came in. The series, which had been in such a slump, came in with a tremendous sale. The readers loved Spider-Man. They empathized with him. And I had found a cast of characters who proved to be the most popular in all of comic bookdom.

Spider-Man existed in the real world. In the old days, a superhero dressed in a costume could be walking unnoticed down a normal city street when he'd spot a ten-foot-tall bug-eyed monster with four arms and scaly skin, breathing fire. The hero would say, "Oh-ho, a creature from another world. I'd better destroy him before he captures mankind." But in the Spider-Man series, Peter Parker would see the monster and say, "I wonder what this nut's advertising?"

We made some of the stories self-effacing or humorous, but they were always realistic. We wrote a drug story in which a friend of Spider-Man's overdosed and thought he could fly like a bird; Spider-Man had to save him before he jumped off the roof of a building. Spider-Man was enough of a teenager to have an identity crisis. He even wondered why he spent so much time being Spider-Man. Was he really trying to do something altruistic or was he just on a big ego trip?

The other characters were also easy to identify. There was J. Jonah Jameson the irascible newspaper publisher Peter Parker worked for. Jameson was a skinflint tightwad who represented the establishment. He really did have a good heart, but it never showed, so he and Peter always fought.

Then there was the black city editor, Robbie Robertson, one of the few times in comics where a black man was given a prestigious job and treated like a normal, capable guy. He became quite popular. And we even gave him a teenage son who was much more rebellious than his father. Whenever the two argued, he would call his father an Uncle Tom.

The Spider-Man series quickly became our biggest seller, with a series under its own name beginning in March 1963. Today, Spider-Man outsells Superman, and it is probably the largest-selling comic book in the world. So much for an antihero.

Stan Lee, a thirty-seven-year veteran of the comic-book business, is now the publisher and creative head of Marvel Comics Group, a company born with the first of Lee's unique comic-book characters, the Fantastic Four. Lee is the author of three books on the origins of Marvel Comics with a fourth, on Marvel's women superheroes, due in 1977. He is currently *collaborating with artist Jack Kirby, creator of Captain America, on an epic-length, 100-page original adventure of Silver Surfer, to be published as a book.★ (courtesy Stan Lee)*

Above: metamorphosis—Peter Parker and the spider (© Marvel Comics).

GEORGIANNA McGUIRE
The Post Peace Corps Blues

I was the only one of the first group of Ghana Peace Corps volunteers to be assigned to a town alone. Peace Corps officials were not sure how volunteers would adjust to a new environment. They thought it would be easier to cope in a new country if one worked with other Americans, but they thought I would be content alone, and I was assigned to a small government school in Tema, Ghana, that had requested only one teacher. I worked there for two years as the English teacher and headmistress for girls.

Some days it was not easy without an American to fall back on. If I needed someone to talk with, I went to a Ghanaian. It worked out well. I became very much a part of the teaching staff of six at the school. We visited together, shared meals, marketed together, and went to movies and dances in town.

I also became close to the students for a number of reasons. It was a new school, part of the Ghana Educational Trust established by President Kwame Nkrumah, and so a new situation for all of us. As headmistress for girls, I was responsible for their safety, and to the extent that I could be, I was their counselor. I am sure that there were problems they did not bring to me because they thought I would not really understand, but there was a closeness and trust on both sides.

Students were in and out of my house constantly. One, in particular, Alice Sika Agudogo, made a strong effort to involve me in the life of the town. She was of the Ewe tribe; her family had been in Tema for years, and she introduced me to grandparents, aunts and uncles, and family friends. She made it clear that it was important that I meet and benefit from the wisdom of the elders, for whom there is great respect in West African society, and I spent hours listening to them talk of the past and the future.

They all took me on in a very personal way. Their attitude was: "Here's a guest in our country; now make her feel a part of our life." Ghanaians have a strong feeling of acceptance and welcome for strangers. It is hospitality in the very finest sense. I was treated in a direct, straightforward manner, with no particular deference to me as a foreigner, although I was respected as a teacher. Students took me to market, hand in hand. I would bargain, but not well, and they would laugh later and say, "That—that is too much. You know, you have been had." It was a pleasant, comfortable, welcoming and learning relationship.

At the time there was a fair amount of anti-American sentiment in Ghana on the part of some government officials and the press. There were newspaper articles that directly accused volunteers of being tools, if not agents, of the CIA. Of course a number of the volunteers also suspected that one or two of us might indeed have been working for the CIA. I have no way of knowing whether that was true, but I am not convinced that it wasn't, either. Although supposedly part of a U.S. mission to help other countries, the Peace Corps was not composed of solely altruistic humans. We had volunteered for the exposure we would get to another culture, for what we could learn from another way of life. There was an expectation on the part of some American officials in Ghana that we should get out there and make friends for America in the great cold war, the struggle for the hearts and minds, if you will. Most volunteers were cynical and resented that expectation. We did not intend to be used in that way, but our very presence contributed to that effect.

I didn't feel any anti-American hostility directed at me, though. It was not part of the Ghanaian culture to be color prejudiced—there was a strong sense of nationalism, and, certainly, resentment of American imperialism and criticism of American racism, but virtually no racial prejudice towards whites.

The two years were good ones, and I felt a real wrench when the Peace Corps truck came to take my shipping crate the morning of my departure. Students had helped me sort and pack things, and we had exchanged many photographs. When I arrived at the airport in Accra, I found that another volunteer, Tom—who was also on his way back to the States—had been accompanied to the airport by his entire school and most of the town. It was a gay, raucous send-off, funny and sad to see. The airline kept paging him to get on the plane so it could leave, and he kept running around saying, "Good-bye, good-bye—I love you all." I was outwardly more sedate until the final moment. Then I broke down and cried bitterly. I was leaving friends and colleagues who had shared their lives with me for two years, and I knew I would always be grateful. I do not cry often or easily, but something very precious was over.

McGuire and panelists discussing the Peace Corps on Washington TV (courtesy Georgianna McGuire).

The real impact of the experience didn't hit me until I returned to the United States. I took a job with the Peace Corps in Washington, D.C. Lillie Gates, a black American who had been on the Peace Corps staff in Ghana came back a month later, and we agreed to share an apartment. We both earned very good salaries and could easily afford a better-than-average apartment, but when we sat down with the Sunday classified ads, Lillie said, "Look, we are going to have problems because you are white and I am black. We are going to find it difficult to find an apartment in D.C." We went through forty-three ads in the *Washington Post.* I called the prospective agents and landlords, and politely explained the situation. I said, "I am interested in your apartment, but there is no point in looking at something that will not be available to us. Will you consider renting to us?" Forty-one people said, "No." Two said they might consider us for other apartments in other buildings, both located in rundown high-crime neighborhoods. Lillie had grown up in segregated Washington, D.C., and though she was angry, she was not as stunned as I was.

Two or three nights later I was on a talk show about the Peace Corps, with Bill Moyers, Sargent Shriver, and several other returned volunteers. They knew what had happened and how angry I was. I think one of them planted a question addressed to me: "What has struck you most about being home?"

On the beach in Ghana (courtesy Georgianna McGuire).

Well, I told them. I launched into a tirade about returning to the land of the free, home of the brave, with brotherhood and justice for all, and coming smack up against the racial prejudice of this society, whereas I had encountered none in "underdeveloped Ghana." I pointed out that I had been sent out to tell others about democracy and this wonderful enlightened country I came from, and damn it, here in this country's capital it was very clear that this country had some very serious, pernicious problems of its own to address. I was quite blunt, and probably effective, because I come across as all-American—everybody's sister, daughter, the girl next door. Shriver and Moyers sat back and let me say my piece. It was close to the end of the show, and there was little left to say. The moderator thanked us, and said, "I think the message is clear. The volunteers are coming back and looking at this country in a different way." He was quite right. For many of us, the Peace Corps was the end of something, and the beginning of something quite new. It forever altered our view of our own country, and more significantly, it altered our perception of ourselves and our responsibilities.

As volunteers, we were thrown into situations where we were expected to act, to do, to contribute to change. When we returned, there was nothing that would make us deferential to authority and accepting of a system that cried out for change.

Peace Corps volunteers came back and got involved—in civil rights, in antiwar activities, in university and political reform—in so many of the battles of the Sixties. And that, I think, is the real significance of the Peace Corps experience. Although those struggles of the Sixties may not have resulted in lasting or basic changes in the society, returned Peace Corps volunteers looked at their own country, analyzed its shortcomings, and tried to improve it.

Georgianna Shine was a Peace Corps volunteer from 1961 to 1963, and a member of the Corps' Washington staff for two years following that. In 1965 she married Mick McGuire, another returned volunteer, and went with him to New York, where she worked in that city's poverty program. Ms. McGuire has been director of an inner-city day-care program in Washington, a consultant to HEW's Office of Child Development/Head Start, and the Education Commission of the State's liaison to the OCD. She is a full-time student completing a master's degree in educational administration, and a full-time mother as well.★
The teacher, left, and the students, overleaf (both courtesy Georgianna McGuire).

JOSEPH HELLER
Reeling in Catch-22

The concept of the novel came to me as a seizure, a single inspiration. I'd come to the conclusion that I wanted to write a novel, and moving back to New York after two years of teaching college in Pennsylvania sent the ambition coursing again. I had no idea what it would be about, however. Then one night the opening lines of *Catch-22*—all but the character's name, Yossarian—came to me: "It was love at first sight. The first time he saw the chaplain he fell madly in love with him."

My mind flooded with verbal images. I got up in the night and walked around, just thinking about it. The next day I returned to the small ad agency where I worked, wrote the first chapter in longhand, spent the week touching it up, and then sent it to my literary agent. It took a year more to plan the book and seven years to write it, but it remained pretty much the same inspiration that came to me that night.

I don't know where it came from. I know that it was a conscious assembling of factors, but the unconscious element was very strong, too. Almost immediately I invented the phrase "Catch-18," which would later be changed to "Catch-22" when it was discovered that Leon Uris' *Mila 18* would be coming out at about the same time as my book. Initially Catch-22 required that every censoring officer put his name on every letter he censored. Then as I went on, I deliberately looked for self-contradictory situations, and artistic contrivance came in. I began to expand each application of Catch-22 to encompass more and more of the social system. Catch-22 became a law: "they" can do anything to us we can't stop "them" from doing. The very last use is philosophical: Yossarian is convinced that there is no such thing as Catch-22, but it doesn't matter as long as people believe there is.

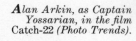

Alan Arkin, as Captain Yossarian, in the film Catch-22 (Photo Trends).

Virtually none of the attitudes in the book—the suspicion and distrust of the officials in the government, the feelings of helplessness and victimization, the realization that most government agencies would lie—coincided with my experiences as a bombardier in World War II. The antiwar and antigovernment feelings in the book belong to the period following World War II: the Korean War, the cold war of the Fifties. A general disintegration of belief took place then, and it affected *Catch-22* in that the form of the novel became almost disintegrated. *Catch-22* was a collage; if not in structure, then in the ideology of the novel itself.

Without being aware of it, I was part of a near-movement in fiction. While I was writing *Catch-22*, J. P. Donleavy was writing *The Ginger Man*, Kerouac was writing *On the Road*, Ken Kesey was writing *One Flew Over the Cuckoo's Nest*, Pynchon was writing *V.*, and Vonnegut was writing *Cat's Cradle*. I don't think any one of us even knew any of the others. Certainly I didn't know them. Whatever forces were at work shaping a trend in art were affecting not just me, but all of us. The feelings of helplessness and persecution in *Catch-22* are very strong in Pynchon and in *Cat's Cradle*.

Catch-22 was more political than psychological. In the book, opposition to the war against Hitler was taken for granted. The book dealt instead with conflicts existing between a man and his own superiors, between him and his own institutions. The really difficult struggle happens when one does not even know who it is that's threatening him, grinding him down—and yet one does know that there is a tension, an antagonist, a conflict with no conceivable end to it.

Catch-22 came to the attention of college students at about the same time that the moral corruption of the Vietnam War became evident. The treatment of the military as corrupt, ridiculous and asinine could be applied literally to that war. Vietnam was a lucky coincidence—lucky for me, not for the people. Between the

Opposite page: Yossarian up a tree at Snowden's funeral —"I don't want to wear a uniform any more." (Photo Trends)

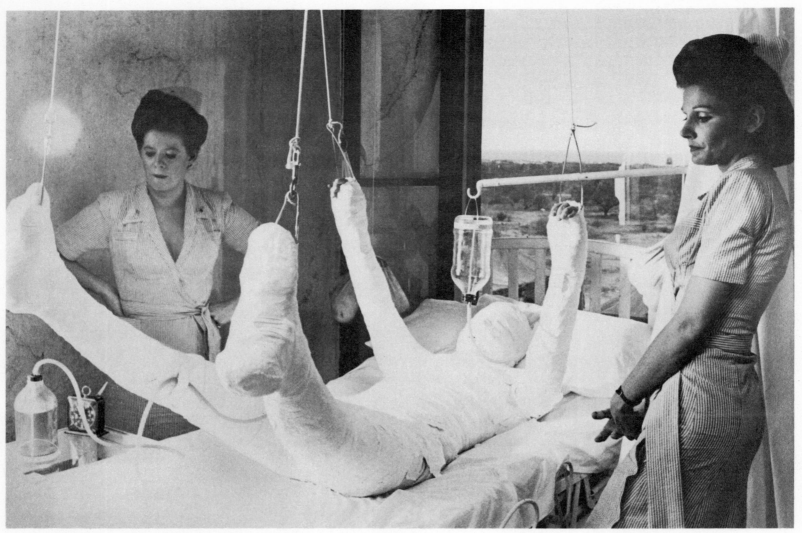

mid and late Sixties, the paperback of *Catch-22* went from twelve printings to close to thirty.

There was a change in spirit, a new spirit of healthy irreverence. There was a general feeling that the platitudes of Americanism were horseshit. Number one, they didn't work. Number two, they weren't true. Number three, the people giving voice to them didn't believe them either. The phrase "Catch-22" began appearing more and more frequently in a wide range of contexts. I began hearing from people who believed that I'd named the book after the phrase.

One way or another, everybody is at the mercy of some context in the novel. I move from situations in which the individual is against his own society, to those in which the society itself is the product of something impenetrable, something that either has no design or has a design which escapes the boundaries of reason.

There is a dialogue early in the book between Lieutenant Dunbar and Yossarian. They are discussing the chaplain, and Yossarian says, "Wasn't he sweet? Maybe they should give him three votes." Dunbar says, "Who's they?" And a page or two later, Yossarian tells Clevinger "They're trying to kill me," and Clevinger wants to know "Who's they?"

It is the anonymous "they," the enigmatic "they," who are in charge. Who is "they?" I don't know. Nobody knows. Not even "they" themselves.

Above: "The soldier in white was more like a stuffed and sterilized mummy than a real nice guy. Nurse Duckett and Nurse Cramer kept him spic and span." (Photo Trends)

Catch-22, Joseph Heller's first novel, has been called "one of the most significant works of protest literature to appear after World War II." It was published in 1961 and a film version of it appeared in 1970. Heller's other works include a play, We Bombed in New Haven and another novel, Something Happened. He is currently living in New York City and completing his third novel.★ (Helen Marcus/courtesy Simon and Schuster)

1962

CALENDAR

January: 1 *Federal Reserve System raises the maximum interest on savings accounts to 4%;* **13** *Chart revival of Chubby Checker's "The Twist" sparks dance craze;* **29** *Test ban talks between U.S., U.S.S.R. and Britain in Geneva collapse after three years;* **31** *Organization of American States votes to exclude Cuba.*

February: 1 *Publication of Ken Kesey's* One Flew Over the Cuckoo's Nest; **10** *U.S. and Russia exchange spies: Francis Gary Powers for Rudolph Abel;* **14** *Jackie Kennedy gives TV tour of redecorated White House;* **17** *"Duke of Earl" leads pop chart;* **20** *John Glenn orbits earth.*

March: *Basketball's Wilt Chamberlain sets NBA scoring record with 100 points in one game;* **9** *Pentagon verifies media reports that U.S. pilots are flying combat missions in Vietnam;* **10** *"Hey! Baby" tops charts;* **14** *Kennedy says he will go to Congress before sending combat troops to Vietnam; Full-scale East-West test ban talks resume in Geneva under UN sanction;* **15** *Defense Secretary McNamara confirms that American soldiers are exchanging fire with Viet Cong;* **30** *Nixon's* Six Crises *is published.*

April: 7 *"Johnny Angel" takes pop chart lead;* **9** *West Side Story wins the best-picture Oscar;* **13** *Steel companies rescind price increases under presidential pressure;* **21** *World's Fair opens in Seattle;* **25** *U.S. resumes atmospheric nuclear testing despite widespread protest.*

May: 7 *Ship of Fools tops fiction list;* **12** *JFK orders 5,000 troops to Thailand during Laotian turmoil;* **18** *Folk queen Joan Baez plays Carnegie Hall;* **19** *Jay and the Americans hit number five with "She Cried";* **22** *Emmys go to The Dick Van Dyke Show and The Defenders;* **23** *Sex and the Single Girl is published; Film release of The Miracle Worker;* **28** *Stock-market prices suffer worst decline since 1929;* **31** *Israel hangs Adolph Eichmann for his part in the Nazi extermination of Jews.*

June: 2 *"I Can't Stop Loving You" brings Ray Charles to top of pop and LP charts, as "Palisades Park" breaks into Top Ten;* **11–15** *SDS national convention at Port Huron;* **25** *Supreme Court bans prayer in public schools.*

Top: JFK congratulates America's first astronaut in orbit, John Glenn (NASA). Center: Peter, Paul and Mary, chart-topping folk singers (Jerry Hopkins). Bottom: the Cabinet meets during the Cuban missile crisis (JFK Library). Opposite page: James Rosenquist tries out his post-pop "walk-through" painting (Bob Adelman).

July: 3 *France declares Algeria independent following plebecite vote;* **10** *Telstar satellite relays first live telecast continent to continent.*

August: 5 *Marilyn Monroe dies of drug overdose;* **11** *Neil Sedaka takes chart lead with "Breaking up Is Hard to Do";* **18** *Rebuffed by U.S. doctors, Sherri Finkbine gets Swedish abortion of baby deformed by thalidomide;* **25** *"Loco-Motion" is number one.*

September: 15 *Tommy Roe's "Sheila" gives way to Four Seasons' "Sherry" as chart leader;* **25** *Sonny Liston takes heavyweight boxing crown from Floyd Patterson in first-round knockout; New York Mets lose 117th game for new league record;* **26** *The Beverly Hillbillies premieres on TV;* **27** *Dylan earns his first New York Times review;* **30** *Cesar Chavez founds farmworker's union.*

October: 1 *James Meredith enrolls as first black at University of Mississippi; Publication of Happiness Is a Warm Puppy featuring Snoopy and Charlie Brown;* **2** *Baseball's Maury Wills steals his 104th base for season record eclipsing Ty Cobb's;* **15** *U.S. pilots in Vietnam shoot first despite orders to fire only in defense;* **18** *Nobel Prize honors discovery of DNA double helix;* **20** *"Monster Mash" captures pop chart lead; Peter, Paul and Mary head LP chart;* **23** *JFK orders blockade of Cuba during missile crisis;* **24** *Film release of The Manchurian Candidate.*

November: 3 *Phil Spector-produced "He's a Rebel" gives Crystals the chart lead;* **5** *Silent Spring, responsible for the pesticide uproar, tops nonfiction list;* **7** *Following gubernatorial loss in California, Nixon tells reporters "You won't have Nixon to kick around any more"; Tale of How the West Was Won unfolds on the Cinerama screen;* **17** *Dulles Airport, first in U.S. designed for jets, opens.*

December: 8 *Printers' strike shuts down all nine New York newspapers;* **15** *Vaughn Meader's The First Family captures LP lead;* **23–24** *The last of the Bay of Pigs survivors are ransomed from Castro;* **26** *Film release of David and Lisa;* **31** *Reports indicate 11,000 U.S. military advisers and technicians are aiding South Vietnam.*

JAMES ROSENQUIST
Art Goes Pop

My first job in New York was painting a Hebrew National salami sign in Brooklyn. I was a member of the sign painters' union, Local 230. I painted huge signs in Times Square. Burt Lancaster's head twenty feet high, Joanne Woodward fifty-eight feet high, huge fields of spaghetti, electric irons, all sorts of things. I was learning about the viscosity of paint and how to work on a really magnified scale, and I got to be very good at it.

One day a UPI reporter came along and asked, "What are you doing?" I got to wondering what the hell I *was* doing, so I stopped working and rented a loft for $50 a month on Coenties Slip, down by the Battery. *Esquire* magazine called it "one of the ten most in places to live in New York" when only a few artists—Bob Indiana and Delphine and Jack Youngerman and Ellsworth Kelly—lived there.

I began doing tough paintings that I thought no one could like. They were either ugly or had some kind of spirit that I was just spitting out. I was a child of the advertising bombardment, and though I hadn't liked the outcome of my work in Times Square, the largeness of it had been a blow on the consciousness. I began to use fragments of realistic images—a huge image of spaghetti, somebody's nose as big as a ski slide with eyes three feet wide. People looking at my pictures could identify the elements *bam bam bam bam,* and the most magnified image, the key to the picture, would hit them last.

I was reacting to the prevailing look of abstract expressionism. To young artists that I knew, drips from a paint can had become a cliché. We had seen that so often that it had become a little stale. Around this time I heard about Roy Lichtenstein. A collector saw one of my paintings and noticed that it didn't have any drips in it, and she said, "Well, there's another person in New Jersey who doesn't have any drips in his paintings either. His name is Lichtenstein and he's doing comic strips."

We were united by a certain focus. We'd looked for dreams and values that could come from a culture in which everything seemed to be immediately obsolete.

The "New Realists" installation—George Segal's The Dinner Table, center (Eric Pollitzer/courtesy Janis Gallery).

There was no art market for younger people; even Willem de Kooning, dean of abstract expressionists, was just surfacing from the underground to have his first show at the Janis gallery where he sold *Woman V* for $1,800 (that painting has since been resold for $850,000 to the Australian National Gallery). So I was surprised when a dealer named Dick Bellamy asked if he could represent me. One day he brought some collectors down to my studio, and they said, "Well, Dick, we want that one." And Dick said, "Well, you can't have it, I sold it last week for $750." I was shocked and kind of angry. I didn't want to sell it, yet I thought, Wow, it's incredible being paid for something you like to do. In February 1962 I had my first one-man show, and the ten or twelve pictures in it sold for $700 to $1,000 each before it opened.

In the fall, Sidney Janis decided to have a show called "New Realists" at his gallery. It shocked the art world because his gallery was a bastion for the abstract expressionist artists. I had two large paintings in there—*Silver Skies,* a fifteen-foot painting, and a magnified trifocal vision called *I Love You with My Ford,* which was divided into a field of huge Franco-American spaghetti as big as fire hoses, two gray profiles and a larger-than-life-sized grille from a 1950 Ford.

Sidney's artists were outraged when they saw all those loft paintings in this exquisite atmosphere. Mark Rothko, Robert Motherwell, and other major expressionists were so upset that they quit the gallery altogether, but de Kooning didn't. He was the only representative of the expressionist school to come to the opening. He paced back and forth for about two hours and left.

Opposite page: Tom Wesselmann perfecting his technique (Bob Adelman).

56

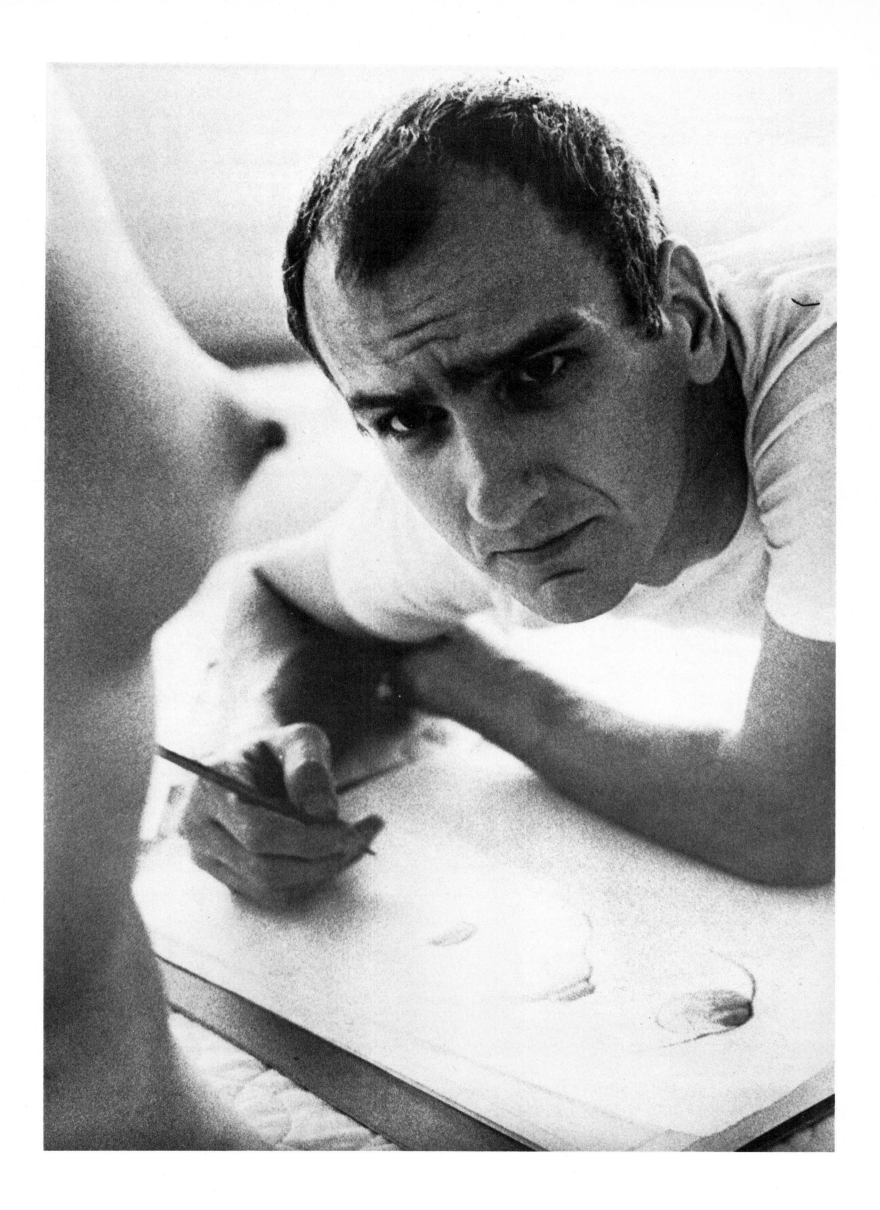

The work of the Americans and some of the English artists in the show seemed very raw. It didn't have the historical patina of the Europeans artists; it didn't have a finish. But it was powerful. Europeans live in an artistic ambiance, and they are accustomed to putting carefully formulated craftsmanship into their work. Americans seem to walk around without an idea in their heads, just doing something and having someone else call it Art. I like the American spirit better. It's less self-conscious, and it's a spirit that can leak out easier. Our realistic imagery was loud and very magnified and disquieting.

Many people hated what we were doing, and the name "pop art" was quickly tacked onto it. People wanted it to be like "popular" music, "popular" psychology. They wanted to get rid of it, and if it was "popular" they thought it wouldn't last. But it continued, continued, continued.

After the opening, Burton and Emily Tremaine, well-known collectors who'd bought some of my earliest paintings, invited me over to their house on Park Avenue. I went and was surprised to find Andy Warhol, Bob Indiana, Roy Lichtenstein and Tom Wesselmann there. Maids with little white hats were serving drinks, and my soda-bottle-and-complexion painting, *Hey! Let's Go for a Ride!* and Warhol's *Marilyn Monroe* were hanging on the wall next to fantastic Picassos and de Koonings.

Right in the middle of our party, de Kooning came through the door with Larry Rivers and another fellow. Burton Tremaine stopped them in their tracks and said, "Oh, so nice to see you. But please, at any other time."

I was very surprised and so was de Kooning. He and the others with him soon left. The artists from the show talked about it later. We said, "Wow, what a strange party!"

Now Mr. Tremaine had never met de Kooning, and probably didn't know him by sight, which was surprising because he had bought some of his paintings, but it was a shock to see de Kooning turned away. At that moment I thought, Something in the art world has definitely changed.

James Rosenquist began classes at New York's Art Students League in the fall of 1955. Two years later he painted his first New York City billboard, and a year after that he was working in Times Square. Since the early Sixties, Rosenquist's work has appeared in shows and permanent collections throughout the world. He is now "doing new paintings about changing star configurations into pigment," and is active in the artists' rights movement.★

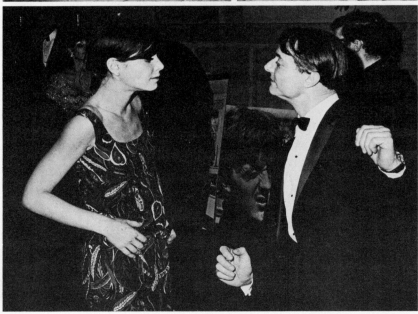

Three artists dancing, clockwise from top left: Robert Rauschenberg, James Rosenquist (both Bob Adelman); Roy Lichtenstein (John Cameola/Globe Photos). Opposite page, clockwise from top left: Claes Oldenburg (Dennis Hopper); Roy Lichtenstein and one of his comic-book heroines (Dennis Hopper); Blam by Lichtenstein (courtesy Sidney Janis Gallery); Warhol in the aluminum-foil bathroom at The Factory (Bob Adelman); Jean Tinguely, a Swiss "new realist" (Dennis Hopper). Overleaf: Rosenquist fitting into his painting Growth Plan, 1966 (Bob Adelman).

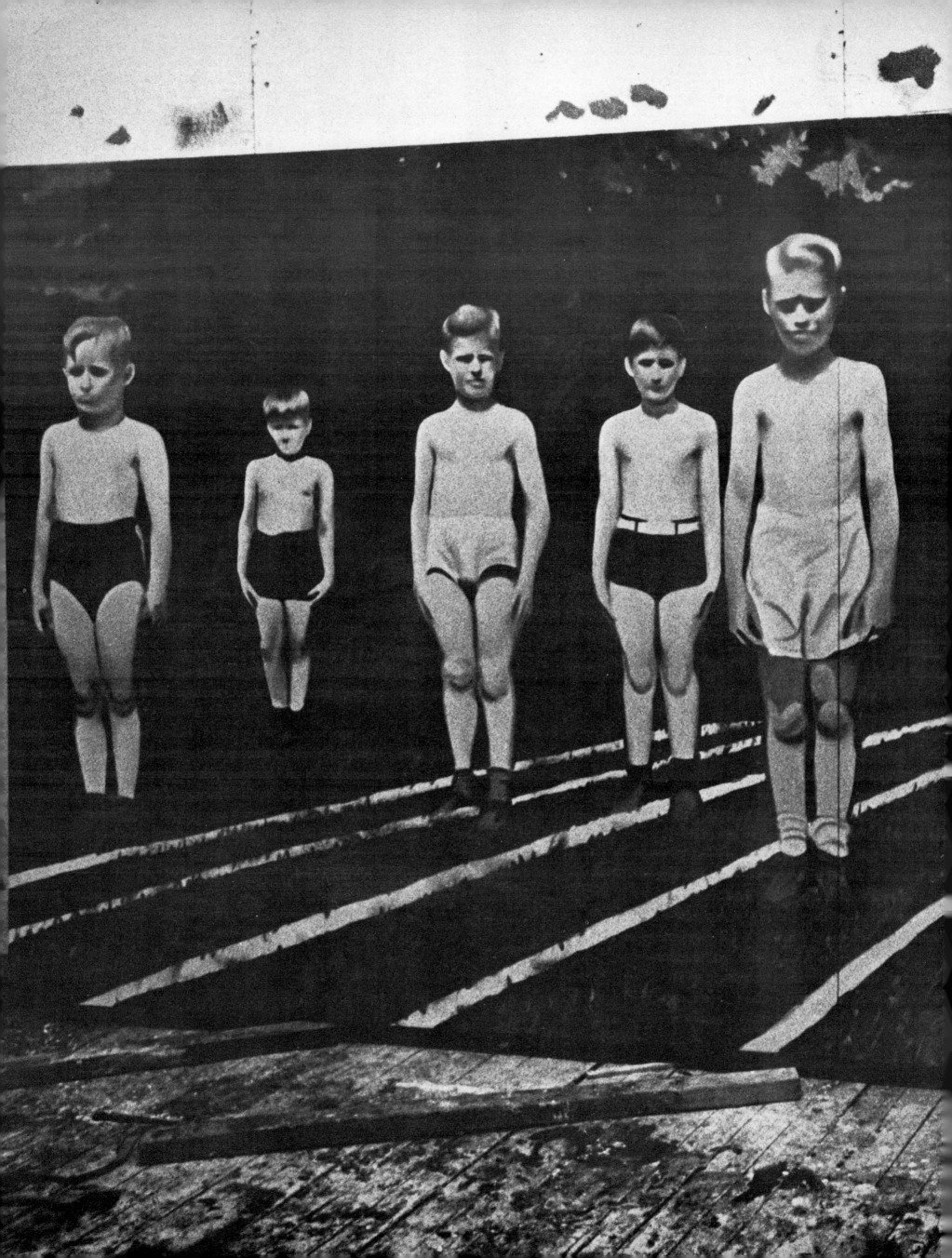

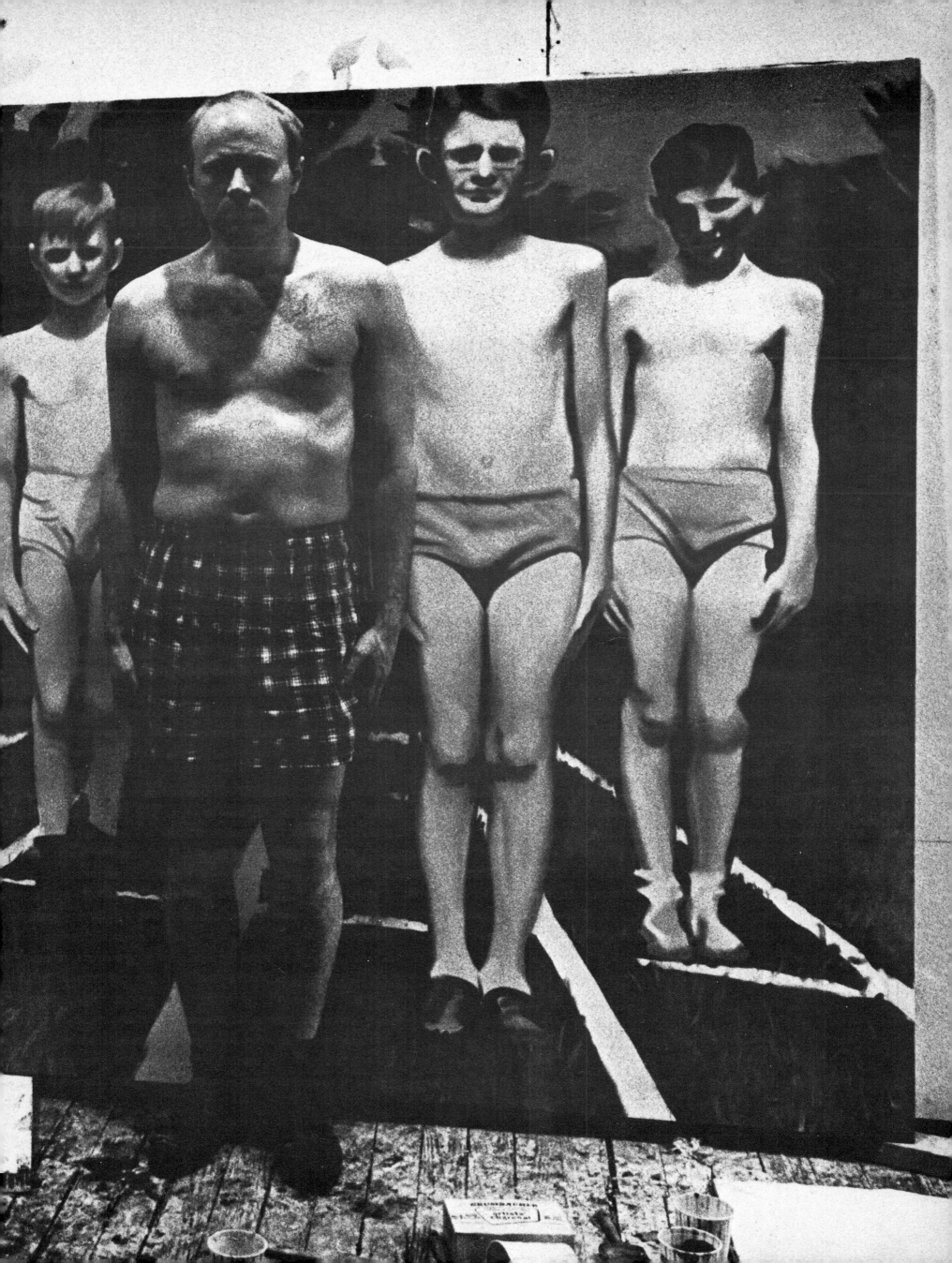

JAMES MEREDITH
The Soldier of Ole Miss

I had just left the Air Force and was attending Jackson State College, a black school, when I first wrote to the University of Mississippi. They had no idea who I was, and replied as they would to any student. Once I sent in my application with the required picture, they saw I was black. They sent me a telegram saying I had applied too late for the winter session. I wrote asking to be considered for the summer session, but received no response.

I finally wrote and accused them of not replying because of my race. Eventually they sent me a letter saying my application didn't meet their requirements. At the end of May I went to federal court and sued them.

To me, it wasn't the specific aim of going to school that mattered; that was just a tactical move. The bigger thing was the struggle between those who were in power and those who were not. I was fighting a war and this happened to be the particular point of battle that was chosen. My objective was to bust the legal system of white supremacy in Mississippi. The immediate objective was to break it at any point; it didn't matter which. Enrolling at the university seemed to be the point where I could gain the greatest support for my case. I was never involved in the civil rights movement. I was involved in a power struggle, to make me and my people a dominant force in the world. The timing of the so-called civil rights movement was coincidental.

I had nothing, no idealism. It was strictly a war game.

Thurgood Marshall, who headed the NAACP legal defense fund, accepted my case, and Constance Baker Motley was my attorney. I had some support from a student group at Jackson. But I never trusted anybody on the inside.

John Doar, later special counsel to the Nixon impeachment proceedings, was my liaison with the Justice Department. I never trusted them either, but I knew they had to uphold the law.

After a year of litigation the Supreme Court ordered the university to admit me. The U.S. marshals arranged for me to be out of Jackson during the week preceding my first attempt to enroll, supposedly for security. I spent the time at a naval air station in Tennessee, reading the newspapers. There was the rigamarole of riots and violence, but it wasn't important to me, and it didn't scare me. I knew that a change always made people react emotionally, that the violence was a necessary element in the change.

James Meredith, University of Mississippi graduate, 1963 (UPI).

When I tried to register in Oxford there were thousands of students outside, but no mobs inside the building. There were some officials, the Board of Trustees and big Governor Ross Barnett. He had issued an executive order relieving the registrar of the university of his duties and appointing himself registrar. He wanted to be the one refusing my entrance.

I went up to him as if I was going to register, but I knew that I wasn't going to. I presented Barnett with my papers. He presented me with a proclamation, signed and sealed by the state. "We have laws still in this state that say that blacks and whites are to be separated, it is the legal law of this land . . ." or something like that—I didn't read it. He made a little speech saying that as registrar of the university he was refusing to register me. But I knew that it was just a procedure, just a game, and I played my part.

I met Governor Ross Barnett for the second time at the state capital in Jackson. It was strictly a show, though nobody told me that. It was five days after my first attempt to enroll and the whole city seemed to be aware of what was going on. Barnett issued a statement declaring "I, Ross Barnett . . . acting under the police powers of the state . . . to preserve the peace and dignity of the State of Mississippi . . . denied to you . . .

Governor Ross Barnett at the Ole Miss campus during demonstrations shortly before Meredith's first attempt to enroll (Dan J. McCoy/Black Star).

Overleaf: Meredith flanked by U.S. marshals during enrollment. John Doar is at right (Charles Moore/Black Star).

admission to the University of Mississippi."

There were mobs of people outside, newspapers, television cameras, jeering crowds. In order for me to get through, Barnett had to order the state police to clear a path through the throng. The entire state legislature, 174 people, was jammed inside the building with Barnett. I was the only black man present. Barnett asked, "Who is James Meredith?" I stepped forward and played the game again.

I was not frightened. It was no different from any other day that I was engaged in war. It made me very aware that my skin was black, but I had no qualms about it. I was a soldier.

Governor Barnett was not all bad. The effect of his attitude was to keep all the attention focused on him, so that the people of Mississippi had no obligation to do anything except wait and see what he was going to do. A previous governor, Theodore Bilbo, incited the people, made them feel that the law was in their hands. It was like, "If you don't want a nigger to vote, then visit him in the morning, you understand?" Barnett was the opposite. He communicated the message "I will handle this, so you don't have to do anything."

The result was that there were no angry mobs in the black neighborhoods, no reports of thousands of blacks abused or killed. The focus was on Barnett.

I actually enrolled a week later, on Monday, October 1.

I flew into the Oxford airport on Sunday afternoon. Marshals met me and escorted me to the campus. The entire student body had caught the "Barnett Special" train to Jackson or found their own means of getting to the football game. We moved into Baxter Hall to spend the first night. I knew the atmosphere was tense, but I sensed that things basically were under control.

When the trouble started, I could not see or hear very much of it. I was awakened several times in the night by the noise and shooting outside as the students battled the marshals. But it was not near the hall and I had no way of knowing what was going on.

I woke up about six-thirty in the morning and looked out and saw the troops. President Kennedy had sent in the Army. There was a slight smell of tear gas in my room, but I still did not know what had gone on during the night. Some marshals came and told me how many people were hurt and killed.

I could never figure out whether my going to school was a point they lost, or if they were just engaging in symbolic opposition. I still don't know.

But even then I knew that there was only one force with a greater potential for violence that the State of Mississippi, and that was the United States government. The only way I was going to go to the University of Mississippi was to get a force on my side greater than the force opposed. The only real task for me was to get the U.S. government on my side, as simple as that. I tricked them, made them do in my behalf what I had not the power to do myself: exert more violent force than the state had the capacity to exert.

In 1966, James Meredith was shot in Hernando, Mississippi, as he led a voter-registration march. He recovered, graduated from Columbia Law School in 1968 and today lives in Jackson, Mississippi, where he practices law.★ (Wide World Photos)

LEE STRASBERG
Miss Monroe

Marilyn Monroe, student (Roy Schatt).

What I remember most is Marilyn Monroe in her first appearance as an actress in the Actors Studio. Live—not just on the screen. I was aware of Marilyn Monroe in the movies, and I enjoyed her, but got no sense of her. You got the glamour, of course, the lights and the makeup. But whenever I think of Miss Monroe, I always bemoan the fact that her audience was not able to see her in person. Because if you thought of her as being glamorous on the screen—the glamour on the stage was simply unbelieveable. It was as if she carried a camera and lights and everything with her.

Many, many people have often expressed a desire to leave Hollywood, which is a place to work but not necessarily a place to develop one's talents. Many people have stated that they are coming to Hollywood only for a certain purpose, and as soon as that's finished they will go back where they belong. Of all the people who have said this, Miss Monroe was the only one who did it—at the moment when she was having the most success in her career and the least personal satisfaction.

It was her contact with Elia Kazan and Arthur Miller—Mr. Kazan, more specifically—which brought her to the Actors Studio. Mr. Kazan told her to come work with me. And the interesting thing is that she did come, she did leave Hollywood, in spite of all the jokes—"will acting spoil Marilyn Monroe?" and that type of nonsense.

She would always sit in the corner of the Actors Studio—in the same seat. She would come sidling in so that nobody would notice. I must say that the people at the Actors Studio were not kind. That doesn't mean they were cruel people. But there was natural resentment, you see. Every actor, if he has any talent, believes or should believe that he belongs in the seat that the other person is sitting in. That was even stronger in the case of Miss Monroe, because they felt she was just a movie star. They knew that the stage was a different thing; nobody can cut out the bad parts, nobody can help you. You have to go on.

You can imagine what it was like for her. The place was quite filled, and she did a scene with Maureen Stapleton, who's no mean actress herself. They did a scene from *Anna Christie,* one of my favorites. Miss Monroe played the young prostitute who comes in looking for her father, and Miss Stapleton, the older woman, immediately sizes her up.

Now, it's very difficult to wipe Maureen off the stage; all you need to do is look at her now on television to know that nobody can completely wipe her off. But our attention was riveted on Miss Monroe. Her part

In class—Marilyn, left, and Strasberg, center front (Roy Schatt).

66

was emotionally deeper and her performance had extraordinary sensitivity. That's one reason she was so shy—she was aware of what you were thinking and feeling without your telling her.

She also did a scene from *Streetcar* with my son John. I must say that I had thought that it was a good scene for her to work on, but not to perform in front of the class—I didn't think she could give a sense of the character of Blanche. Oddly enough, it turned out to be *more* believable than any Blanche I'd ever seen. Miss Monroe's own natural sensuality and sexuality, together with the sensitivity which she created and conveyed on the stage, made you understand the woman almost more than the woman understood herself.

These two scenes live in my memory not just because they were memorable performances, but because it was such a tragedy that the audience and many of the people who became "experts" on Miss Monroe could not see these rare, rare moments. After the *Streetcar* scene, the people in the Actors Studio were very different towards her. There was still, naturally, the jealousy, but there was also a strange kind of respect for what they recognized as a talent that deserved to be there.

It's sad for me to remember that I once told her: "Whenever you are ready to be a member of the Actors Studio, write me a letter." Her position entitled her to it, and what we saw in the Actors Studio was almost like an audition. Just before she died, she did write me a letter, which she didn't sign. It was supposed to be delivered to me when she came to New York a few days later.

She stood for a whole kind of feminine sensitivity and sexuality. She was naive, not sophisticated in the intellectual sense, but in a flirtatious sense. Also, she had "experience" knowledge, and she always spoke out of that, never pretending to anything that she did not, herself, experience. That's very rare, and people found her very exciting to be with. These qualities keep her alive for so many people. They call her "Marilyn." If you say, "Marilyn who?" they look at you—there's some other Marilyn?

At the Actors Studio she was also "Marilyn," but in a different way. Once she was doing a scene with a young man, and they were supposed to rehearse. She called him up, and said, "This is Marilyn." The fellow said, "Marilyn who?" And she said, "You know, Marilyn. The girl from the class."

Lee Strasberg, president and artistic director of the Actors Studio, is responsible for the international acceptance of Method acting, making him the world's best-known acting teacher. His work with the Group Theatre and the Actors Studio has influenced the great performers of recent decades, among them: Marlon Brando, James Dean, Ellen Burstyn, Robert De Niro and Al Pacino.★ (Peter Basch/Globe Photos)

Above, left to right: Monroe in Bus Stop with Don Murray; in Marilyn; and with her second husband, Joe DiMaggio (all photos Photo Trends). Opposite page: the girl from the class (Photo Trends).

TOM HAYDEN
Writing the Port Huron Statement

Most of the people who came to form Students for a Democratic Society did so out of personal experiences rather than a political background. Students were beginning to feel that the university was an empty place. Conditions on campus like standardized dress and food and dormitory regulations brought it home. Concern was growing about the bomb and disarmament. A certain politicizing had arisen from Kennedy's inauguration of the Peace Corps. But most importantly, there was the civil rights movement.

Al Haber, an activist I had met in Ann Arbor, and I and others formed SDS into an information and support network for civil rights workers, though we also wanted to explore the whole question of human and economic rights in the context of a student movement.

We believed students could be the catalysts for change in the world. They were volunteering for the Peace Corps, they were the moving force in the civil rights movement, they were shaking up governments around the world. It seemed that students could awaken other classes of people to participate in the democratic process.

SDS president, Al Haber (courtesy Al Haber).

By early 1962, SDS had a National Executive Committee made up of about forty or fifty students and nonstudents from SDS chapters around the country. We decided to draw up a document that would express our ideas and our vision, and we planned a week-long meeting in June to debate and refine the first draft of that document. The meeting took place in Port Huron, Michigan, at an AFL-CIO camp. It was a logical spot because the League for Industrial Democracy was our parent organization, and we received our funding from liberal labor-union groups.

I was given the task of preparing the initial document. By then I was living in New York, in a small "railroad" apartment on West 22nd Street. I shared the place with three other people who tried to live normal lives while I locked myself in my room with stacks of books and articles. About a month before the meeting I began to write. Pages and pages, just knocking it out.

We took it to the Port Huron convention, which turned out to be a very euphoric communal experience. It was a beautiful setting, right on Lake Huron. We had one large meeting room, which could comfortably accommodate a plenary session, and there were lots of little cabins.

The work was very, very hard. There were about sixty people, and we worked all day and all night. One night I was so tired that I put my sleeping bag across the kitchen doorway so that the people walking over me to breakfast would force me to wake up.

To do the work we broke up into several groups—for instance, one on the question of values and another on the question of the economy. The groups would talk and argue and write and then come back with a redraft in substance that a later group would put into a better style and format. It was amazing. In five days we had a finished version.

The Port Huron Statement might not seem so radical today, but for 1962 it was a pretty advanced document. It began by stating the need for values rather than immediately offering political programs and making legislative demands. It broke with cold war ideology—we got into a lot of trouble with our liberal sponsors because we blamed the United States, not just Russia, for the arms race. It was the first major call for a focus on the neglected problems at home after a generation of cold war obsession.

We had a concept—participatory democracy—that enabled us to begin with immediate grievances and yet aim for more far-reaching changes, thus allowing us to be both reformist and revolutionary. It was a call to action when students wanted to take action. We asserted that students had a role in history at a time when parents and administrators treated us like children. The pride we stirred in students was important.

The people at Port Huron were a healthy group of human beings, healthier than many of the radicals of later years. I'm not sure why. I think it's partly because we were straight out of the mainstream. A few of the people were "red diaper babies," whose parents had been on the left in the Thirties, Forties and Fifties, but most of us were people whose background was apolitical and middle American. We were very natural and original. We had to be. We weren't following anybody; we weren't echoing anybody, we didn't speak out of rhetoric or abstraction. We spoke out of our experience.

We took a lot of heat from the old leftists who were still reliving battles between communists, Trotskyites, and social democrats from the Thirties. We thought they were totally incomprehensible. A lot of the socialists were more anticommunist than anything else. It wasn't a debate about ideas, really. There were two very different kinds of consciousness staring at each other, an uncomprehending conflict. It showed something that I've learned over and over again.

There's always a radical group that, once established, tries to control the gate through which all new ideas pass. We had to break through that. More than anything else, this situation created a sense of "them"—the old leftists—and "us." Now we were embattled. They—not the right wing—were trying to prevent the growth of a new radical force. The names they called us reinforced our new left identity. It got so bad that summer that twenty-five of us, living together in a few apartments, struggled to decide whether we were going to leave the parent organization, the LID, or negotiate and stay.

It was like reliving the Thirties. The LID people locked us out of our offices, summarily fired staff members, and cut off our funds. We finally broke away—our connection with LID became a formality. It was that positive communal experience at Port Huron, followed by this struggle for our own identity, that created such a sharp definition of ourselves. It's a unique experience to feel that you yourself are an agent of change. We felt "this is our destiny." Later generations couldn't feel that.

Tom Hayden's involvement with SDS began while he was a journalism student at the University of Michigan. Since then he has been a labor and antipoverty organizer, and an activist in the antiwar movement. One of the Chicago 8, he was tried in connection with the riots that occurred during the 1968 Chicago Democratic Convention. He and his codefendants were later cleared. Hayden is now a part of the Campaign for Economic Democracy, an organization that grew out of his 1976 U.S. Senate campaign.★

Hayden in the mid-Sixties (Alan Copeland).

NORA EPHRON
The Pill and I

I moved to New York in 1962, just graduated from Wellesley, suddenly embarked on a new life. I had to do something about birth control. I had just read *The Group*, so I knew that the Margaret Sanger clinic was this place that you could go to get birth control.

The clinic was in a brownstone on 16th Street. The reception room was small, and had a few white chairs and a little table at the front. There was a desk next to a stairway, staffed by a very austere nurse type who did not look like the kind of person who wanted to know you were single—which was ridiculous, of course, because you could've said you were a hooker and they would have given you a package of pills. But what did I know? I was so dopey that I told her I was engaged.

Taking the pill (Bob Fitch/Black Star).

I was escorted into a little room with about eight or ten other women. A nurse came in, carrying a very dignified-looking attaché case. She sat on the table in front of us and went "Click, click" to the case and it fell open. It was filled with this insane rubber relief of the inside of a lady. (I always wanted to find one of those; I'm sure you can buy them somewhere.)

Anyway, she opened it and explained the four methods of birth control that the clinic prescribed. She demonstrated three of them. First, she shot a little contraceptive cream into the attaché case. Next she inserted a diaphragm into the attaché case. It was fabulous. Finally, she inserted a coil into the attaché case. So I chose birth-control pills.

All I knew about the pill was that it had been tested on several thousand Puerto Rican women and not one of them had had a child in years. They contained a larger dose of estrogen than they do now, and they were also larger pills. Nobody was sure if they caused blood clots or prevented them, or if they caused breast cancer or prevented it. By now I've read almost everything written about them, and I still don't know much more than I did in the beginning. But it began a long and happy relationship between me and birth-control pills.

When I first started with the pill, I would stop taking them every time I broke up with someone. I had a problem making a commitment to sex; I guess it was a hangover from the whole Fifties virgin thing. The first man I went to bed with, I was in love with and wanted to marry. The second one I was in love with, but I didn't have to marry him. With the third one, I thought I *might* fall in love. It was impossible for me to think that I might be a person who "had sex," so whenever I had no boyfriend it was always a terrible emotional mess. I couldn't start sleeping with someone until I could begin the pill's cycle again. It was awful. Finally, my new gynecologist explained it all to me: "Dahlink, who knows what's coming around the corner?"

Nora Ephron is a contributing editor of Esquire *magazine, and is the author of* Wallflower at the Orgy *and* Crazy Salad.★

Nora Ephron's college yearbook picture, 1962 (courtesy Nora Ephron).

JIM BOUTON
A Rookie in the World Series

I wasn't surprised to be in the World Series against San Francisco. We were the Yankees and we expected to be in the World Series. But it was really exciting for me—my first time in the big leagues—being escorted in the morning from the hotel to the ball park by police with sirens, roaring through the town, passing red lights, like we were chiefs of state or something.

I remember being very much in awe of the other players, because they were all very famous—a whole team of famous players: Mickey Mantle and Roger Maris, Elston Howard, Whitey Ford, Bobby Richardson, Tony Kubek, Bill Skowron and me, little old me. I walked around a lot with a stupid grin on my face, and I enjoyed calling my teammates by their nicknames in conversations with my old friends. I'd say, "The other day, Whitey was saying to me . . . then the Mick said . . ." It was fun to be able to talk about them like that.

There were three of us who were new to the team that year: me, Phil Linz and Joe Pepitone. We definitely didn't know our place. Rookies are supposed to be seen and not heard; we were seen and heard plenty. After a while, guys like Bill Skowron would comment about our clothes or hair or something. Once Skowron made a crack at Pepitone and Pepitone said, "Buzz off, buster, I'll have your job by the end of the year."

Left to right: Roger Maris, John Blanchard, Elston Howard, manager Ralph Houk, Ralph Terry and Yogi Berra celebrate the Yankees' 1961 American League pennant victory (courtesy N.Y. Yankees).

When we won the pennant, the three of us ran around like maniacs, pouring champagne on each other. We figured that was what you were supposed to do. The veterans were more blasé about the whole thing. They were worried that we would splash some of it on them. Their big concern with the Series was getting enough tickets for their families.

Opposite page: Whitey Ford, starting pitcher in three of the 1962 World Series games (UPI).

The '62 Series was a closely fought battle. The Yankees were ahead 3–2 going into the sixth game. Then it began to rain. And it rained. For three days—everybody was starting to build an ark—that's how much it rained. After it finally stopped, the Giants tied up the Series 3–3.

The night before the tie-breaking seventh game, San Francisco fans yelled and chanted outside our hotel, trying to keep us up. Whitey Ford had gotten a sore arm, and I was being considered to replace him in the pitching rotation. But the rain gave Ralph Terry, our best pitcher that year, a chance to rest, so Ralph pitched the seventh game instead of me.

It would have been pretty exciting for a young kid to pitch in a World Series his first year up. It would've been tremendous. But in a way I was almost as glad that I didn't pitch. It was a one-run, low-scoring game, and I'm not sure that I would have won. I really didn't want to lose the seventh game of the World Series on national TV. Also, if I lost, the Yankees might decide that I wasn't Yankee material.

Before the game, I was so excited that I walked to the wrong bullpen. I saw all these Giant uniforms and I made an abrupt U-turn and ran across the field to my own bullpen. The players in the dugout saw me and hollered, "You're in San Francisco, rook!" I needed a tag on me—"This man's name is Jim Bouton. If he gets lost, send him to the Yankee bullpen."

I finally found my way. I sat on the bench with Ralph Terry—one of the few Yankee veterans who was really nice to the rookies. The fans were making a lot of noise. There were 40,000 people there, with a band playing in the stands, but Ralph didn't even look nervous. I was excited and smiling to myself. I looked over at him, and I said, "Hey, you know something, Ralph? Whether we win or lose today, this is a lot of fun." He said, "Yeah, sure it is." And that's exactly how I felt. It was just fun to be there.

The game was close going into the bottom of the ninth. We were ahead 1–0, the Giants had two outs and runners on second and third. Willie McCovey was hitting against Ralph Terry. He looked like he was going to tee off, and he did—he rifled a tremendous shot right to second baseman Bobby Richardson. Our hearts sank. It was one of those moments when you're terrified and thrilled in the same second. Terrified when I saw McCovey swing and heard the crack of the bat, thrilled when I saw it go right into Richardson's glove for the last out. We ran from the bullpen, the players swarmed out of the dugout, and we carried Ralph off the field on our shoulders.

The locker room was a madhouse—with a lot more reporters than players. The famous players were mobbed by press. Terry was twelve people deep. Champagne was flowing over people's heads. I was giving interviews to journalists from Japan and Australia—they interviewed anyone with a Yankee uniform. The veteran Yankees were taking champagne bottles and putting them in their coats. They'd been through this before; some of them had lived through ten World Series victories in sixteen years. To them, it was just another day. There were angry that it had to go seven games, so they couldn't get back to hunting or fishing or whatever they did in their off-season.

Every time a team wins the World Series, they get a gift—a World Series ring or trinket like that. Some of these guys had so many rings that they began to insist on bracelets, silver service sets—they were running out of ideas. Yogi Berra had rings for every member of his extended family. One more World Series victory and the baseball commissioner was going to have to build them a garage to hold all their World Series loot.

Jim Bouton spent six years with the Yankees, winning twenty-one games during his second year with the club and playing in two World Series. He worked as a sportscaster from 1970 to 1974, wrote a book called Ball Four *and starred briefly in a TV series based on its story. He is presently getting his pitching arm ready for another season of baseball.★ (courtesy N.Y. Yankees)*

Opposite page, clockwise from top: the Yankees' heavy artillery, left to right, Roger Maris, Yogi Berra, Mickey Mantle and Bill Skowron (Bob Olen/N.Y. Yankees); catcher Elston Howard; Tony Kubek, shortstop; second baseman Bobby Richardson (all courtesy N.Y. Yankees); center: Ralph Houk with Mickey Mantle (Photo Trends).

VICTOR MARCHETTI
The Missile Crisis at the CIA

I was working in the Office of Current Intelligence, one of the CIA's research and analysis centers, and had been watching Cuba for some time. We were distressed by its growing military capabilities and the economic assistance which the Soviets were providing, yet we would have argued against the Bay of Pigs invasion, but nobody asked our advice until it was too late. Now the Cuban government was convinced that the United States was intent on destroying it. It was my opinion that Castro was not a communist, but was being driven into the arms of the Soviet Union by the ham-handed activities of the Kennedy Administration.

Our office first became aware of an unprecedented military build-up in Cuba during the summer of 1962. Various technical and research methods (none of which, incidentally, bore any similarity to Leon Uris' spy novel *Topaz*) indicated that there were frequent shipments of arms to Cuba. The Air Force and the Navy photographed ships sailing from Soviet military ports to confirm the analysis.

Another fellow and I had invented an esoteric art we called "crate-ology"—*crate* as in large boxes. Nobody had any faith in it except us, but we could examine photographs of crates and make pretty good estimates of what was inside. We thought there were bombers, torpedo boats and the like being delivered by Soviet ships.

For more than a year the Warhawks in the Pentagon had been screaming that there were missiles in Cuba. They were hysterical and deliberately manipulated information to justify action against Castro. At the time the charges were false, and I spent at least half of each day disproving them.

But by the latter part of August, we became quite disturbed by the military build-up, so we began writing top-secret reports to the director of the agency. We said that we'd never seen anything comparable and that we didn't know what it meant. As far as we could tell, the equipment was largely defensive—land armaments, motor torpedo boats and fighter aircraft—but some of the weapons could be considered offensive, like the Ilyushin bombers.

Ironically, the Warhawks remained strangely unexcited, and Pentagon agencies like the National Security Agency and the Defense Intelligence Agency began publishing evaluations contradicting our findings. They claimed that the assistance being shipped to Cuba was largely for agricultural and economic purposes. Their position was ridiculous in view of the facts. We were watching entire boatloads of young Soviets arriving in Cuba wearing only two kinds of sport shirts; it smelled of an unsophisticated Soviet attempt to introduce military personnel.

Fortunately for us, John McCone, then director of the agency, saw some value in our reports. He was briefed and our arcane art of crate-ology was explained and he accepted it as a valuable analytic tool. However, when McCone requested briefings from the crate-ologists, the CIA hierarchy raised its ugly head. Instead of reporting directly to McCone, I had to brief one of my superiors and he would report to McCone. He would be ushered into McCone's office while I waited outside. Every time McCone had a question my boss would run out, get my answer and then run back in. But because of our reports McCone began to suspect the unthinkable.

In 1962 no reasonable person believed that the Soviets would introduce nuclear missiles into Cuba. We had them outgunned ten to one in strategic strike capabilities. We had the Polaris submarine, the B-52 bomber armed with hound-dog missiles, and a huge ICBM advantage. Khrushchev was under pressure from his political opponents and the Soviet hawks to do something about this imbalance. He didn't want to waste too much money on military hardware, so he hit on a scheme that would help him bridge the missile gap quickly and cheaply. If he could slip shorter-range missiles, like the ones we had in Italy and Turkey, into Cuba, he could double his strike capability. He would still be outgunned, but he would be more of a threat.

By September, the first U-2 reports came back. They showed seven or eight surface-to-air missile sites being built in Cuba. The interesting thing about the sites was their pattern. Instead of ringing Havana or Cienfuegos in the usual defensive manner, they were spread over a large area. It was a puzzle that we, as analysts of Soviet military activity, couldn't quite figure out. McCone was the first to voice an answer. He said that if the Soviets were creating an area, and not a point, defense, then they were readying the whole island as a strike base against the United States—whether it be by missile, submarine or bomber.

It was hurricane season and for a couple of weeks clouds covered the island. The U-2s and other photographic reconnaissance were of no use, and we had no idea what was happening. The White House wanted answers, so the *crème de la crème* of the CIA and other intelligence agencies prepared a report on the situation. In essence they said that, yes, the situation in Cuba is serious and possibly very dangerous, but they did not believe that the Soviets would be so foolish as to install offensive nuclear weapons.

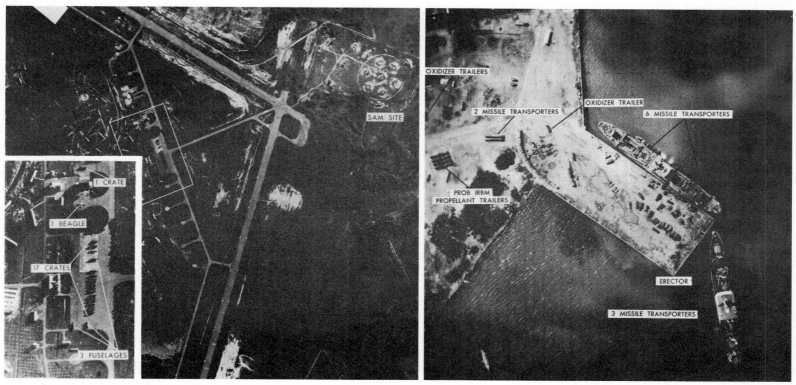

*O**pposite page: A crate-laden Soviet ship (U.S. Navy).
Above: aerial photos of Russian arms deliveries and military
installations in Cuba (left: Photo Trends; right: U.S. Navy).*

In the meantime, we crate-ologists began to notice a new type of vessel making arms deliveries to Cuba. These were "large hatch" ships with huge holds beneath their decks. The Soviets had been carrying their bulk military cargo on deck, which meant we could identify it, but now the decks were relatively clear. Despite their attempt at subterfuge, they underestimated our analytical capabilities. A few things were left on deck. We would eventually associate them with the delivery of strategic missiles and realize that the missiles themselves had been hidden in the holds.

When the cloudy weather broke, the U-2 flights resumed. They brought back clinching evidence. We saw sites, like at San Cristobal, still in the early stages of development, but which we could confidently identify as field missiles sites. We acquired corroborating information from other technical sources and the background reports of Colonel Oleg Penkovsky, an officer in the Soviet army and a spy for the West. Then we saw the arrival of the equipment necessary to support the sites: fuel propellant trucks and rings used for firing purposes. They were building into a ready position.

There was no longer any doubt that Cuba was to be a base for strategic missiles. The entire United States, except for a small corner of northwest Washington State, was vulnerable. It was still a week before the actual crisis erupted, when Kennedy declared that we would not tolerate the introduction of offensive weapons into Cuba.

The Soviets denied everything, but we watched them hide their Ilyushin bombers in the mountains and their "large hatch" ships kept coming. Then we saw a couple of very strange-looking ships set sail for Cuba and some inexplicable construction begin at the Havana harbor. We soon concluded that the ships were carrying nuclear warheads and that the harbor was preparing to receive them. We were getting close to panic time.

The Soviets continued to play innocent and the week of secret meetings commenced in Washington. Kennedy and his closest advisers were locked in, trying to determine our options.

By this time we were working in the war room at the CIA. To enter you had to press a certain combination of buttons at the door. Inside it looked much like it does in the movies. Huge wall maps monitored the traffic in the Caribbean. We received information and analyzed it as fast as it came in. People were scurrying around trying to put it all together, and the big bosses were running in and out to find out what was going on. There were calls from the director: "Where do we stand now?" The Soviets were proceeding with their plans.

My fellow crate-ologist and I were taking turns manning the war room, and we became worried. We had concluded that we were on the brink of a war and would be incinerated as soon as those missiles reached Washington, D.C. We told our families to load up a station wagon full of necessities, and if they didn't receive a call from us at a certain time every night, they were supposed to drive north to Pennsylvania. The area is heavily strip-mined and looks like it has already been bombed. At least they would be safe.

We were in the war room when Kennedy announced the blockade; the atmosphere was quite depressing. We could literally watch its success or failure on the maps on the wall.

There was a deafening silence as we watched the first ship approach the blockade. It was Romanian and we knew it was innocent, carrying no arms. But anything could have happened. The Navy handled it well, under strict orders from the White House. Instead of seizing the ship, there was a polite exchange in which the Navy requested permission to board and check the manifest. Then the ship was allowed to pass.

The real scare came hours later. We were watching the progress of a group of ships that we suspected were carrying warheads. The atmosphere tensed as they sailed closer. Suddenly they slowed and then went dead in the water. We didn't know if this was temporary or permanent, but we deduced they were receiving instructions from Moscow. Then one turned about-face. We knew then it wasn't going to run the blockade. You could hear the sighs of relief. Another ship turned in its tracks. Kennedy had called Khrushchev's bluff.

After leaving the CIA in 1969, Victor Marchetti wrote The CIA and the Cult of Intelligence *with John Marks, and a fictionalized version of life at the CIA called* Rope-Dancer. *He continues as a critic of the CIA and an advocate of reform in the intelligence-gathering profession.*★ *(Stanley Tretick/People Weekly © Time Inc.)*

1963

CALENDAR

January: 2 *UPI reports that 30 Americans have died in Vietnam combat;* **7** *First-class mail costs 5¢; Travels with Charley is best-selling nonfiction and Fail-Safe and Seven Days in May are one and two on fiction list;* **8** *France loans the Mona Lisa for exhibit in Washington;* **11** *Whiskey-a-Go Go in Los Angeles is America's first discotheque;* **22** *English version of Solzhenitsyn's* One Day in the Life of Ivan Denisovich *introduces him to American readers;* **28** *Last holdout, South Carolina, peacefully begins school desegregation.*

February: 9 *"Hey Paula" takes chart lead as "You've Really Got a Hold On Me" enters Top Ten;* **11** *Julia Child debuts as* The French Chef; **19** *Publication of* The Feminine Mystique; **25** *Supreme Court reverses South Carolina riot conviction, declaring that states cannot legislate against peaceful protest.*

March: 1 *Major civil rights groups coordinate Mississippi voter-registration drive;* **18** *Supreme Court rules poor are entitled to free counsel;* **20** *American socialite Hope Cooke weds Sikkim's crown prince;* **21** *U.S. closes Alcatraz prison;* **28** *Film release of Hitchcock's* The Birds; **30** *Chiffons top chart with "He's So Fine."*

April: 2 *Martin Luther King spearheads massive assault on Birmingham, Alabama, segregation;* **8** *Best-film Oscar to* Lawrence of Arabia; **10** *USS* Thresher *and crew lost in first nuclear sub disaster;* **27** *"I Will Follow Him" is number one single, with "Baby Workout" climbing both pop and R&B charts;* **30** *McDonald's has sold more than one billion 15¢ hamburgers.*

May: 4 *Beach Boys come to prominence as* Surfin' U.S.A. *enters LP chart;* **18** *"If You Wanna Be Happy" leads pop chart;* **27** *Harvard fires Richard Alpert for his LSD experiments and dismisses Timothy Leary at semester's end;* **29** *James Bond first comes to the movie screen in* Dr. No.

June: 1 *"It's My Party" jumps into chart lead;* **5** *Britain's war secretary John Profumo resigns amid sex scandal;* **11** *Buddhist monk sets himself afire to protest religious persecution in South Vietnam;* **12** *The lavishly produced, long-awaited* Cleopatra *premieres; civil rights worker*

T*op to bottom: Baez and Dylan (USIA); JFK in Berlin (JFK Library); blacks and whites join hands during the March on Washington (John A. Kouns); Joseph Valachi, holding glass, at the Senate hearings on organized crime (Wide World Photos). Opposite page: John Kennedy campaigning for the presidency that ended in his assassination (Photo Trends).*

Medgar Evers is murdered; **17** *First woman in space is Russian Valentina Tereshkova;* **20** *California courts label Lenny Bruce a narcotics addict;* **21** *Election of Pope Paul VI follows the death of John XXIII;* **26** *JFK delivers his "Ich bin ein Berliner" speech at the Berlin Wall;* **28** *First American publication of* Fanny Hill *triggers numerous antiobscenity suits;* **29** *Peter, Paul and Mary make Dylan's "Blowin' in the Wind" a commercial success.*

July: 1 *Postal zip code goes into use; James Baldwin's* The Fire Next Time *leads nonfiction list;* **20** *"Surf City" is first surfing song to reach number one.* **26-28** *Newport Folk Festival crowd hails Bob Dylan, Joan Baez, Pete Seeger and Phil Ochs.*

August: 2 *Elephant jokes are the rage;* **5** *U.S., Russia and Great Britain sign first nuclear test ban treaty;* **9** *President Kennedy's second son dies two days after premature birth;* **28** *Rev. King's "I have a dream" speech concludes the March on Washington;* **30** *U.S.-U.S.S.R. hot line is installed;* **31** *"My Boyfriend's Back" supersedes Stevie Wonder's "Fingertips—Pt. 2" as top single.*

September: 7 *Freewheelin' is Dylan's first LP chart entry;* **15** *Church bombing in Birmingham kills four black girls;* **27** *Joseph Valachi tells Senate crime hearings about "Cosa Nostra."*

October: 6 *Sandy Koufax leads Dodger four-game sweep of World Series;* **7** *Bobby Baker, an LBJ protégé, resigns government post amid charges of influence peddling;* **12** *"Sugar Shack" and "Be My Baby" head chart;* **21** The Group *is best-selling novel.*

November: 2 *South Vietnamese President Ngo Dinh Diem and his brother are killed in coup;* **16** *"Deep Purple" tops pop chart;* **19** Look *magazine spotlights innovative education at Summerhill;* **20** *American military personnel in Vietnam number 16,800;* **22** *John F. Kennedy is assassinated in Dallas;* **24** *Jack Ruby kills alleged assassin Lee Harvey Oswald;* **29** *President Johnson appoints Warren Commission.*

December: 2 *Nonfiction best seller is Jessica Mitford's* The American Way of Death; **4** *Ecumenical Council votes to permit the use of vernacular in Catholic mass;* **7** *Singing Nun's "Dominique" tops chart with "Louie Louie" second.*

DAVID HALBERSTAM
The War Will Be Over by Christmas

I was the *New York Times* man in Vietnam. A typical day in Saigon would begin about 3 A.M., when I'd fly out of the city to an operation in the Mekong Delta. At 4 A.M., breakfast would be served in Tan Son Nhut airport. The thought of combat always cut my hunger, so I would only be able to manage a cup of that terrible Army coffee. At five, the sun would come up. How beautiful the farmland was: the rice paddies, the water buffalo, the ducks, orange and coconut trees. Horst Faas, the great AP photographer, once said that it was like a page out of the Bible, and it really was.

Suddenly, I'd be landing in a helicopter, hurled into the war. People would be shooting, running, trying to find cover. I'd have no idea where the fire was coming from. It was terrifying, feeling so naked. I'd run out of the helicopter and into the paddy for cover. I always remember the first splash of landing. We'd be spinning, it would be hard to get footing, my mouth would always be so dry. I'll never forget how breathless I was, how my heart pounded and how parched my throat was. Once I'd come out of cover, I'd never know if there'd be fighting or merely a hot walk in the sun. I'd never know if or when I might be hit. I will never forget that fear.

At four o'clock the operation would be over. I'd return to Saigon for an incredible French meal. It was a goddamn eerie world, yet somehow romantic. Behind us always was the sense of some darkness to come.

When I first came to the country in 1962, I felt the American policy was probably worth pursuing. I wasn't an ideologue, but I thought that the country would be better off without Communism than with. Years later, researchers at Columbia University asked me which intellectuals influenced me on Vietnam. "Hell," I answered, "I was a twenty-eight-year-old kid, catapulted out of a helicopter into the war—to find out it didn't work."

Halberstam, left, with colleagues Neil Sheehan, right, and Malcolm Browne in Vietnam (courtesy David Halberstam).

There is a wonderful story about my predecessor, Homer Bigart, going down to the same area in the delta with Neil Sheehan, the reporter who later broke the Pentagon Papers. Homer is probably the greatest correspondent of our time, and they were covering what was supposed to be several days of famous victories. The American PIOs had really laid it on. They watched the first operation go fairly well: a few VC were killed.

But the second operation wasn't at all successful, and the third day they watched the ARVN do nothing at all. An obvious fraud. On the way back with Homer, Neil, who was only twenty-five and pea-green, gnashed his teeth, mumbled and snarled. Finally Homer said, "Mr. Sheehan, Mr. Sheehan, what is the matter? Are you disturbed?"

Sheehan mumbled that it seemed a waste.

"What do you mean, Mr. Sheehan, that it is a waste of time?" asked Homer.

"Well, you know," answered Neil, "three days down here and no story."

"No story, Mr. Sheehan? What do you mean no story? There is a story: It doesn't work. That's your story."

That's what we were finding out. We had been sent out to cover something—victory in a very small war—and it wasn't there. Even when the ARVN could muster up a few victories with the help of the bright new American equipment, they'd kill maybe a hundred VC. We'd hear that the VC had been wiped out of the area. Then I'd talk to a very honest American, who'd say, "There's no victory at all."

"Why? Haven't the VC been routed?"

Opposite page: a Vietnamese woman whose U.S. field medical card reads "extensive wounds to forehead and eye" (© Philip Jones Griffiths/Magnum). Overleaf: a GI in a "liberated" Saigon home during the recapture of that city after a North Vietnamese attack, 1968 (© Philip Jones Griffiths/Magnum).

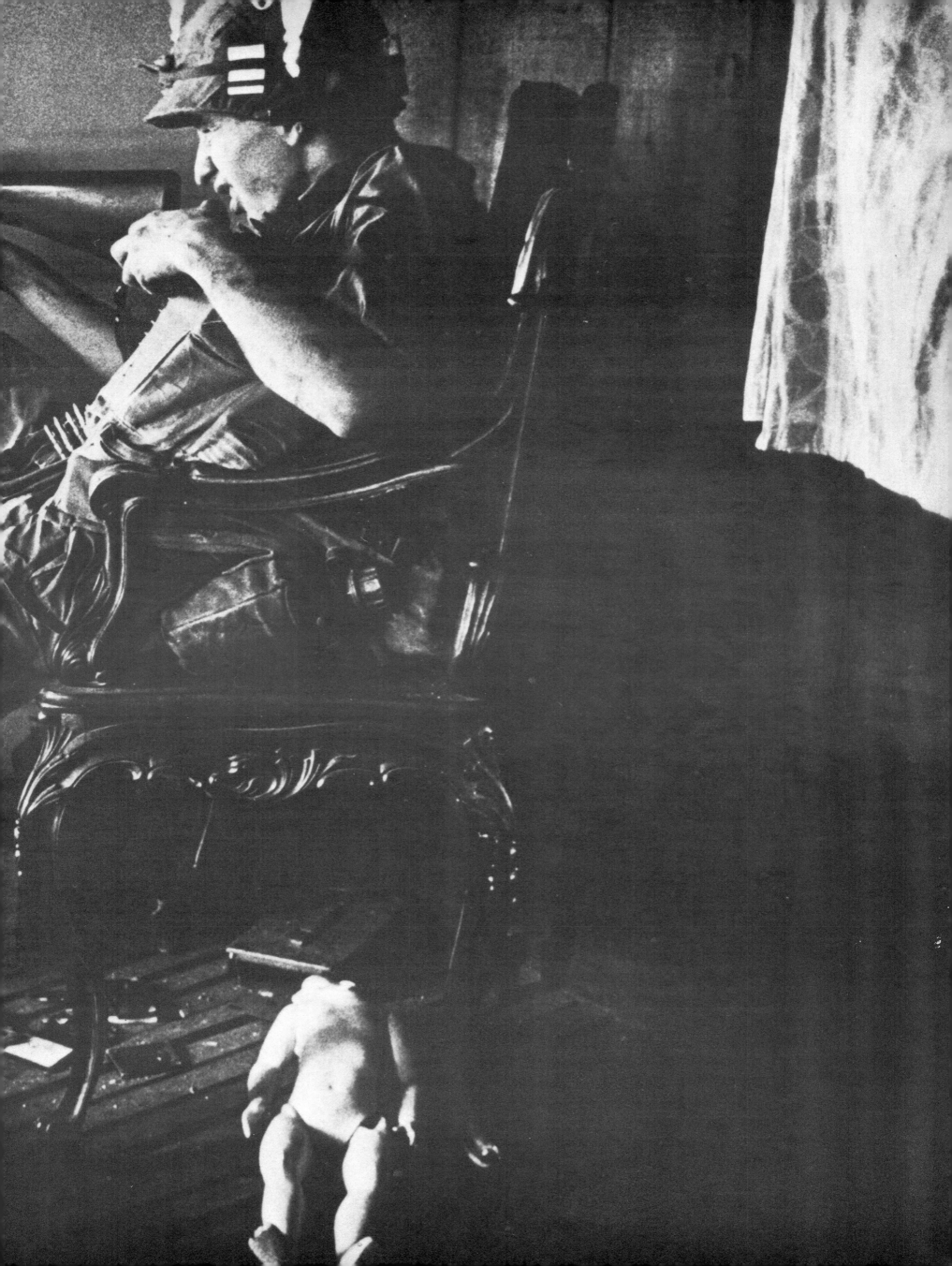

"No. We've killed a thousand, and they've recruited a thousand."

And that's exactly what it was all about. I began to get a sense of what so few American generals and officials were seeing. We were fighting the birth rate of the society. We could kill them, but they would replenish themselves. The Americans and their proxies had a kind of military superiority, but the VC had a total political superiority. They were the descendants of the men who had fought the French out of the country, and the ARVN were the people who had either stood on the sidelines or fought with the French. This is the crucial factor. Most ARVN high officials were former French corporals who represented the upper class. They had contempt for the peasants and spoke French as a first language, and if they'd been

trained at all, they'd been trained by the French or the Americans.

On the other side was the VC commissar. He'd been fighting in that area, spoke a local dialect, and was one of the peasants. He understood them, understood their grievances. And he had been fighting a revolutionary war for twenty years—always on the winning side.

At this time in the American war effort it was very radical to write that the war wasn't working. The *Times* was uneasy about it. They kept wishing our sources would identify themselves. Why won't your colonels identify themselves? I found a number of good people who would talk to me, but with discretion. I worked at an obvious disadvantage: anyone who wanted to make a pro-government statement about how the war was going on would be delighted to be quoted by name. No one else would.

Late in 1962 General Harkins of the Military Assistance Command in Vietnam met with McNamara. "Everything is going to be okay," he reported. "We'll have it over by Christmas."

McNamara asked if there were any problems. Harkins answered: "The only problem I have is with the American press."

It was always that way. The American ambassador, Fritz Nolting, a pleasant, mediocre, miscast man, once flew into a terrific rage at me. I kept saying that it wasn't working. "Mr. Halberstam," he began,

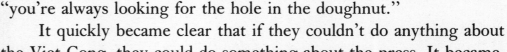

"you're always looking for the hole in the doughnut."

It quickly became clear that if they couldn't do anything about the Viet Cong, they could do something about the press. It became, to an uncommon degree, a public relations war: if enough high-ranking officials were flown out and said in interviews at the airport that it was going well, then the war would be going well. The public would sit in Washington and read that so-and-so said the war was going well and believe it. It was a bullshit machine, semi-automatic, incredible.

Neil and I used to cover these press conferences together. As a new State Department type would declare, "We see the light at the end of the tunnel . . ." Neil would nudge me and whisper, "Another foolish Westerner come to lose his reputation to Ho Chi Minh."

I began filing negative stories within three months of my arrival. I was wary of being too pessimistic, but everything that I saw on the field reinforced my worst fears. The day after New Year's, 1963, the battle at Ap Bac took place. That was the first time all the factors I'd been writing about came to a head: the failure to fight; the pillow-punching staged operations; the fraud; the bad leadership. Everything that was wrong in the country was present in the defeat.

I seized on the battle at Ap Bac. You could only write so many stories on how the wily VC got away again, but Ap Bac was a real battle. The ARVN had a whole VC battalion cornered on three sides. American fighter-bombers, armed helicopters, armored personnel carriers were everywhere.

At three o'clock, the ARVN commander had the chance to close off the fourth side by bringing in a reinforcement, but we suddenly saw that he had deliberately left the VC an escape valve. Instead of bringing

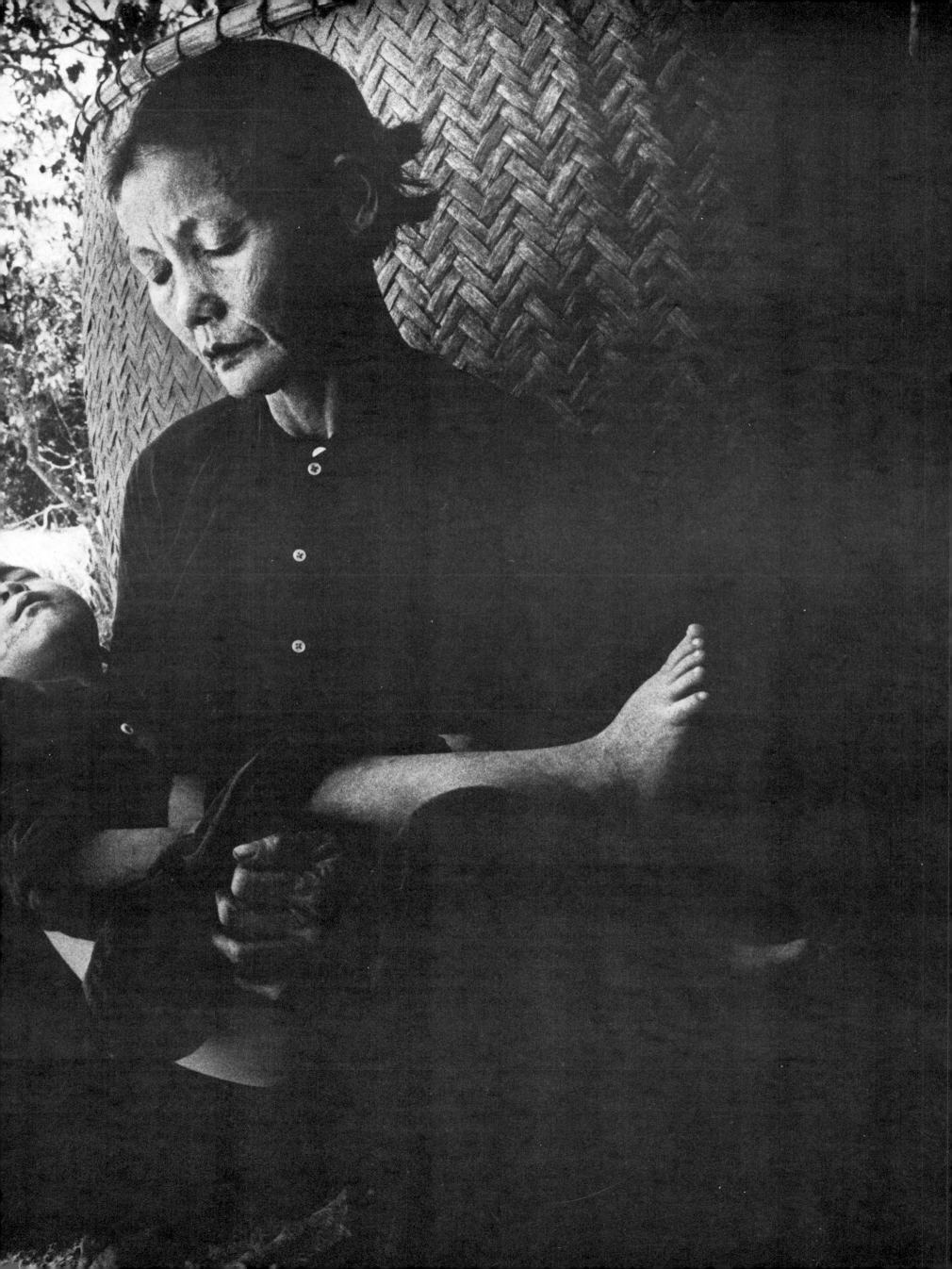

on the troops, he deliberately allowed the VC an exit route, and they were able to get out by nightfall. In the meantime, the VC had fought furiously. They'd shot down five American helicopters and killed three American and many Vietnamese soldiers. An entire ARVN armored brigade stood by, afraid to charge across the paddy field toward the tree line. They just wouldn't do it. They refused their commands.

The next day I ran into General Harkins at the site. "Gentlemen," he addressed a few reporters, "this is a great victory. We have them in a trap, and we're just about to spring it." The enemy was long gone and the ARVN were killing their own men by blind shelling. I'll never forget it . . . "A great victory." I never knew whether he believed it or was lying.

This caused some problems for us with our colleagues, not just with the foolish, hawkish ones like Joe Alsop who were always wrong—it was literally a matter of faith for him to be wrong—but with decent, intelligent, honorable men who stayed in Washington and saw the war through the prism of Washington events. They simply could not believe that the government would lie. Not the American government they knew. This was true of many editors—it was almost a generational problem.

Neil Sheehan, Charley Mohr and Mert Perry (both of whom quit *Time* because their editors did not accept their version of reality), Peter Arnett, Mal Browne: we were quite embattled. We needed to be one another's friends; we sure had enough enemies. We were embattled with the American mission. With people like Harkins who sent CID investigators after our sources. With our colleagues. With the U.S. government in Washington. President Kennedy tried to get Punch Sulzberger to pull me out because of my stories, and Lyndon Johnson used to tell other reporters not to be like Neil and me because we were traitors to our country.

We had huge battles merely for access to the front. The American embassy had arranged a waiting list to get on the helicopters, and sometimes we had to wait up to three weeks. Neil and I started taking taxis to the war. You could pay a Saigon cabdriver 150 piasters and he would drive you to the battle area in his beat-up Buick or Chevrolet.

I wasn't disillusioned, partly because I had few illusions. I just thought that the people in charge, like Harkins and Nolting, weren't very good or honest. I didn't think of it as an American failure. I hadn't yet traced it all back—saying that Harkins wasn't very good because McNamara and Taylor weren't very good; Nolting wasn't very good because Rusk and Kennedy weren't very good. I did not yet see the Mission as an extension of American politics. I believed then that if we told the truth, people would listen. I wasn't sophisticated enough to know that they weren't telling the truth out there because they did not want to hear the truth.

* * * *

I have a young friend named Brendan Smith. Once, about 1970, when he was around seven, I wore a tie made out of camouflage material to his house. Brendan looked at it and asked me: "Were you in the war?"

For my generation, being in the war always meant World War II. That was a real war, and ours was a kid's war. I thought about it and I thought of those years in Saigon, all those struggles, and I said, "Yes, I was in the war."

In 1962, David Halberstam became the New York Times *correspondent in Vietnam after fifteen months of reporting on the war in the Congo. In 1964 he won a Pulitzer Prize for his coverage of the war in Vietnam, and with Neil Sheehan and Malcolm Browne, he received the Louis M. Lyons award for reporting "the truth as they saw it in Vietnam . . . without yielding to unrelenting pressure." His many books and articles include* The Making of a Quagmire *(1965) and* The Best and the Brightest *(1972). He is currently working on* The Powers That Be, *a book about the rise of modern media in America.★ (Waring Abbott/Photo Trends)*

Opposite page: A Marine in Hue, after the Tet Offensive, 1968 (McCullin/Magnum). Overleaf: comrades-in-arms, left to right, Lieutenant General Chae Myung Shin, commander of Korean forces in Vietnam, General William Westmoreland, commander of U.S. forces in Vietnam, 1964–1968, and Lieutenant General Nguyen Huu Co, South Vietnam's deputy premier, before his dismissal on charges of corruption (© Philip Jones Griffiths/Magnum).

RALPH ABERNATHY
Martin Luther King's Dream

The day of the March on Washington was a mammoth occasion. The coordinators had worked very hard; as a result, more than a quarter of a million people were gathered in front of the Lincoln Memorial to ask for jobs. It was a summer day, so bright and sunny that people removed their shoes and splashed in the pool in front of the memorial.

All the early keynote speakers spoke beautifully. A. Philip Randolph of the Pullman Porter's Union, Whitney Young of the Urban League, John Lewis of SNCC, Roy Wilkins of the NAACP, Bayard Rustin of CORE and I all contributed. The audience was totally integrated; people who were poor and middle class and rich were together in one massive body. Mahalia Jackson sang "Move On Up a Little Higher" and "Nobody Knows the Trouble I've Seen," and the audience held hands and sang along in a close affirmation of faith.

But the climax of the day came with a speech I had heard briefly the night before the rally. Dr. King and I had met with some members of the SCLC staff at the Willard Hotel in Washington, and he'd read me a draft he was working on. The famous "I have a dream" line was in there, but the bulk of the speech was about the problems that faced the people in the country: poverty, disease, hunger, the denial of the right to vote, the desperate need for jobs. I told him that I was praying for him and that, as usual, I thought he would steal the show.

Dr. King was the last speaker. He'd been nervous that not many people would show up. He craved large groups to inspire him. When he saw the size of the crowd, he was confident he could take the mass of people higher than any of the other speakers had.

Dr. King never tried to get away from his calling as a minister of the gospel, and at this moment I really think he felt that his congregation was the whole nation. He was speaking to the corrupt and unjust power structure, and to the oppressed people all over the country who needed to be given hope and courage.

It is the usual custom of a preacher as he finishes a prepared text to say some other words. Here he establishes eye contact with his audience. On this day, Martin Luther King's speech really began when he left his text. He said, "I have a dream," in a very musical voice, and he lifted his hands in oration. As he lifted his hands, the people lifted theirs, and he went on.

"I have a dream that one day on the red hills of Georgia, the sons of former slaves and the sons of former slave owners will be able to sit down together at the table of brotherhood . . . I have a dream that my four little children will one day live in a nation where they will not be judged by the color of their skin, but by the content of their character . . ." People were standing on their seats, yelling "Amen!" and those who were not standing began to applaud. He was calling for integration at its best, for the tearing down of the walls of an unjust system. He was expressing the longings, hopes and dreams of every person in that assembly of 250,000 people. He took the audience higher and higher, and as he left, the entire group rose to its feet. It was one of the greatest moments in the history of our nation.

I embraced him as he left the podium. I told him how great his speech had been, and how thrilled and moved I was by it. He said that the Holy Spirit had moved him, and he was not arrogant about it at all. Actually, he was very humble. I don't think he yet realized the greatness of the speech.

I had loved him ever since I first got to know him in Montgomery nine years before. But at that moment I loved him even more.

Martin Luther King delivers his "I have a dream" speech, above (Bob Adelman), during the Lincoln Memorial rally that climaxed the March on Washington, opposite page (Robert W. Kelley/Life, © Time Inc.).

Birmingham

Martin Luther King came to Birmingham, Alabama, in the spring of 1963 to force the desegregation of its public facilities. His strategy was confrontation: nonviolent mass demonstrations and civil disobedience. Although the demonstrators were at first arrested peacefully, the police later used dogs and fire hoses. The confrontations ended with a federally enforced truce that promised, but did not guarantee, desegregation.

In the fall, Governor George Wallace closed Birmingham schools to prevent court-ordered integration. The President intervened, and schools reopened. Five days later a black church was bombed and four children died.

Above: the funeral of one of the four children killed in the Birmingham church bombing (UPI).

Gatefold: fire hoses batter black student marchers in Birmingham, 1963 (Bob Adelman). Opposite page: a policeman surveys the damage at the site of the church bombing (John A. Kouns).

That afternoon I returned to the grounds of the Lincoln Memorial with Dr. King. The contrast was almost frightening. Just hours before we'd heard those profound utterances and so many cries of "Amen!" and Mahalia Jackson's singing. Such massive sounds had come from in front of that historic monument, and now we stood there, thinking we were all alone. There was nothing but a stillness and a serenity.

Then it seemed the statue of Abraham Lincoln was speaking to us. It seemed that Lincoln was saying, "Free at last! Free at last!" The whole atmosphere was full of freedom—the freedom that our ancestors had fought and died for, that Lincoln had been assassinated for. Though the Emancipation Proclamation had not brought total freedom, it seemed that Lincoln was now telling us that we had broken the shackles of fear by our words.

Then there was silence, and we saw how the wind was blowing the programs about, and we watched the tracks of people being covered by the sands. But as we turned to leave, the silence seemed to be broken again by a voice. I heard: "You're free now, because you have a dream."

*Ralph Abernathy and Martin Luther King, Jr.,
were young ministers in Montgomery, Alabama, when
Rosa Parks refused to give up her bus seat to a white passenger
in 1955. They organized the successful 381-day Montgomery
bus boycott and a year later formed the Southern Christian Leadership
Conference. Abernathy was national financial secretary and became
SCLC national president after King's assassination in 1968.
He coordinated that summer's Poor People's Campaign, when mule trains
full of job-seekers converged on the capital to camp in the
shadow of the Washington monument.★
The Reverend Ralph Abernathy and wife, Juanita,
at an SCLC benefit, 1968 (Globe Photos).*

CHARLES EVERS
My Brother's Keeper

I never wanted to be a big shot. All I ever wanted to be was my brother's keeper. Medgar was my younger brother and my only whole brother. He and I were bedmates, and teammates, and schoolmates. We went into the Army together.

I was the naughty boy of the crowd and Medgar was the good guy. We had the same goals, but our methods of getting there were different. He always felt that he should be willing to give rather than to receive, and I was the reverse. He was willing to give until it hurt; I believed in giving until it was enough.

Medgar was the first black man to apply to Ole Miss, in the late fifties. They turned him down for "technical reasons." Later he became field secretary for the NAACP, and he was very busy with voter registration and organizing chapters throughout the state. I did most of the hustling and wheeling and dealing, making the money for us. It's still the thing I do best. I always used to tell him, "You do the civil rights and I make the money."

I'd been in the funeral business, with a restaurant and cab business on the side, but I got into trouble with the White Citizens Council in Philadelphia, Mississippi—they're the Klan without sheets. They harassed me until they finally broke me. I got in such bad financial shape that I told Medgar, "Look, you stay here. I'm going to make some money, and I don't give a damn how I make it." I left him with twenty-seven dollars and a brand new '56 Ford and drove to Chicago.

The first job I got was as a washroom attendant. I mostly worked the Ambassador East Hotel, a fancy place on the North Side. I got to talking to some of the men who came by, and finally I started finding some of them some girls. That wasn't enough, so I got another job carrying meat at the Swift Packing Company across town. I had worked there about six months when I saw a friend of mine who knew I had a degree in education. He said, "What are you doing here?" I said, "I can't get no job, nowhere." He found me a low-paying teaching job. It wasn't enough. I started running policy for the numbers players, and gradually I decided to do it for myself. I made enough money to open a small nightclub, the Club Mississippi, and then another, the Palm Gardens. I was just beginning to make real money.

Then one night in June 1963, I came in from my club at two A.M. I'd had a good night, and left the club early. I was tired, I'd made a lot of money, so I headed home. I saw lights on all around my apartment, and thought, What the hell's going on here? I went up on the big old porch we had, and looked into the window of the living room. There were all these people in my apartment. I thought something must be wrong with my daughter. I rushed inside. "What's wrong? What are you all doing in my house this time in the morning?" I never had visitors much. Someone said, "Your wife Nan wants to see you."

Nan came up to me and said, "Come on, Charlie. Come on." She was looking all funny. "What's wrong with our daughter?" I asked. She said, "Nothing wrong with Pat." Then I said, "It's Medgar."

He and I had talked the Sunday before. We both broke down on the phone because he was afraid that I was having trouble with the Syndicate. He said, "Charlie, be careful, they're gonna kill you." I said, "Don't you worry about me and those hoods; you with them damn crackers down there." We both started crying right there on the phone.

I asked Nan, "What happened?" Nan said, "They shot him." I said, "Oh, well, they can't kill us Everses, they probably just winged him." She said, "No, Charlie, he's dead."

Medgar Evers (Wide World Photos).

Medgar was shot in the back as he was going into his house in Jackson. He was coming back from a civil rights rally and some vulture shot him in the back, I guess from across the street. He'd been trying to desegregate all the utilities and the lunch counters. He helped them try to desegregate the library. His main thing, like mine and all the rest of us, was to make life better for black people and poor folks. And for that reason, and that reason alone, he was killed.

I don't remember what I did after Nan told me about Medgar. She said I came into the bedroom and packed my clothes. When I came to, you know where I was? In Jackson, at his house. I don't remember how I got on the plane, and I don't remember the trip.

I wanted to go to the morgue, and they tried to stop me. I wanted to cry with him when nobody was around. I wanted to fix his hair. I went down and stayed with him for a long time—just the two of us. I said, "I'm never gonna let you die in vain. I'm gonna get even with him if it's the last thing I do."

Evers' funeral with full military honors in Arlington (Wide World Photos).

Racism is a sickness that eats away at a person, white or black. Right then, I really wanted to kill white folks. I meant to go out and kill them by the dozens, 'cause one of them had shot Medgar in the back. But in the morgue that night, just me and him, something kept telling me, "Charlie, you ain't to worry. You're not going to do anything but get yourself killed. There are only two of us. You're not going to accomplish anything for Medgar like this."

When we were very young, we'd agreed that if anything happened to either of us, the other would carry on. The next day I went down to Medgar's NAACP office, and I said, "I'm taking over." I've been here in Mississippi ever since. I figured that the least thing I could do is to keep his name and what he did alive.

Charles Evers became the NAACP's Mississippi state field secretary after his brother Medgar's murder on June 12, 1963. He led economic boycotts, sit-ins and voter-registration drives that helped desegregate Mississippi and transformed its electorate from predominantly white to 28 percent black. In 1969 he was elected mayor of Fayette, becoming the first black mayor of a biracial town in Mississippi. He ran unsuccessfully for governor in 1971 and today still presides as mayor in Fayette.★ (Carl Robinson/Photo Trends)

BENJAMIN C. BRADLEE
The 22nd of November

The last time I saw Jack Kennedy was two weekends before he died. My wife, Tony, and I visited his home in the Virginia countryside. It was a brisk autumn afternoon. Jackie and Caroline were out riding in the fields below the terrace. A typical Sunday afternoon of reading the paper and talking. Jack was mentioning something to me when Leprechaun, the pony, got loose and came after us on the terrace. We leaned against the house to get out of his way, but Leprechaun would not leave Jack alone.

He kept bobbing his muzzle up and down against Kennedy's ass and rolling him over, literally rolling him over like a log. We all got the giggles, everyone was laughing. Kennedy was shouting at the photographer: "Be sure to get this. We're about to witness the President being trampled by a pony." It was gay, warm and uncomplicated.

All of the subsequent questions and hassles about whether or not I was too close to Kennedy seem so remote when I think about that afternoon. It was just a nice way for adults to spend a day.

Kennedy was due to see Johnson in Texas in two weeks. They'd recently discussed the trip. He liked Johnson, but they were not close friends. Kennedy liked anybody who would run for election; whether that person won or lost, Kennedy had respect for him. But the two staffs never got along. Johnson's staff never quite realized that Johnson himself had a hell of a lot of style: they were embarrassed because Texas style didn't have the national acceptance that the "Playboy of the Western World" style had. It turned out to be a fatal flaw in Johnson, because he always appeared insecure in front of Kennedy, though he was a strong and powerful man.

As I understood it, the Texas trip was intended to heal a catfight in Texas politics—Yarborough versus Connally and LBJ. It was the kind of fight that Kennedy instinctively understood—two wings of the party at war. Adlai Stevenson had just been to Dallas and had been jostled and spat upon. Kennedy didn't really want to go, but he always liked the adrenaline of contact, and he'd persuaded Jackie to go.

Jackie had just lost little Patrick Kennedy a day or two after he was born. She had gone to rest and recuperate on Onassis's yacht, and it had aroused a lot of publicity, not all of it good. Jack had been understanding, but he wanted a favor in return. One night when Tony and I were visiting, he asked, "Maybe now you'll come to Dallas with me."

I used to think it was strange that everybody remembers where he or she was when Kennedy was killed. Perhaps it tells us something about how we place and measure ourselves. I was browsing in a bookstore near the National Press Building during lunch hour. I heard whispering. Suddenly, the whispers grew louder, and I heard separate words: Kennedy. Shot. Assassination.

I rushed back to my office at *Newsweek*. Everyone was grouped around the ticker. It didn't seem possible that such a hopeful man had been killed. I got into a terrible fight with a friend who kept saying to me, "He's going to die. Going to die." I knew he was going to die, but I got so angry at this guy's telling me. And then of course he did die.

It was Friday-night deadline, and we had to tear up the entire magazine. So, in addition to getting control of myself, I had to attend meetings and conferences to decide who was going to do what, and then cry a little. Oz Elliot assigned me to do an "appreciation." He said I should because I knew him in a special way. I could not write it. I was too emotional.

Above, left to right: Mike Mansfield, Sam Rayburn, John Kennedy, Lyndon Johnson, one month after election (Photo Trends). Left: Lee Harvey Oswald (UPI). Opposite page, top: Leprechaun nuzzles the President, Tony Bradlee steps in (Cecil Stoughton/JFK Library). Bottom: Kennedy visits relatives in Dunganstown, Ireland, during a 1963 state visit (Photo Trends).

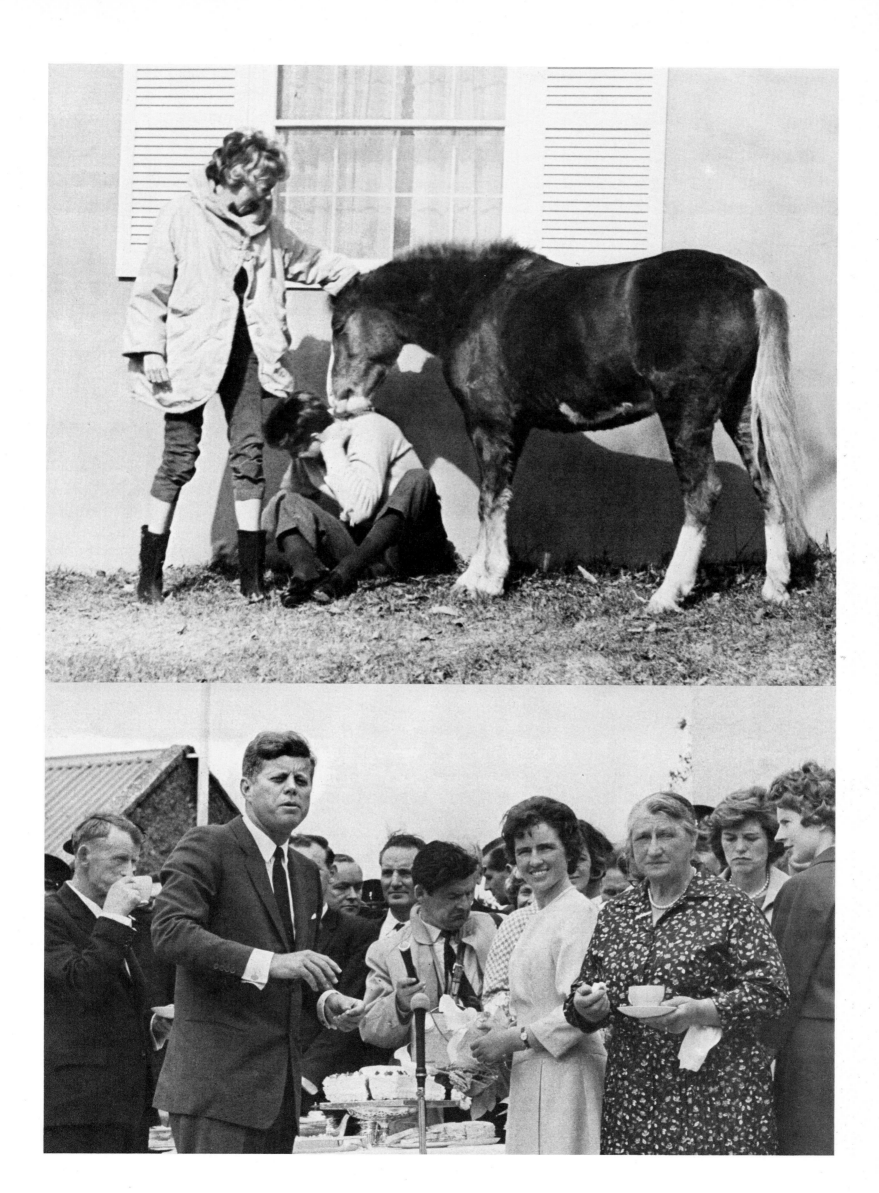

Jackie's secretary, Nancy Tuckerman, called to ask if Tony and I would come to the White House and stay until Jackie came home with the President's body. She wasn't sure where the plane from Dallas was headed. We waited a while at the White House with Jack's sisters Jean Kennedy Smith and Eunice Kennedy Shriver. Finally, we were told that she was flying to Andrews Air Force Base and would be driven from there to Bethesda Naval Hospital.

We all climbed into a White House limousine and took off with a motorcycle escort on the most hair-raising ride I have ever taken. The police must have thought there was some therapy to driving fast, and, Jesus, we literally flew. At one staggering moment, the motorcycle escort skidded and we were sure he was going to die. Somehow he regained control and we arrived at the hospital. It was surrounded with people, television cameras, and eerie light. We waited around in a suite. Then Jackie came into the room.

It was a terrible sight, this wounded bleeding bird in a pink wool suit that was still covered with the President's blood. She happened to gaze around the room; then she came to Tony and me. She threw herself in our arms. She looked at me and said, "Oh, Benny, do you want to hear how it all happened?" And I said, "Yes, of course," or something. I was just scared to death. And then she said quietly, "But not for publication."

Mostly I remember her hands describing how part of his brain had flown out onto her hand. It seemed so unreal.

The Irish Mafia was in and out of the suite trying to make a wake, but they didn't believe in it. Us Wasps weren't used to wakes. I remember Bobby asking everybody where they thought he should be buried. There was a move for Boston—he was their pride and joy. Most people thought that wasn't right—he was a Bostonian by accident. He'd lived in New York when he ran for Congress, and he belonged in Washington.

Jackie was in a separate world. The doctors were trying to get her to go to bed, but she wouldn't. Friends told her to change her clothes, but she wouldn't do that either. Kenny O'Donnell was sent on a mission to retrieve her wedding ring, which she had placed in the coffin in Dallas. It was a dreadful time. We were all struggling for control. There was no sobbing. It was too incomprehensible. Americans don't get assassinated; Europeans do. That's how they solved problems.

I was an usher in the church for the funeral. It was a hell of an audience, all the heads of state. I couldn't get a seat, so I stood in the aisle. I stood and watched everyone enter, then: President Lyndon Johnson. The line stopped. I remember just looking at him. He was wearing a cutaway coat. That's when I cried. He looked so mournful, what we later came to recognize as his "shame" expression. Then we headed for Arlington.

It was the beginning of a long lousy slide. A certain letdown came over me. I don't know if it was the assassination or just that I was getting older. I was jolted into realizing that maybe we didn't have any answers, maybe we didn't have the system. Kennedy had never been a revolutionary, in any sense of the word. Bobby was much more of a gut liberal than Jack. But life was never the same after Kennedy was assassinated. That's for goddamn sure.

Benjamin C. Bradlee first came to know John Kennedy when they were neighbors in Washington, D.C., while Kennedy was a senator from Massachusetts. During Kennedy's Presidency Bradlee was the Washington bureau chief for Newsweek *magazine. Since 1965, he has been with the* Washington Post, *where he is now executive editor. Mr. Bradlee is the author of* That Special Grace *and* Conversations with Kennedy. *Bradlee with the President's son, John-John (Cecil Stoughton).*

Above, top: The motorcade in Dallas (UPI). Center, left to right: Kennedy being interviewed in 1958 by Tom Wolfe, then a Springfield, Mass., reporter (Wally Huntington/Globe Photos); Jack and Jackie (Photo Trends); the President and Khrushchev in 1961 (Wolf/Globe Photos). Opposite page: JFK campaigning for the Presidency at FDR's retreat in Warm Springs, Georgia, in 1960 (Photo Trends). Overleaf: President Kennedy's burial at Arlington National Cemetery (Photo Trends).

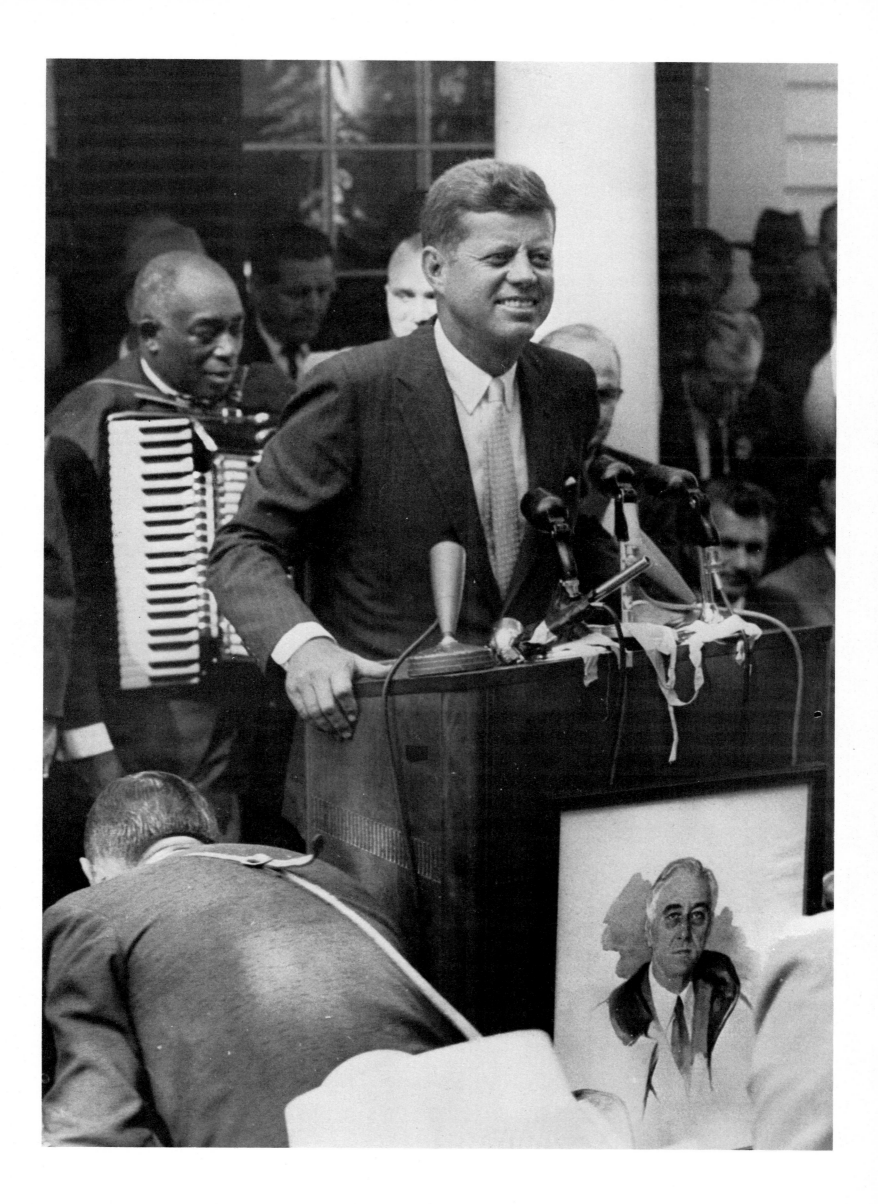

READERS OF ROLLING STONE
Where We Were

ROLLING STONE Our college radio station wasn't very powerful, and I guess we didn't have many listeners. But we did our best to put classical music and a few original programs over as much of Pittsburgh as our limited FM transmitter could manage.

Around one-thirty on the day Jack Kennedy was killed, the UPI Teletype was clacking out commodity prices from Chicago—the kind of stuff that wound up in tiny type on the financial pages of newspapers—when the bell inside rang ten times.

Ten bells! Flash! The highest-priority signal there is. This means something really big, like war being declared. Guys had worked in newsrooms for years and never heard ten bells.

The machine was silent for a few seconds. Then the keys hit the paper in a short burst: JKWIUFG P4UIT KRG½M SNH9BJQ.

Somebody on the UPI system was transmitting on top of the guy in Chicago, and the machine was printing gibberish. Ten bells rang again. The machine seemed to hesitate. Then it came: FLASH. SHOT FIRED PRESIDENT'S MOTORCADE. GET OFF THE WIRE. Then the bells went off again.

FLASH. KENNEDY SHOT. KENNEDY SHOT. FOR CHRIST SAKE GET OFF WIRE.

Chicago stayed off. And bit by bit, in staccato snatches, UPI's Dallas man sent it out as fast as he got it from his reporters around town. Dealey Plaza. Texas School Book Depository. Parkland Memorial Hospital. Governor Connally. J. D. Tippit.

We were studying journalism, and this was the first test of whether we could do what they'd told us journalists have to do: Shove the shock and the emotion out of the way and get the story out. So we did. Even though we knew our handful of listeners had probably turned us off and snapped on the TV.

By five-thirty that evening most of the Duquesne students had gone home, and only a few of us remained behind to keep the station on the air till sign-off time. It was understood that the station director—a veteran of earlier days in broadcasting—would replace me behind the microphone for the six o'clock news. I sat down to write the story for him, and he began with: "The President of the United States is dead."

That's what I remember most vividly about November 22nd, 1963. Typing out that sentence. Because even after all the shocks of the afternoon, it still seemed unreal, and I felt a quiver as my fingers touched the keys. I can remember those words appearing on the yellow copy paper in my typewriter then as clearly as I watch these words fall onto this paper right . . . now.

—Dennis L. Foley

ROLLING STONE I went to a crowded Catholic parish school in West Philadelphia where a lot of kids from the black and ethnic ghettos in that part of the city went. My fifth-grade nun was Sister Maria Inviolata, a dark woman who cursed and prayed in Polish and who never once pronounced my name right that whole year. Her nickname was Kong, and there was definitely a resemblance between her and the big guy.

Kong was tough; everybody knew it and tried to keep on her good side, except Gary Bard, a small black kid who didn't care because he was equally tough. He was a jitterbug. He was the kid who made cologne and Cuban heels with cleats popular in our class.

One day Kong and Gary Bard had a showdown. We were taking our Friday geography test. Gary was turned almost all the way around looking at my answers and laughing a little because he couldn't quite read my writing. (Actually, he couldn't quite read.) Kong must have been watching him from her desk the whole

time. While everybody had their heads down in their test papers, she quietly took the wooden yardstick she used as a pointer and threw it like a spear at Gary. It hit him in the back of the head, not very hard, but he owwed very loudly and everybody looked up at once.

Gary shot up out of his seat and glared at Kong. She smiled at him. Gary picked up the yardstick and walked slowly up to Kong's desk, his cleats making an extra-loud noise that echoed throughout the room. Gary stood directly facing Kong, broke the stick over his knee, and put the pieces on her desk. The kids in the back of the room were standing on their seats by now. We were hypnotized, waiting for the next move, cringing with the fear of Kong that Gary Bard didn't show at all.

Suddenly a voice came out of the intercom box on the wall, and everyone—Gary and Kong included—jumped. It was the voice of the Mother Superior, the school principal. "Sisters and teachers, boys and girls. I have just been told by the Monsignor that something very tragic has happened. President Kennedy was killed this afternoon in Texas, just a little while ago. Monsignor wants all of us to say a special rosary for the repose of our President's soul and for his family and for our country, which is in grave danger now . . ."

By the time the voice box went off, Kong was crying, and she looked as though she'd forgotten that Gary Bard was standing in front of her desk. She clutched her rosary beads and waved her arms, shouting something at all of us in Polish. We looked around at each other, wondering if anybody knew what she was telling us to do. I noticed that Gary Bard was back at his place in front of me, taking his rosary out of his desk. Kong was clapping now and finally saying in English, "Turtle position, get into turtle position. Monsignor says our country is in grave danger! We have to pray for the President!" So we all curled up under our desks in turtle position—just like in air-raid drills—and Kong led us in praying the rosary. She had squatted under her desk, too.

We were all scared, I think, even Gary Bard. He and I kept looking at each other from under our desks, wondering what was going to happen, and I kept losing my place on the beads.

—Frank DiOrio

ROLLING STONE We were known as the Prescott Junior High School Rebels of Baton Rouge, Louisiana, and boy, did we ever live up to our name on November 22nd, 1963. Negroes attend Prescott now, but when I was in the seventh grade in 1963, we had no Negro pupils; and if we had had Negro pupils I'm afraid that they would have been lynched.

Immediately after lunch we were allowed to go out into the schoolyard for a recess. Rumors were thick during recess.

"Kennedy's been shot."

"Is it true?"

"Are you sure?"

"I hope it's true."

"Let's give a medal to whoever shot him."

"Yeah! I hope that nigger-loving son of a bitch is dead."

Groups of students began doing different things. Some students sang choruses of "Glory, glory, hallelujah." Others cheered "Hip! Hip! Hooray!" Everyone was happy, laughing, putting their arms around each other, slapping each other on the back. It really seemed like a joyous occasion. The teachers who were standing by their classroom doors did nothing to stop the celebration. They only smiled at our antics.

—Gary Dale Babin

ROLLING STONE It was cloudy and cold outside as our second-grade class watched a truck pulling a house drive by. The secretary in the office announced that someone named Kennedy had been shot in Dallas. Everybody started talking about this. Another kid and I started drawing pictures of spies shooting Kennedy in his car. A few minutes later the secretary announced that the President was dead. We stopped drawing our pictures. It was my first Kennedy assassination.

—Dennis Sullivan

These essays are part of a participatory journalism experiment conducted by the editors of Rolling Stone in 1973.

1964

CALENDAR

January: 3 *Russia buys its first U.S. wheat;* **8** *President Johnson declares war on poverty;* **10** That Was the Week That Was *joins TV season;* **11** *Surgeon General concludes cigarette smoking is a health hazard;* **16** Hello, Dolly! *opens on Broadway;* **27** *Defense Secretary McNamara reports Vietnam combat has claimed 101 American lives;* **29** *Film release of* Dr. Strangelove.

February: 9 *Beatles take America by storm: "I Want to Hold Your Hand" and* Meet the Beatles *rule record charts, and Ed Sullivan hosts their U.S. debut;* **17** *Supreme Court's "one-man-one vote" rule orders reapportionment to equalize population in congressional districts;* **25** *Heavyweight boxing crown passes to Cassius Clay, who adopts the Muslim faith and becomes Muhammad Ali.*

March: 9 The Spy Who Came In from the Cold *tops fiction list;* **15** *Elizabeth Taylor marries Richard Burton ten days after divorcing Eddie Fisher;* **21** *"She Loves You" continues the Beatles' chart dominance;* **23** *Publication of* John Lennon In His Own Write; **26** *Broadway opening of* Funny Girl *makes Barbra Streisand a star;* **27** *Good Friday earthquake hits Alaska.*

April: 4 *John, Paul, George and Ringo have top five singles and top two LPs;* **13** Tom Jones *takes best-picture Oscar;* 8½ *wins best foreign;* **22** *New York World's Fair opens;* **24** *President Johnson tours Appalachia.*

May: 16 *"My Guy" is top single;* **22** *LBJ coins "The Great Society";* **24** *First issue of the L.A. Free Press sparks a trend toward underground newspapers;* **30** *A. J. Foyt sets Indy 500 record but two drivers die in pileup.*

June: 7 *Dionne Warwick moves into the Top Ten with "Walk on By";* **19** *Carol Doda makes entertainment history by dancing in Gernreich topless bathing suit;* **21** *Jim Bunning pitches the first perfect game in the National League since 1880;* **22** *Hemingway's A Moveable Feast becomes the leading best seller;* **27** *Peter and Gordon's "A World Without Love" leads singles chart, and the Rolling Stones' first LP enters chart as they tour U.S.*

July: 2 *Johnson signs the first broad-based civil rights bill;* **3** *Georgia's Lester Maddox urges*

Top: LBJ, President and candidate (Bob Adelman). Center: Johnson hands out the pens he used to sign the 1964 civil rights bill (Wide World Photos). Bottom: the Warren Commission (Wide World Photos). Opposite page: Beatles in the sky with wires on (Photo Trends).

use of axe handles against blacks entering his restaurant; **4** *Beach Boys' first number one is "I Get Around";* **15** *Barry Goldwater accepts Republican presidential nomination;* **27** *U.S. ups Vietnam troop commitment to 21,000;* **29** *Civil rights movement splits over issue of election-year ban on demonstrations;* **31** *Ranger 7 sends first closeup photos of moon.*

August: 4 *Bodies of three missing civil rights workers found buried in Mississippi;* **7** *Senate passes Gulf of Tonkin Resolution;* **11** *Beatles offer A Hard Day's Night;* **20** *LBJ signs antipoverty program, which includes VISTA;* **22** *"Under the Boardwalk" makes Top Ten;* **24** *Publication of* Games People Play; **26** *Democrats nominate LBJ;* **31** *Johnson signs food stamp bill.*

September: 5 *Supremes' first number one hit "Where Did Our Love Go" is replaced by "House of the Rising Sun";* **15** Peyton Place *comes to TV twice a week;* **16** *TV's Shindig brings go-go dancers into our homes;* **22** The Man from U.N.C.L.E. *premieres;* **24** *Warren Commission concludes Oswald acted alone.*

October: 5 *57 escape East Berlin by tunnel before discovery;* **14** *Nobel Peace Prize goes to Rev. King;* **15** *Political shakeup in Russia: Kosygin and Brezhnev replace Khrushchev;* **16** *China explodes its first atomic bomb;* **17** *"Do Wah Diddy Diddy" leads charts, Motown classic "Dancing in the Street" is second, and "Oh, Pretty Woman" is third;* **18** *U.S. swimmer Don Schollander wins a fourth gold medal in the Tokyo Olympics;* **24** *212 Americans have died in Vietnam combat.*

November: 3 *Democrats have landslide day at the polls; Robert Kennedy becomes senator from New York;* **9** *Bellow's Herzog tops fiction list;* **24** *Maximum interest on bank accounts is raised to 4½%;* **28** *"Leader of the Pack" takes chart lead from "Baby Love."*

December: 3 *Berkeley Free Speech Movement sit-in ends with 796 arrests;* **5** *LBJ awards the First Congressional Medal of Honor since Korea; "She's Not There" and "You Really Got Me" hold steady in the Top Ten;* **11** *Sam Cooke dies in shooting;* **17** *Film release of* Zorba the Greek; **25** *War games like Risk and Diplomacy are Christmas hits.*

SID BERNSTEIN
The Beatles Take New York

In the fall of 1962 I was working for General Artists Corporation, a booking agency in New York, and studying at the New School for Social Research. One of my courses was American civilization with Max Lerner. During one lecture, he suggested we pick up an English newspaper or two each week, to see how the British form of government compared to ours, so I started a varied diet of newspapers: the *London Times,* the *Daily Telegraph,* the *Daily Express,* the *Observer,* the *People.*

Some time very late in '62 I noticed a story about the Beatles, and because of my work in the music business I was, of course, interested. I started to search each week for stories on them. Gradually the headlines got bigger and bigger, and when I saw a story on page 3 of the *London Times,* I decided that it was time to strike. The Beatles were going to happen.

Early in '63 I went on a search for Brian Epstein, their manager, and finally got him on the phone at his parents' home. He said that it would be futile to bring the Beatles to America without radio airplay. He stressed their importance in England, but said that he'd gotten no reports on any airplay whatsoever in the United States. I simply said, "It's going to happen, Mr. Epstein. I feel it's going to happen."

Epstein asked where I proposed to play them. I ad-libbed. "The ideal place would be Carnegie Hall." By accident, the timing was impeccable. He had recently watched a picture called *Carnegie Hall,* a film about the tradition of the great artists who'd played there, on the BBC, and he got carried away by the idea.

I said, "Let's take February 12th. It's Lincoln's Birthday, that's a holiday for school kids, and it's far enough away for us to have the Beatles mean something in America." He asked about money. Again I ad-libbed and said $6,500 for two shows, for a matinee and an evening show. He said, "That sounds fair, let's make a deal."

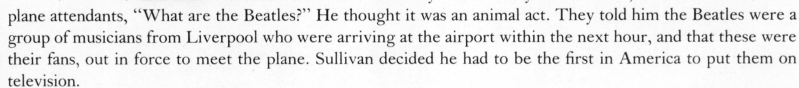

Ed Sullivan and Paul McCartney (Photo Trends).

Then in the summer of '63, so the story goes, Ed Sullivan was changing planes in London while on a European vacation with his wife, and saw thousands of kids with banners: "Hi, Ringo"—"We Love You, George"—"Hi, John"—"Hello, Paul"—"We Love You Beatles." Naturally his curiosity was aroused, and he asked the airplane attendants, "What are the Beatles?" He thought it was an animal act. They told him the Beatles were a group of musicians from Liverpool who were arriving at the airport within the next hour, and that these were their fans, out in force to meet the plane. Sullivan decided he had to be the first in America to put them on television.

He booked them for three dates in February, one Sunday before and two right after my date. When I learned about it, I knew that the success of my Carnegie Hall date was insured, because anyone who appeared on *The Ed Sullivan Show* two weeks in a row automatically became a hit. I became a promotion man of sorts for the Beatles, trying to work up enthusiasm.

Somewhere around November of '63, the first record came out in the States, but it wasn't until "I Want to Hold Your Hand" in January 1964 that the Beatles took hold here. Suddenly Bob Hope was wearing a wig and doing Beatle jokes; the Beatles became a household word. Right on the heels of the first record, two more came in: "She Loves You" and "Please Please Me." By the time I put my tickets on sale, they had the number one and two records on the charts.

My ticket prices were quite low—$3.50, $4.50 and $5.50—and we sold out in no time at all. By the time I got to the box office to pick up the tickets I had put away for myself and friends, I saw speculators selling tickets for $50 and $75 to kids who had been turned away from the window.

The Beatles during the shooting of Help! *in 1965 (Photo Trends).*

112

A few weeks later I was in a taxi on my way down to my office on 57th Street. On the radio the arrival scene at Kennedy Airport was being broadcast. The announcer said, "The Beatles are now leaving the airport in four separate limousines, provided for their safety, heading for the Plaza Hotel." I asked the driver to drop me at the Plaza—remember, I had never met them, or Brian Epstein—and there was a replay of what Ed Sullivan must have seen in London. Thousands of kids were crammed behind barricades, with signs and flags saying "We Love You Beatles."

The show at Carnegie Hall was an event like no one had ever witnessed before. The audience was well behaved, well mannered—it was Carnegie Hall and there was tradition to observe—but the screams must have penetrated to the tenth floor. The next day the lady who booked the hall said, "Mr. Bernstein, we would be very glad never to have you play here again." A year earlier, when she had asked me who the Beatles were, I'd said, "It's a phenomenon," never describing what this phenomenon was. She'd bought the explanation, probably thinking it meant a phenomenal violin player.

The show was also the turning point in my life. Carnegie Hall has a fire rule: If you have five or more players on the stage, you can't have a seat on it. But they were just four, so we had three hundred chairs on that stage, many of them there for press people that I couldn't accommodate elsewhere. Everybody was within touching distance of the Beatles. Up until this concert, I was just another schnook, another guy in the business. Suddenly I found myself a minor celebrity, with press from all over the world interviewing me as though I was an expert on the Beatles. It gave me worldwide publicity. It was a very, very special day in my life, and certainly in my career.

Of course, it was only the beginning for the Beatles. After we'd sold out Carnegie Hall, I told Brian, "You know, we could fill Madison Square Garden. I've already checked with them and they tell me their people could print a set of tickets in twenty-four hours." Epstein was curious, so I took him over to the Garden. He was impressed—I felt sure he was going to say yes—and I knew we could sell those 18,000 seats because we had turned that many people away. But Epstein looked at me and said, "You know, Sid, we proved our point at Carnegie Hall. I think we'll do it another time."

They did come back the next year—to play Shea Stadium. By then, Madison Square Garden was too small.

Since the early Sixties, Sid Bernstein has been involved with the popular music business. As a manager and promoter he has handled such artists as the Rascals, Laura Nyro, Smokey Robinson and the Bay City Rollers. He now heads Sid Bernstein Productions in New York City. ★
(Chuck Pulin)

The Fab Four arrive in New York before the Sullivan show and the Carnegie Hall concerts, above (Harry Benson). In the midst of Beatlemania in San Francisco later that year, opposite page: Cow Palace ticket taker in Beatle wig, top; Beatles under siege, below. The hysteria was so intense the photographer was unable to shoot without being jostled (Erik Weber).

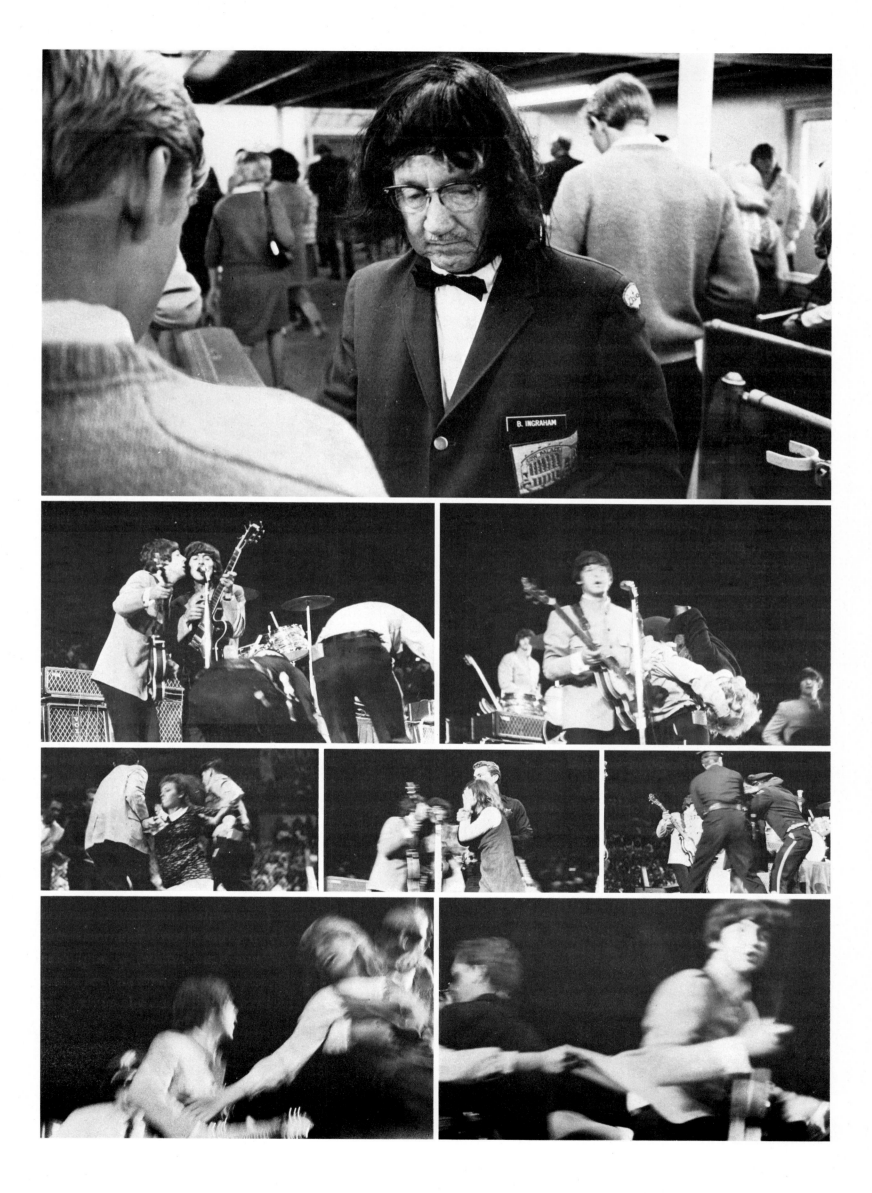

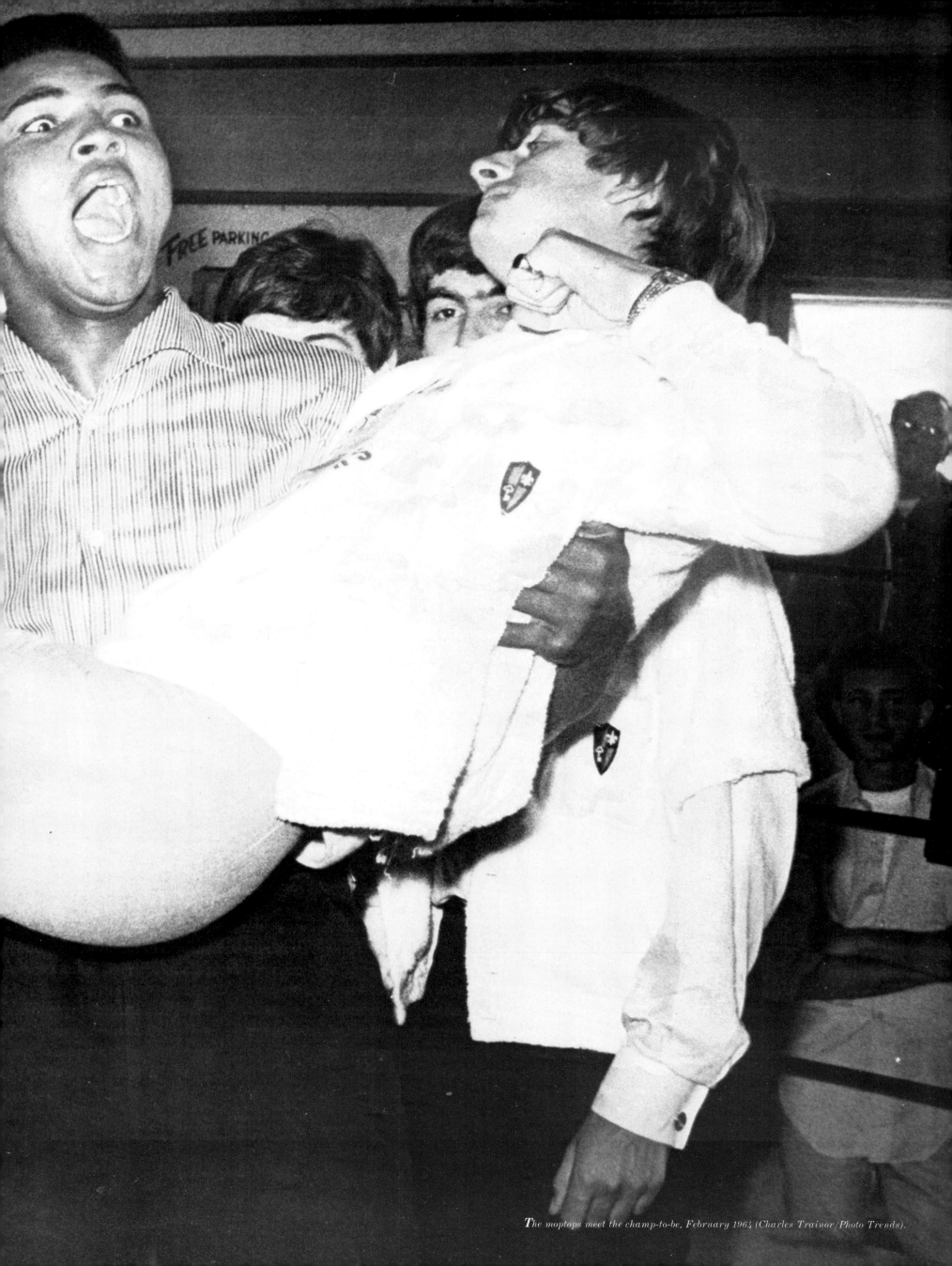

The moptops meet the champ-to-be, February 1964 (Charles Trainor/Photo Trends).

Liverpudlians welcome the Beatles home, 1964 (Photo Trends).

TONY SCHWARTZ
The Bomb, the Daisy and Barry Goldwater

It was one of the most political commercials ever made. I had been working in advertising for twenty years when one day in September I got a call from Aaron Ehrlich, a producer at the advertising firm of Doyle, Dane, Bernbach. Ehrlich told me he had a special project for me, but that we had to discuss it in person, not over the phone.

We met, and he took out a photograph of President Johnson, held it up before me, and said, "Will you work for this product?"

I agreed, and he explained that he wanted me to work on the sound for a number of commercials. I work with the sound of words. Advertising writers work only with the literal meaning of words, but I deal with the *effect* of what you hear, with the interplay of visuals and sounds. Sound is an emotional thing.

Ehrlich had seven or eight spots for me, some better written than others, but most of them requiring that I come up with appropriate voices. In one, the writers wanted the *look* of poverty and the *sound* of opulence. So I used the voice-over of children talking about middle-class life, including a kid talking about his three power lawn mowers, and set it against a visual background of sharecropper children.

Another spot consisted of five minutes of alternating Russian and American atom bombs exploding, with voice-over countdowns alternating faster and faster. They liked that a great deal, and wanted me to do a one-minute version of it. I told them I had the perfect thing.

I had previously made a sound track of a little child counting up to ten, which dissolved into the countdown for an atom-bomb explosion. It symbolized at once the simplest and most complex use of numbers

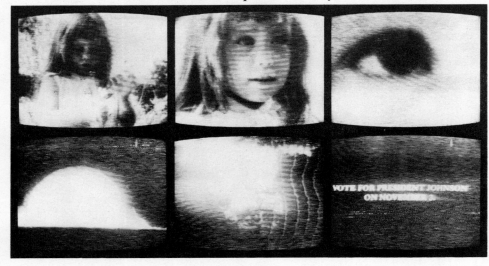

The medium—photographs of the daisy
ad on TV, left (courtesy Tony Schwartz)—
and the message—a woman at the 1964 Democratic
Convention, opposite page (Bob Adelman).

in the world. I showed it to Ehrlich *et al.,* and said, "You have a little child pulling the petals off a daisy. The camera goes in on the center of the daisy, and that becomes the explosion when it detonates."

They thought it was fantastic, and I went ahead and listened to all the recent tapes of Johnson's "Rose Garden speeches" to find the right sound symbol. I found a quote that didn't make much sense on paper, but that worked emotionally on the listener. Cut to the right length, it read: "These are the stakes: to make a world in which all of God's children can live, or to go into the dark. Either we must love each other or we must die."

I added it to the end of the film.

They flipped for it. They chose a little girl, and filmed her picking the daisy and counting to ten while walking along the Henry Hudson Parkway north of New York City.

The spot ran only once, on "Monday Night at the Movies" the night of September 7th, but it created a great stir. It never ran again as a commercial, but it made the cover of *Time,* was the subject of a feature in

The New York Times Magazine, and ran as a news item on almost every television station in the world.

The spot played on the underlying public feeling that Goldwater spoke for the use of tactical atomic weapons whereas Johnson was against the use of any nuclear weapons. When people hear "atomic" weapons, they don't hear the word "tactical." Goldwater's name was never mentioned, but the spot made people think, "Whose finger do I want on the trigger?"

Goldwater could have defused it by saying, "I think that the danger of total nuclear war should be the theme of the campaign this year, and I'd like to pay half the cost of running this commercial." If he had, the commercial would not have been perceived as being against him. He would have changed the feelings and assumptions stored within us. Instead, it was like the woman who goes to the psychiatrist and is shown a Rorschach pattern and says, "Doctor, I didn't come here to be shown dirty pictures!" The daisy commercial evoked Mr. Goldwater's pro-bomb statements. They were the dirty picture in the public's mind.

Tony Schwartz has created commercials for products as diverse as Coca-Cola and presidential candidates. He is a veteran of over two hundred political campaigns, working for Humphrey-Muskie, Ted Kennedy, and most recently, Jimmy Carter. His book, The Responsive Chord, *is about the theory and practice of electronic communication.★ (courtesy Tony Schwartz)*

TOM RUSH
How Success Spoiled the Folkies

The Cambridge-Boston folk-music scene was at first an amateur scene—amateur in the original sense of the word. In the early Sixties the musicians, and even the coffeehouse owners, were in it for love, not for money. In fact, there was very little money to be made. At the Alhambra, Tulla's Coffee Grinder, the Golden Vanity and the Salamander the emphasis was on coffee; the music was a sideline, something to lure potential coffee drinkers. Then as the balance shifted in favor of the music, they began to charge a cover—fifty cents, perhaps a dollar. The performers were paid a maximum of ten dollars for a night's work, and nobody worked more than one or two nights a week.

You couldn't make a living as a folk singer, and nobody tried. We were all involved in other things— being students or typewriter repairmen or molecular biologists. Most of the music was played in people's living rooms; if someone had a gig that night, the party would move down to the coffeehouse.

The coffeehouses themselves were constantly in financial peril. During the final days of the Golden Vanity the electric company shut off the juice, so the owner set up a gasoline generator in the basement. It powered the sound system and a single light bulb, and whenever you hit a high note the light would go dim. The generator, which was louder than the music, would jig its way across the basement floor and pull out its wires; then the show would stop until the owner went downstairs with a flashlight and wrestled it into submission.

The Club 47, which was to become the center of the folk scene, started out as something of a crash pad. Its proprietors and friends were living there surreptitiously, sleeping on the stage or fixing motorcycles in the basement.

Not only were we unprofessional, we were militantly antiprofessional. We were traditional music devotees, purists. If we were to sing a song it had to have been handed down for generations from father to son via the oral tradition, with Woody Guthrie's music being the only exception. The watchwords were "ethnic" and "commercial," which were synonymous with "good" and "bad." Leadbelly was "ethnic"; the Kingston Trio were "commercial."

There were certain ethical questions raised by this attitude. We were vaguely embarrassed by the discrepancies between the music we had adopted, the music of the poor and illiterate, and our parents' swimming pools or our college courses. There was much agonizing over whether a white boy could really

sing the blues.

Attitudes started to change around 1960 as Joan Baez began her ascent to stardom and as Byron Lord Linardos took over the business affairs of the Club 47. Byron, who had co-owned another establishment, the Unicorn, had a more businesslike approach to coffeehouse management, and his rules and regulations were resented. Yet the

Maria Muldaur at the Club 47 in the Kweskin Jug Band days (Dick Waterman).

club, which had been on the verge of bankruptcy, began to prosper. Byron established a following for the artists by having the same act appear on the same night every week. The public began to identify Wednesday, say, with the Kweskin Jug Band or Tuesday with Jackie Washington. At the same time, in the wake of Joan's success on Vanguard Records, the Charles River Valley Boys and I each put out records of our own on what were virtually "vanity" labels. They were only distributed locally, but it somehow legitimized us, making it easier to cultivate a following, draw more paying customers and make more money. We began to realize that we might be able to make a living playing music. Professionalism was rearing its ugly head.

The audience for folk music was growing rapidly, and the coffeehouses started featuring out-of-towners as well as local talent. Most of them came from New York City, the other large folk scene. The Club 47 and the Unicorn, which had emerged as the more serious establishments, started bringing in Judy Collins, Dave Van Ronk, Jack Elliott, Eric Andersen and Bob Dylan. The record companies began to realize that something was up. Joan Baez's success was phenomenal. Paul Rothchild, the producer of the Charles River Valley Boys' album, went to work for Prestige Records and signed up half of Cambridge. Geoff Muldaur, Eric Von Schmidt, the Charles River Valley Boys, myself, Bill Keith, and Jim Rooney all went with Prestige. In a hot bidding war, Vanguard got Jim Kweskin and his Jug Band. Both Vanguard and Prestige had courted them. Paul Rothchild and Maynard Solomon, the head of Vanguard Records, fell all over each other at a Cambridge party lighting Jimmy's cigarettes or bringing him more beer.

A lot of players had more than one gig going. Bill Keith was in both the Jug Band and the Charles River Valley Boys as well as being half of Keith and Rooney. Geoff Muldaur was a solo act as well as being in the Kweskin band. Fritz Richmond, master of the jug and washtub bass, worked with everybody. The result was a great deal of song swapping, record borrowing, and lick stealing. Perhaps the prime artistic mover was Eric Von Schmidt. Eric was first and foremost an illustrator, doing books, posters and album covers, but he had an uncanny knack for spotting good songs on scratchy Library of Congress field recordings, and he wrote some wonderful ones of his own. Everybody owed a lot to Eric, including Baez and Dylan.

The professionalism that developed turned out to be the death of the coffeehouses. As audiences came to recognize and appreciate individual artists, they lost interest in the "hootenannies" and in folk music for its own sake. They wanted to hear Judy Collins, Jim Kweskin—"name acts." These acts were playing colleges and public concerts and getting used to better pay than the coffeehouses could offer. With audiences dwindling and acts harder and harder to find, one by one the coffeehouses began to close.

Tom Rush released his first album on a national label in 1965, the same year he was voted most promising new male folksinger by Billboard *magazine. His latest album is* Ladies Love Outlaws *and he is touring when not at home on his 600-acre New Hampshire farm.*★
(Dick Waterman)

PETER TOWNSHEND
Talkin' 'Bout My Generation

The Mod movement in England has always been one of the things that impressed me most in life. It was a movement of young people, much bigger than the hippies and the underground, a powerful, aggressive army of teenagers with their own transport and their own way of dressing. It was acceptable—this was important—their way of dressing was hip, it was clean, and it was groovy. You could be a bank clerk and people would think, "Well, there's a smart young lad," but you could also be fashionable. That was the good thing about it.

To be a mod, you had to have short hair, money enough to buy a real smart suit, good shoes, good shirts, plenty of pills all the time, and a scooter covered with lamps—and you had to be able to dance like a madman.

If you were a mod, you liked the Who. That's how we happened. The Who could invoke action. The phenomenon, considering that most mods were lower-class garbagemen, was that four mods could actually form themselves into a group that sounded quite good. Mods weren't the kind of people that could play the guitar.

As individuals, these people were nothing. They were England's lowest common denominators. Not only were they young, they were lower-class young. They had to submit to the middle class's way of dressing and speaking and acting in order to get the very jobs which kept them alive. That made their way of getting across that much more effective, because they were hip and yet, as far as Granddad was concerned, still exactly the same.

As a force, they were unbelievable. They were the Bulge, the result of all the old soldiers coming back from war and screwing until they were blue in the face. Thousands and thousands of kids—too many kids, not enough teachers, not enough parents, not enough pills to go around. The feeling of being a mod among two million mods was incredible. It was as if you were the only white man in the Apollo, then someone suddenly came up and touched you and you became a black. It covered everybody, everybody looked the same, everybody acted the same and everybody wanted to be the same.

It was the first move toward unity I have ever seen—unity of thought, drive and motive. Youth has always got some leader or other, some head man. The head man was Mr. Mod. It could have been anyone, any kid, however ugly or fucked up, if he had the right haircut and the right clothes and the right motorbike. He was mod! It affected me in an incredible way; it teases me all the time, because whenever I think, "Oh, youth today is just never gonna make it," I think of that fucking gesture that happened in England. It was the closest to patriotism that I've ever felt.

In 1963, Peter Townshend joined with Keith Moon, John Entwistle and Roger Daltrey to form the Who, a band described by one critic as "the best known and most brilliant expression of Great Britain's Mod movement." Townshend, the Who's lead guitarist and guiding force, is also a lyricist and composer, and the author of such rock and roll classics as "I Can See for Miles," "My Generation" and the first rock opera, Tommy.★

Left: The boys in the band, left to right, vocalist Daltrey, bassist Entwistle, guitarist Townshend, drummer Moon. Opposite page: Peter Townshend in 1964. Overleaf: "To be a mod, you had to have short hair . . . and a scooter covered with lamps . . ." (Photo Trends).

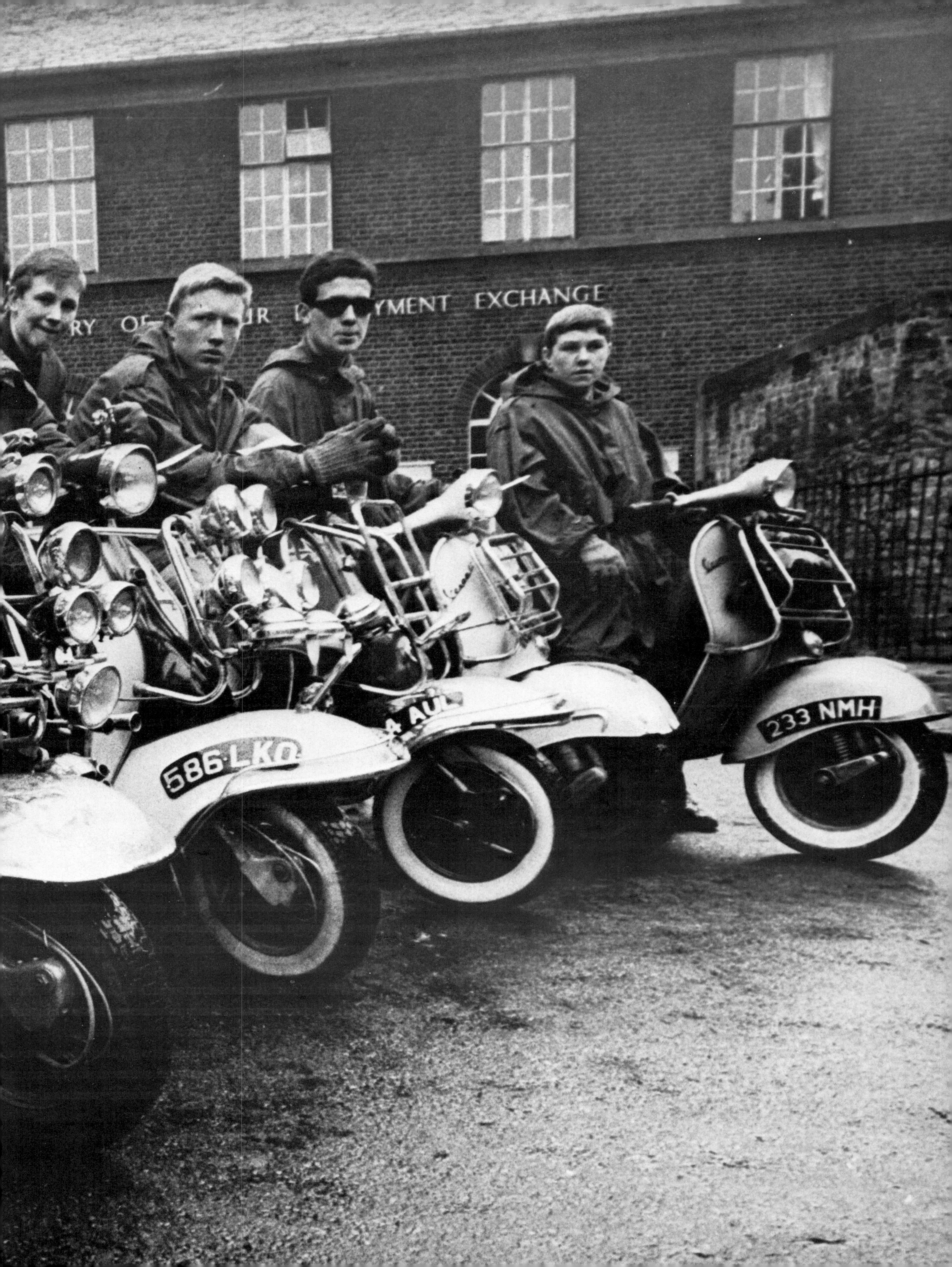

YMENT EXCHANGE
586·LKO
233 NMH

DANIEL ELLSBERG
The Curious Case of the Tonkin Gulf Telegrams

It was summer, and I was just beginning my job as special assistant to Assistant Secretary of Defense John T. McNaughton, whose main task was to manage Vietnam affairs for Secretary McNamara. On Monday, August 3rd, I started reading the cables on Vietnam. Reading cables in the Pentagon means literally being wired into a particular area, where you intercept the daily flow of telegrams from the fleet in the Pacific, the forces in Vietnam, the embassy, the CIA. When you have all that inside dope and all those secrets to keep, it separates you from the readers of the *New York Times*—it makes it impossible to listen seriously to anyone who doesn't have that information, to learn from them or to tell them the truth.

A lot of the cables that day dealt with an attack the day before, August 2nd, on a U.S. destroyer which had been patrolling close to the shores of North Vietman in the Gulf of Tonkin. Two North Vietnamese torpedo boats had been severely damaged and apparently one had been sunk. Hanoi claimed that our destroyer had been inside their territorial waters, and that there had been covert U.S. attacks in the vicinity of the destroyer the preceding night. The United States denied both charges.

On Tuesday morning, the fourth, cables from two destroyers, the *Maddox* and the *Turner Joy,* reported that they were under continuous torpedo attack. There was a twelve-hour time difference between Washington and the Pacific. The cables arrived after the action had actually finished, but they came in sequence, which made reading them almost like watching the action. In the western Pacific, it was a moonless, starless night. The seas were stormy. Our destroyers reported torpedo after torpedo coming at them from North Vietnamese patrol boats—they recorded twenty-two in all. The sea seemed to be filled with them.

 As I was reading the cables, McNamara and others from the National Security Council were at the White House with President Johnson, deciding what to do. I didn't know it, but a tentative decision was reached then to execute bombing attacks against North Vietnam at first light in the Tonkin Gulf.

Suddenly a cable came in from Captain Herrick, commander of the task force, who was on the *Maddox.* I will never forget the substance of that cable—the actual text was later published:

> Review of action makes many recorded contacts and torpedos fired appear doubtful. Freak weather effects and overeager sonar man may have accounted for many reports. No actual, visual sightings by *Maddox.* Suggest complete evaluation before any further action.

Two carriers in the Pacific—the *Constellation* and the *Ticonderoga*—were preparing to execute the strikes at first light. But the order had not yet been given, and Herrick's cable was, of course, a recommendation to wait for light to see if there was any wreckage or oil spots or signs—as there were on August 2nd—that the ships had actually been under attack. Meanwhile, more cables came in. One said the destroyer *Turner Joy* "also reports no actual visual sightings or wake . . . the entire action leaves many doubts except apparent attempt to ambush at beginning. Suggest thorough reconnaisance by aircraft at daylight."

A later one said all reports of torpedos after the first one "are doubtful, in that it is suspected that sonar man was hearing ship's own propeller beat."

The President had scheduled an announcement to the nation for nine-thirty that night, but the *Constellation* was not yet in position. The time of the launch kept getting postponed and so did the President's speech. He didn't want to make a statement to the public until enemy radar tracked our attack planes; otherwise he might be accused of warning the enemy and endangering our aircraft by his announcement. But he also wanted to reach the Eastern Seaboard television audience before midnight that night. If he waited until the next day, it would be hard to justify proceeding without congressional approval or an investigation.

During the night, I sat in Assistant Secretary McNaughton's office with staff people and various military men from the Joint War Room. There was a great flurry of excitement when we realized there was a confusion about time zones in the Pacific. We might have been off by an hour in our understanding of the time of the launch.

Finally, President Johnson chose not to wait any longer—even though the planes were still taking off. At 11:37 P.M., he announced to the American people that, although we sought no wider war, we were at that moment carrying out strikes against North Vietnam. Johnson described this mission to Congress as a response to an unprovoked attack on our vessels, which were carrying out a routine mission in the Gulf of Tonkin. He chose Senator Fulbright to manage the passage of the Gulf of Tonkin Resolution, which he proceeded to treat as "the functional equivalent of a declaration of war." It was the only basis he ever asked or was given for the subsequent bombing of North Vietnam, which started in early 1965, or for our ground invasion in the south, which started later, in the spring.

Except for the Herrick cable and the follow-ups to it, I knew no more than the public: there had been an attack and we had responded. It helped the President politically. It later served as a declaration of war and contributed to his victory in the election. It demonstrated that he could be as tough as Goldwater proposed to be, and yet restrained in his "response." I could only assume at the time that the doubts raised by Herrick had somehow been resolved in communications I hadn't seen, but it left questions in my mind that I had to

wait years to resolve.

Within a week or two, though, I learned from reports in the Pentagon that the Hanoi charges had been correct, our denials false. Clandestine CIA attacks against North Vietnam, totally controlled by the United States, had preceded the August 2nd attack on our destroyers, and similar U.S. attacks had occurred again on August 3rd—

before the supposed North Vietnamese attack of August 4th. Moreover, I learned that our destroyers were in fact on a deliberately provocative intelligence patrol close to the shores of North Vietnam. It took seven years to prove that there had been no attack on our destroyers the night of August 4th, after all.* But within the month, because of Herrick's cables and the CIA raids, I knew that Secretary McNamara's assurances to the Senate—that the attack was unequivocal and unprovoked—were both untrue. Senator Fulbright said years later that if he had the Herrick cable in 1964 or if he had known of the CIA covert raids, he would never have floor-managed the Gulf of Tonkin Resolution. Senator Gruening told me, at the time he appeared to testify for me at my trial in 1973, that if he had known either of these facts, the resolution would never have gotten out of committee and could never have passed. Wayne Morse told me the same.

But regrettably, when I read the Herrick cable on my second day on the job in 1964, it would never have occurred to me to have handed a copy to Morse and Gruening. It wasn't until I finished reading the Pentagon Papers in September '69 that I saw the information in the whole context, and understood what I ought to do. In November I started giving papers to Senator Fulbright, and the chapter on the Tonkin Gulf was the first batch that I handed him. Some time after that, in 1970, the Fulbright Committee, and later the Senate, voted to repeal the Tonkin Gulf Resolution. But the bombing went on anyway. It lasted eight years in all. Seven and a half million tons.

* See Anthony Austin's *The President's War*.

During the Sixties Daniel Ellsberg worked for the Rand Corporation and the U.S. government analyzing and dealing with problems in foreign policy and defense. In the fall of 1969 he gave copies of the Pentagon Papers—a top-secret Defense Department study of U.S. decision-making in Vietnam—to the Senate Foreign Relations Committee, and in June 1971 he gave copies to various newspapers. He was then indicted on charges of violating espionage, theft and conspiracy statutes for a maximum sentence of 115 years. The charges were later dismissed on the judge's finding of numerous acts of illegal misconduct against Ellsberg and his codefendant, Anthony Russo, by the U.S. executive branch. Ellsberg now lives in San Francisco, lecturing and writing.★

Opposite page: The USS Maddox *(U.S. Navy). Top: Captain Herrick, left, and the commanding officer of the* Ticonderoga, *on the lookout for PT boats (U.S. Navy). Above: Senator William Fulbright (Photo Trends). Left: Daniel Ellsberg (Annie Leibovitz).*

BARBARA GARSON
Free Speech Comes to Berkeley

At Berkeley, the traditional way to collect money or pass out leaflets was to sit at one of the many tables set up at the corner of Bancroft and Telegraph right in front of the campus. The Berkeley police issued permits for the available space, and the campus political groups divided them up amiably. But when we returned from our summer vacation in 1964, we were told that we could no longer use the area. It had been "discovered" that it was university, not city, property. At first the school maintained that traffic was being blocked and that too many leaflets were being dropped in the street. Then, very stupidly, they said we could use the space, but we couldn't advocate direct action of any kind. In other words you couldn't say "Let's go down to the *Oakland Tribune* and picket."

That was the beginning of the Free Speech Movement, which turned out to be the first big student "revolt" of the Sixties. Our demands were simple: No rules were to be made regarding students that didn't apply to other citizens.

People continued to use the tables, and the administration collected names of violators. Some of us decided not to give our names. If it was illegal to leaflet on campus, let them arrest us then and there.

Jack Weinberg was at the CORE table when a dean asked him his name, which he refused to give. The Berkeley police drove on the campus and put him into the car, and then—hundreds of people claim to have started it—someone sat down in front of the police car so that it couldn't move. Before long, people were all around and over it. Soon Sproul Plaza was covered with thousands of people.

Jack sat calmly in the car. He knew immediately that the moment was going to last a long time; he stopped eating and somehow got a bottle to piss in.

Sproul Hall, the administration building at Berkeley, and the focal point of the Free Speech Movement demonstrations (© Paul Kagan).

That evening Mario Savio emerged as a leader. Like a lot of us, he'd just returned from the South and was infuriated with having to face this petty harassment while trying to collect money for SNCC. It was the classic miracle—the boy who stuttered stood up on the police car and fluently expressed all our deepest sentiments: that our protest was not only for CORE and SNCC but for us students as well. We would not let the big corporations use us as educated tools to manipulate their blunter tools. The university had an entire institute to serve the state's agribusiness—and here we were, forbidden to raise nickels and dimes at the campus gates for striking farm workers.

The next night, Clark Kerr, the president of the university, promised student delegates that he would negotiate with us if we dispersed peacefully. Family Day began the next day, and he didn't want a police car surrounded by hundreds of people to greet the parents. I argued against dispersal, knowing how much Kerr wanted to avoid an incident, but the crowd acquiesced. Did I think that was a sell-out!

Kerr's approach actually turned out to be most instructive for everybody involved. We entered into constant negotiations over the tables and our rights. We were constantly betrayed. Three months of this helped most people overcome their naiveté, and after a while we began to hold noon rallies on the Sproul Hall steps every time the administration double-crossed us and constant meetings in classrooms across the campus; they weren't authorized, but the janitors opened the buildings for us.

At the end of November the Board of Regents, the group of industrialists and other "distinguished" citizens that governed the entire state university system, made it clear that they would not negotiate the FSM demands. At Thanksgiving they began "disciplinary action" against Mario and three others. I don't think

Opposite page: Mario Savio in Sproul Plaza, 1964 (© Paul Fusco/Magnum).

Clark Kerr wanted to do that. He was an astute manipulator—"the captain of the bureaucracy" (his own phrase)—but the Regents refused even to appear willing to negotiate with students. The leader of this hard-core wing, I am told, was Mrs. Hearst. Yes, Patty's mommy.

That really set it off. At massive meetings, all the options were presented. Sometimes thousands of people voted. The political process was out in the open in Sproul Plaza twenty-four hours a day, culminating in the December decision to sit in.

On the Sproul Hall steps, Mario got up and gave the speech that has become so famous: "There's a time when the operation of the machine becomes so odious, makes you so sick at heart, that you can't take part . . . and you've got to put your bodies upon the gears and upon the wheels and you've got to make it stop." Joan Baez sang, "How many roads must a man walk down, before you call him a man," and as she sang, those that thought this was the road they had to walk began to walk into Sproul Hall. About a thousand of us marched into the Administration Building and sat on the gears.

It was euphoric: we fixed endless peanut butter and jelly sandwiches; we sang rock and roll and our FSM Christmas carols. I personally hate singing "We shall not be moved." It always means to me that we are about to be moved.

Which we were. The Oakland and Berkeley police forces came that very night. They moved from floor to floor, clearing out the building. People outside said, "Oh, God, I missed it. I just left to get a soda." Around 800 of us were arrested in turn, everything orderly. The faculty bailed us out at enormous cost and from that moment on were with us. After all this time, they were suddenly horrified, "Police brutality! Police on campus!" which was hardly the central issue.

Three days after the arrests, with an effective strike in progress and a faculty senate meeting scheduled for the next day, Clark Kerr held a huge meeting in the Greek Theater. He said, "We must decide to move ahead or to continue anarchy." He told us we could solve this together.

At the end of the speeches we sensed that something was missing from the "togetherness"—*us*, the Free Speech Movement. As Kerr left the podium, Mario Savio walked up the aisle and onto the stage. The whole audience was galvanized. At the exact moment he began to speak, a policeman grabbed him around the neck and dragged him off the stage.

The next day, the faculty senate voted overwhelmingly to support the full demands of the FSM. I felt almost annoyed—what a lot of pushing we had to do to get those liberals to finally vote their own consciences. Most of the students, however, felt immensely relieved now that the grownups were on our side.

Somehow or other, the faculty vote tipped the balance. The administration decided not to enforce their old regulations. The next term, we came back and used our tables. I guess that's how all revolutions are won—they don't get fought out to the bitter end. The army comes over, then the navy; somebody gets frightened, and the czar runs away.

Barbara Garson is the author of the play MacBird!, *which was originally created for a teach-in at the Berkeley campus. Her most recent works are a book,* All the Livelong Day: The Meaning and Demeaning of Routine Work, *and an Obie award winning children's play,* The Dinosaur Door. *During the Vietnam War, she worked in an antiwar GI coffeehouse near Fort Lewis army base, and in 1964 on the Berkeley campus, she edited the FSM Newsletter.★*

Above, left to right: Jack Weinberg, trapped in the police car; the sit-in at Sproul Hall that followed—students hearing reports of their action and preventing a police officer from locking the doors (all © Paul Fusco/ Magnum). Left: Garson and her daughter, Juliet (Zara Pippitt).

1965

CALENDAR

January: 2 *Rev. King makes Selma the focus of a concerted drive for voting rights;* **20** *Inauguration of Johnson; Ex-DJ Alan Freed dies;* **23** *"Downtown" takes chart lead from "I Feel Fine."*

February: 6 *"You've Lost that Lovin' Feelin'" is leading single;* **7** *Johnson orders first sustained bombing raids against North Vietnam;* **21** *Assassins gun down Malcolm X in New York;* **27** *U.S. issues white paper justifying bombing attacks on grounds that North Vietnam is the aggressor.*

March: 8 *LBJ sends first ground combat troops into Vietnam, raising troop count to 27,000;* **13** *"My Girl" holds pop lead; "Shotgun" is top R&B;* **21** *National Guard protects Selma-Montgomery Freedom March;* **24** *University of Michigan stages first antiwar teach-in;* **27** *"King of the Road" rules C&W chart;* **30** *HUAC begins its first noncommunist investigation—of the KKK.*

April: 5 *My Fair Lady takes Oscar honors;* **9** *Houston opens its Astrodome;* **20** *The Pawnbroker is first film containing nudity to receive production approval;* **24** *Wayne Fontana and the Mindbenders' "Game of Love" reaches top of chart;* **28** *U.S. Marines are ordered into Dominican Republic as civil war erupts.*

May: 1 *"Mrs. Brown You've Got a Lovely Daughter" moves into pop lead;* **15** *Antiwar protests mark Armed Forces Day.*

June: 3 *Edward White is first U.S. astronaut to walk in space;* **14–18** *856 arrests result from voting protest in Jackson;* **19** *Nguyen Cao Ky is appointed South Vietnamese premier despite U.S. and Buddhist opposition;* **19** *"I Can't Help Myself," "Mr. Tambourine Man" and "Wooly Bully" vie for pop lead;* **28** *U.S. ground troops officially engage in battle.*

July: 8 *Arrests mount in Chicago during school integration protests;* **10** *"(I Can't Get No) Satisfaction" moves into chart lead;* **12** *The Source is best-selling novel;* **15** *Mariner 4 transmits first Mars pictures;* **21** *Defense Department reports 503 Americans dead in Vietnam combat;* **23** *LBJ signs bill to replace silver quarters and dimes with alloyed ones;* **24** *"Like a Rolling Stone" enters chart the day before Dylan's electric debut at New-*

port; **30** *LBJ signs Medicare bill.*

August: 6 *LBJ signs Voting Rights Act;* **13** *National Guard intervenes on third day of Watts riot; The Matrix opens in San Francisco with Jefferson Airplane as the house band;* **14** *"I Got You Babe" introduces Sonny and Cher; "Papa's Got a Brand New Bag" heads R&B chart;* **16** *Publication of Manchild in the Promised Land;* **21** *Stones' Out of Our Heads jumps to LP lead;* **23** *Help! premieres;* **31** *It's illegal to burn your draft card.*

September: 15 *TV debut of I Spy;* **16** *Chavez's UFW votes to strike against Delano, California, grape growers;* **18** *Get Smart! premieres . . . would you believe?* **25** *Dodger pitcher Sandy Koufax overcomes an arthritic elbow to set season strike-out record; "Eve of Destruction" takes pop lead.*

October: 1 *Publication of Dune and reissue of the Lord of the Rings trilogy;* **2** *Dylan's electric album Highway 61 Revisited hits the chart;* **9** *"Yesterday" moves ahead of "Hang On Sloopy" to top chart;* **10** *Yale claims their Viking map of Nova Scotia predates Columbus;* **15–16** *Weekend antiwar protests in 40 cities nationwide;* **26** *Queen Elizabeth makes each Beatle a Member of the British Empire; "Rescue Me" leads R&B chart.*

November: 1 *Wham-O files patent on the Frisbee;* **2** *John Lindsay wins New York mayorship; a Quaker burns himself to death in front of Pentagon as war protest;* **6** *"Get Off of My Cloud" is leading single;* **8** *Publication of The Autobiography of Malcolm X;* **9** *Electrical failure blacks out Northeast U.S.;* **13** *American release of Juliet of the Spirits;* **15** *Breedlove sets world land speed record of 600.001 mph in Utah;* **18** *1,095 Americans have died in Vietnam combat;* **27** *Ken Kesey hosts first public acid test;* **27** *Whipped Cream (and Other Delights) is Herb Alpert's first number one LP.*

December: 4 *U.S. troops in Vietnam total 170,000;* **6** *Maximum bank account interest now 5½%;* **13** *A Thousand Clowns opens;* **18** *Having a Rave Up With the Yardbirds is released;* **22** *Film premiere of Dr. Zhivago;* **24** *LBJ orders Christmas bombing halt;* **27** *Broadway debut of Marat/Sade.*

Top: the Beatles and their MBE's (Photo Trends). Center: Sandy Koufax in motion (Bud Gray/Photo Trends). Bottom: a Buddhist demonstration in Saigon protesting Ky's appointment as South Vietnam's premier (Tim Page). Opposite page: a Selma constituent (James H. Karales).

Selma

In March 1965, civil rights demonstrators twice tried to march from Selma, Alabama, to Montgomery in support of black voting rights. Both attempts failed—the first was turned back by state troopers with tear gas and night sticks, the second ended in compromise and death. As hundreds of people converged on Selma to demand an end to the violence, President Johnson went before Congress to introduce voting rights legislation. On March 21st, 3,000 people walked out of Selma protected by federal troops, and five days later reached Montgomery. In four and a half months the Voting Rights Act of 1965 was law.

Clockwise from top left: Brown's Chapel in Selma—the starting point of the Selma to Montgomery march (© Norris McNamara); James Baldwin and Joan Baez on the way to Montgomery; a Canadian contingent lends its support; the march approaches its destination—the capitol in Montgomery, March 25, 1965 (all James H. Karales).

Opposite page: the man with one leg who walked the 54 miles from Selma to Montgomery. On the following pages: the march begins; entering Montgomery singing "We Shall Overcome" (all James H. Karales).

TOM WOLFE
The Pump House Gang

The Pump House Gang was just an anonymous group of surfers, called that because they hung around a concrete blockhouse used by the La Jolla waterworks. The blockhouse was just a landmark, a place to hang out. They arrived every morning at Windansea Beach, and some went out to surf.

I must have been a sight, when I look back on it. I looked tremendously old to them. I was thirty-four. I turned up every day in a seersucker jacket, white ducks, white shoes, white shirt and occasionally a necktie. I hadn't been out in the sun since '61, and I wasn't about to go out in it again. (I like the ocean air, but that's about all I like about the shore.) I was out there in my Eastern garb like Ruggles of Red Gap. I never pretended for a second—or even could have pretended—that I was a part of their world. I was like the man from Mars.

What's really amazing, though, is that if you stand around like the village information gatherer, people will come up and vounteer the most extraordinary things. Like the story of Donna, a twenty-one-year-old and her eighteen-year-old boyfriend who killed themselves in a murder/suicide pact on the steps of the Pump House. The local explanation was that she couldn't see anything beyond surfing. Her life had come to an end because she was now twenty-one. Another girl, Jackie, who was fourteen, gave me a composition she'd written after surfing with her boyfriend on twelve-foot waves at dawn which was full of poetry about "reverse stances" and "fast-flowing suction." They had their own vocabulary. "Bitchin" meant terrific. "Hang ten"—the best there was—was taken from how surfers put their toes at the very tip of the surfboard. "Hair-out" meant yellow—if you were unable to do some very dangerous surfing, then you "haired out."

The Volkswagen van had replaced the Woody, a station wagon with wooden sides, as the main mode of surfer transportation. All the wood on the Woodies had rotted out, so there were no more left. You could live in the van and still transport boards to and from the beach. And for the Pump House Gang, they were very easy to fix.

If the motor died, they waited until two or three in the morning, when they could spot another Volkswagen on a dark street. Then they exchanged motors. They didn't just steal the motors, they replaced the new motor with their own and wired it all up. They maintained that this was very thoughtful. The owner never had to face the humiliation that his motor had been stolen. He'd just figure it had conked out, and got it fixed.

The first surfers I ever met furnished their garages in the same way. I was supposed to meet them at my hotel at eleven-thirty one night. I walked up and I noticed something coming out of the casement windows. It was a huge portrait of a Spanish grandee that I remembered hanging over the mantel in the hotel lobby. Next came a big brass bowl full of magnolia blossoms. Then a piano stool with a plum-colored cushion. There in the gloaming I saw four or five boys in baggy shorts, windbreakers, and tennies, and I knew who they were. I asked, "What are you guys doing?" They said, "Well, we figured if we were going to take you down to see our garage, we ought to fix the place up a bit."

The surfer garages were the site of the first communal living I'd ever seen. The garages were mostly in alleyways near the beach. The beds were mattresses thrown over old carpeting, and electrical appliances were plugged in everywhere, attached to cords attached to lamps. There were some stuffed couches and armchairs, and "Coors Beer" signs on walls—spontaneous pop art, you might say. One of the boys had been kicked out of a garage. He and his pals were debating whether or not to go over to the garage, reinfiltrate it

Above and opposite page: the Pump House and the gang at Windansea Beach, La Jolla (© Bruce Davidson/Magnum).

142

and hold a destructo. "Destructo" was their update of an old, old word for a party involving demolition and carnage: namely, a "rout."

They were listed in the La Jolla phone book under "Meda, Mac," for the Mac Meda Destruction Company, which was the name they used when they invited people to parties, and they'd had decals made with a mushroom cloud and that name.

The Pump House Gang was not all male, by any means. There were some absolute knock-outs among the girls, many of whom had that pre-Raphaelite look of undone natural hair parted down the middle. In fact they went in for many styles that became common in the hip world two or three years later, such as fur jackets with the sleeves cut off and jeans with boots.

To keep up their reputation on Windansea, the group had to have some pretty good surfers, since Windansea was one of the best surfing beaches in the area. But no one in the group except, perhaps, a fellow named Artie Nelander was of championship caliber.

At Windansea, if you looked out about a thousand feet, there seemed to be huge pink shells bobbing up and down over the water. These were the backs of the surfers hunched over as they sat astride the boards looking out to sea, waiting for the swells that might build into a really good wave. Then it would be beautiful to watch. You'd see a good surfer get wrapped up in the curl of a wave and stay just far enough in front of it to keep from being pounded into the floor of the ocean.

It began to dawn on me that this surfing was just 25 percent sport and 75 percent way of life. It was a curious thing to build a communal life around, since riding a surfboard was so hard to do. But I got on terrifically with them because I never indicated that I knew the first thing about any of it. How could I? What could the man from Mars know?

Tom Wolfe first wrote about the surfers he met in Southern California for the New York World Journal Tribune's Sunday magazine, *New York, and that essay later appeared in his second book,* The Pump House Gang. *Wolfe's latest, and seventh book,* Mauve Gloves and Madmen, Clutter and Vine, *was published in 1976.★ (© Bruce Davidson/Magnum)*

The endless summer boys, above, and opposite page, a surfer girl (all © Bruce Davidson/Magnum).

144

DIANA VREELAND
Chatting about Style

I went to *Vogue* in 1962, as editor-in-chief, and almost immediately things took off into the real, swinging Sixties. It was the best time to be a journalist in fashion because with fashion goes the ambiance of a time—it's more than just the clothes. I was in the perfect place at the perfect time. The Kennedy White House gave style and good taste a good name. The whole thing was too delightful, and I was the most fortunate person in the world.

A youthquake was starting. High society had disintegrated incredibly. "Society," in the old sense, had to have a center: great houses to go to, private places to be seen in. High society was a private world, but suddenly it seemed everyone had gravitated to his own private world and the center was lost. Meanwhile, the young did things their way, without regard to the old world. And anyone who wasn't with them made no difference at all.

Top model Jean Shrimpton—the Shrimp (David Montgomery/ Photo Trends).

I saw the first traces of the change with the Twist. My son took me to the piers in South Philly, where all the rock and roll was playing, to watch this dance. Things were really cooking. Within weeks all of New York was twisting at the Peppermint Lounge. I remember even Mrs. Lytle Hull, the *grande dame* of New York society, brimming with curiosity and venturing there to see why everyone was twisting. She was very amused.

Internationalism had everything to do with it. The two most important factors were the Pill and the jet plane. Suddenly, women were freed sexually and fashion was transformed. All over the world, beautiful girls, photographers, and kids were flying to Nepal, Afghanistan, Katmandu. They would see things that other generations only read of as scholars. All of this had an enormous effect on the imagination. Night-blooming jasmine, lotus flowers, sun. Under the equator, the moon is in a different position. Everything was suddenly available.

Then photographs started coming in to me with the new English look. I loved it instantly. I published photographs of the Beatles in 1964 with their clean, sweet Eton-boy image. Then David Bailey sent me pictures of his new girl, Jean Shrimpton, who quickly became a top model here. Later that year he sent me the Rolling Stones. Mick was kind of stout, with a huge mouth, and a much bigger face. Not the beauty that he is today.

England became the trend-setter for the rest of the world. I get on with the English well—I was born English. I never fail to remark on how they buck up and take advantage of any situation and then turn it their way—often into a bizarre form of expression. It was a very interesting social picture there for a moment.

The idea of beauty was changing. If you had a big nose it made no difference, so long as you had a marvelous body and good carriage. You held your head high, then you were a beauty. The throat was long, the wrist slim, the legs long. You knew how to water-ski, snow ski and how to take a jet plane fast in the morning to go anywhere, be anyone when you got off.

By the mid-Sixties, we'd introduced two major looks in the pages of *Vogue*. With Courrèges, the English minijupe ascended to *haute couture*. The minijupe had started with the little girls of London. With their beautiful complexions and their long swinging hair, they strolled Knightsbridge in these little dresses.

Mary Quant had helped it along; Courrèges took it over from a clean, athletic, aesthetic point of view. He turned out big bubble hats, bubble glasses, and it looked like we were going to the moon. In a minijupe, one wore short white boots and delicious little white gloves—marvelous, ravishing.

Part of my family lived in Rabat, the capital of Morocco. Every time I was in Paris, I'd take the Friday plane right down. In two hours, I was in the world of the caftan and the jhelaba, and I found it the most delightful way to dress. The jhelaba is the Moroccan outdoor costume for men and women. You put it over your head. It's like a caftan, but not open to the ground. In the streets, everyone wears a jhelaba, from the king to the silk merchant. All of North Africa has worn it forever.

I brought it to *Vogue* by having all sorts of luxurious European princesses and contessas pose in caftans—I sent to Rome for seventeen- and eighteenth-century caftans for Elizabeth Taylor.

British designer Mary Quant (John Cowen/Photo Trends).

Whenever I wanted to introduce a style, I always used the Italians, with their *je ne sais quoi,* their special extras: five languages, marvelous manners, lunch at half-past three and dinner at half-past eleven. The Italian movie, Fellini; the Italian beauty, Magnani; were the curtain raisers of the period. One must never forget the ones who do the warming up. It's easy for everyone to join, but who establishes it? It comes from nuance here and there.

Makeup went the whole way, then, didn't it? You could use anything: yellow, orange, silver and gold on one eyelid. I also introduced the unmade-up mouth, which took three-quarters of an hour to put on. When

our new styles arrived in the provinces, though, then the deluge came, with letters reading: "When are you going to publish the clothes for real women?" Real clothes for real women, that was the cry. R–E–E–L— that's how I spelled it.

By this time, the magazine had become accustomed to the, shall we say, eccentricities of the editor-in-chief. The advertising department kept saying, "You're keeping the magazine so young. It's wonderful."

But I never knew how to reply to that. I've never thought of fashion as being anything but young, because when it's old, it's a compromise. Then it's no longer fashion, it's merchandise.

Above: youthquake specials (all Photo Trends).

For over thirty-five years Diana Vreeland reported and popularized the fashions of the day: first as fashion editor at Harper's Bazaar and then as editor-in-chief at Vogue. When she left Vogue in 1971, she became special consultant to the Costume Institute at New York's Metropolitan Museum of Art and organized five shows: "The World of Balenciaga," "The Ten, the Twenties, the Thirties," "Romantic and Glamorous Hollywood Design," "American Women of Style," and "The Glory of Russian Costume."★ (Caterine Milinaire)

DAVID BAILEY
Coming of Age in Swinging London

It was late spring when Chrissie Shrimpton announced that she had a man who was going to be bigger than the Beatles. He was performing on an island in the Thames, and Chrissie was only about fifteen. Her father was very unhappy about her sister Jean being with a married photographer, and I had been threatened with a shotgun all the previous year. Now I was accepted—just. I thought that someone with even longer hair who sang for a living would be considered worse than someone who was paid to take snaps. Chrissie's father didn't know that no one would let his or her daughter marry a Rolling Stone, but I think he had his suspicions.

I first met Mick at the Shrimptons' farm; he had long hair, big lips and not much dialogue. I'm not sure who thought who was square. Later he thought I was a star-fucker, but that was just his conceit. He was giving Chris a hard time, so a photographer friend of mine named Duffy said we would give him a going over, cut some of that hair. But we were more talk than action.

Mick and I became friends. I think I was lacking in his eyes because I was not a musician, but I became his link to another world—and I knew that this rude, long-haired git was on his way. By this time I was a man of the world, so when Mick wanted to go to a proper restaurant I took him to the Casserole, which was, and still is, a little bistro on Kings Road. He slopped his food like a good lower-middle-class boy. I, being working class, noticed bad manners more than most. To Mick's amazement I told him he had to leave a tip of 15 percent. I think that was his first realization of things to come.

Terry Stamp had taken Jean and me to a place in the sky called the Ad-Lib. It was a Soho penthouse converted into a discotheque with loud music, mirrored walls and a huge window looking down on London. The clients were pop stars, young actors and actresses, artists and photographers. I took Mick, and soon, like a Fifties debutante, he came out with a little help from his friends.

I met the rest of the Stones when I shot the cover for their second album up at Vogue Studio. I never got paid—in those days things were done out of friendship. Charlie Watts made a great impression on me because he was a fan of Charlie Parker and knew who Irving Penn was, which made him quite rare in that time and space. I never really became friends with Bill or Keith. But I later became friends with Brian, of whom I felt protective. He was really a little prince.

Mick came to Paris with me on an assignment for French *Vogue*. Even though he was known in England, he could have been a creature from the black lagoon to the French. But I took some pictures of him, and Diana Vreeland, who with her usual insight loved his face, used them in the American edition of *Vogue*. Later we were thrown out of our hotel for making too much noise. Flying back to London in the tourist section I first realized that fame embarrasses me. The air hostesses were English and recognized Mick. They asked if we'd like to sit in first class. We drank the free champagne, but stayed where we were.

Going through customs, a fake Battle of Britain type in a blue blazer and Royal Air Force badge asked Mick, "Who on earth do you think you look like?" Mick replied in his usual suave way, "As long as I don't look a cunt like you I'm all right." The first of many heads turned. Now I see Mick maybe twice a year and love him very much, partly because you love people the longer you know them, partly because he hasn't changed that much and still resents that 15 percent service charge.

Londoner David Bailey was one of the foremost photographers and trend-setters of the Sixties; his fashion photographs of Jean Shrimpton, Marisa Berenson and others made them the stars of the modeling world. He is currently producing documentaries and TV commercials—and continues to do fashion photography.

Bailey and Jean Shrimpton (Photo Trends). Opposite page: Jagger, 1965 (© Jim Marshall).

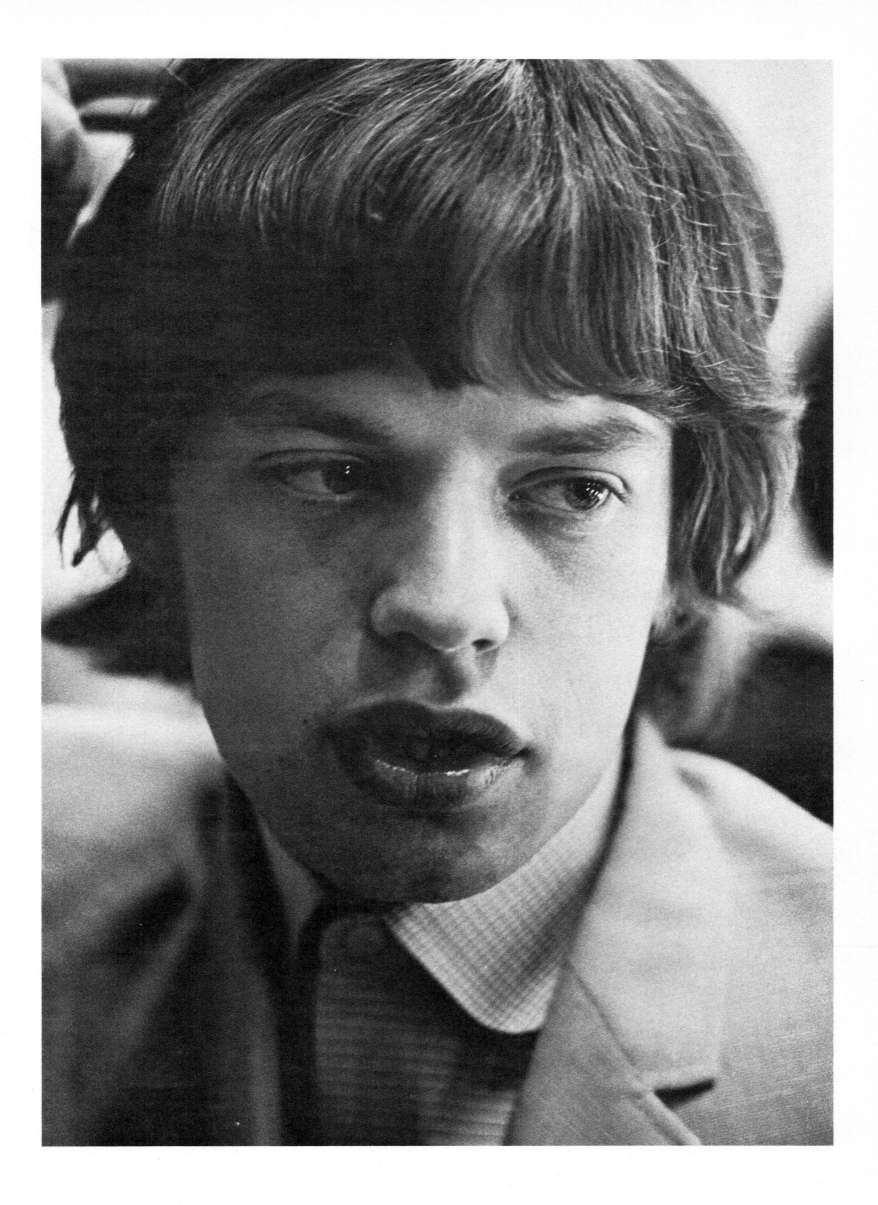

MICHAEL BLOOMFIELD
Dylan Goes Electric

The Folk Establishment at Newport was selling fewer and fewer records because rock and roll was getting more popular. They'd embraced Dylan a few years before as the youngest member of their camp, saying, "You weren't with the Weavers, but you knew Woody Guthrie. You are a real folkie, Cowboy Bob." And then Dylan went out and played rock and roll.

To the folk community, rock and roll was greasers, heads, dancers, people who got drunk and boogied. Lightnin' Hopkins had made electric records for twelve years, but he didn't bring his electric band from Texas. No, sir, he came out at Newport like they had just taken him out of the fields, like the tar baby. This guy's an incredible modern street guy, and he came out there like Stepin Fetchit. It was ridiculous, but the folk style was "relevant." It was image. To them, it was more romantic than rock and roll. They wanted Dylan to wear Iron Boy overalls and sing songs about Hattie Carroll.

Dylan might have been just as content to do an acoustic set. He spent the whole day in the sound truck, with his bodyguard and Bobby Neuwirth, getting high and fermenting in his brain. He probably had a few apprehensions. Maybe he even knew that it might not go over.

I just never dreamed it wouldn't. I played with the Butterfield Band—six amplified instruments—before Bob played. The audience loved it. That was always the highlight of the evening—when people could get up and boogie. I thought that when Bob played, it would be the best boogie yet.

Something ridiculous happened the day Butterfield played, which should have tipped me off. We played amplified music very expertly, but when we showed up at a workshop Alan Lomax, the folklorist, gave us a really bad introduction. It was like, "Well, Newport's finally reduced to bringing this sort of stuff to the stage." Our manager, Albert Grossman, the Grey Cloud, went up to him and said, "Hey, you know something? You're a real prick. How could you give an introduction like that for these people?" And Lomax said, "Hey, I'm not gonna take your lip!" and shoved Albert. And these two older, nonviolent people started duking it out. They were rolling on the ground, rolling in the tumbling tumbleweed.

Albert Grossman a few years after Dylan's electric debut (Baron Wolman).

I was cheering. I said, "Kick that ass, Albert." Wow. Albert put his body on the line to defend our right to boogie and rock and roll anywhere.

Albert was also Dylan's manager, and I'd played on Dylan's new electric album, *Highway 61,* so Barry Goldberg, some guys from the Butterfield Band, Al Kooper and I rehearsed a set with him.

By the next night, the momentum had built up. The festival had bodies out there as far as you could see—except it was dark and you couldn't see anything. They kept saying, "Bob's gonna come out." The festival was leaving him for last.

Then we came out. I was wearing Levis, a button-down shirt and a sports coat. The black guys from the Butterfield Band were wearing gold shoes and had processes. Dylan wore rock and roll clothes: black leather jacket, yellow pin shirt without the tie. And he had a Fender Stratocaster. He looked like someone from *West Side Story.*

We didn't electrify any of his old songs, we played the new things from *Highway 61,* songs like "Maggie's Farm." But it might as well have been old acoustic Bob, old Ramblin' Bob, the way he ignored the musicians. It could have been the Stones behind him. At most, he'd tighten his jaw and move just a little.

We finished with "Like a Rolling Stone," Dylan's hit single. I thought we were winning the crowd over. I thought we were boffo, smasheroo. After it was over, I said, "Bob, how do you think we did?" And he

Opposite page: Bob Dylan in 1965 (© Lisa Law).

150

said, "They were booing. Didn't you hear it?" I said, "No, man. I thought it was cheers." He didn't seem pissed, he seemed perplexed. He was a guy with a hit single, and they were booing him.

Then Peter Yarrow from Peter, Paul and Mary came out and said, "Well, come on, let's hear it for Bob." And all he heard was "Booo! Booo!" He was up there pleading for about ten minutes, and then in the back room he said, "Oh, Bob, go out and do one of your old numbers. Come on, Bob, you don't want to let your fans down."

In penance—in penance!—Dylan put on his old Martin and played. But he sang "It's All Over Now, Baby Blue." You know, "The sky is falling down on you, It's all over now, Baby Blue."

The Newport establishment—Theo Bikel, Odetta and Pete Seeger—felt betrayed. These people had embraced Bob as a prophet, and when his music no longer reflected their kind of social content, they felt politically and personally betrayed. His audience was just small-minded and rigid. You know why? Because they were more interested in idolatry than music. Many people who went through very poignant life changes used Dylan's old music as a background track for their lives. They said, "You show us the way." But he probably was just a poet making product, and when his way differed from their concept of "The Way," they were angry.

Dylan should have just given them the finger and said, "Hey, this is what I do. It's all over now, Baby Blue."

 Michael Bloomfield was one of the first white rock musicians to fuse electric guitar playing with the blues of Chicago's South Side. He joined the Butterfield Blues Band in the mid-Sixties, founded the Electric Flag in 1967 and later teamed up with Al Kooper for Super Session *and* The Live Adventures. *Today he plays the San Francisco Bay Area club and concert circuit, and his latest album is* If You Love These Blues, Play Them as You Please, *on Guitar Player Records. He thinks it's his best record.*★

CARL BERNSTEIN
New York Blacks Out

I was living in Manhattan, but I was working for a small paper in Elizabeth, New Jersey. I was supposed to have dinner with my former next-door neighbor from high school days, Ben Stein, who subsequently went to work in the Nixon White House as a speechwriter. He was going to Columbia at the time, and he lived on the twelfth or thirteenth floor of a big old building on Broadway. I hadn't been there more then five minutes when the lights went out. It was just about dusk.

We waited for a couple of minutes for the lights to go back on. They didn't, and when we looked out the window we saw that there were no lights at all. We walked one flight up to the roof and heard hollering from all the elevators. From the roof we could see that all the lights were gone. All there was was New Jersey; it was like this beacon, you couldn't see any of Manhattan. We put on a portable radio and there was a lot of talking going on there, about how a blackout had followed a grid pattern down from Canada. I figured this was going to be some story, so I said, "Well, I'll see you around, Ben," and I left.

I got a cab and rode—I didn't know where I was going to go, so I just rode down Broadway. There were crowds starting to gather all over, and some people were lighting candles. The streets were lined with people, and even in the first hour in the traffic I could recognize a feeling of shared experience. It wasn't like the normal New York attitude, you know, "Get out of my way so I can get downtown quicker."

We rode further down Broadway, and there were still no lights. The signs were off. It was amazing.

Finally I said to myself, "I guess the thing to do is go to the *New York Times.* They'll know what's going on." The cabbie let me out at Times Square, and I groped my way down to the *New York Times,* and I walked in. I had never been to the *New York Times* in my life. I went up a few flights of stairs, and some editor was yelling at a head copyboy, "Go out and buy more candles." He was taking dollar bills out of his pocket so this guy could buy more candles for the *New York Times* newsroom.

The whole place was a fire hazard; there was paper scattered all through the place. It must have been after the first deadline and people were trying to work with white candles on their desks. There were reporters all over the place, and it was apparent that they had no idea of what was going on except that all the lights were out. Nothing except the telephones worked, and it was mass confusion. It was as if the greatest news organization in the world knew absolutely nothing. I wondered if it was sabotage.

Two blackout scenes—selling magazines in a darkened subway station . . .

I decided to go out on the street. One of the first places I went to was Grand Central Station. It was just a madhouse, with everybody heading for the bars. You could see immediately that this was going to be the greatest adulterous affair there ever was. Nobody had to explain why they weren't coming home, right? People who I am sure had never in their lives messed around were dry-humping all over the place. It was wall to wall with stalled commuters, really something. ("Here's to the 7:02!")

I went down into the subways. A lot of people were stuck for hours, but they were singing songs like "I've Been Working on the Railroad." I interviewed people as they were led off the trains; everybody was making jokes and having a great time. The people from the subway were truly confused. They were under the impression it was a subway failure, and then they came up and saw that it wasn't the subway that failed. It was the universe.

I left Grand Central and started to hitchhike; you couldn't get a cab. The first ride I got was on the back of a little Honda, and I went to the Waldorf. It was getting very cold out. I had seen people come out of the subway, and now I wanted to see what the fancy people who were probably wearing tuxedos were doing. The Waldorf bar was absolutely jammed, and I did the requisite talking to the bartender and the customers. Again, there seemed to be a tremendous amount of commerce between older businessmen and young secretaries. It was a big holiday. People were really getting drunk. It was incredibly noisy, and coats were flying all over. You got the feeling that this might turn into the biggest binge since Prohibition.

. . . and preparing dinner by candlelight (both photos Bill Ray/Black Star).

I went downtown; I didn't know downtown New York, but it was somewhere around the Brooklyn Bridge or the Manhattan Bridge. By that time, people were trying to get uptown, and it was apparent to them that they were not going to get cabs, so they were hitchhiking. It was joyous. People felt safe in a way they never had. You're taught, especially in New York, "Don't talk to strangers; anybody that talks to you on the street is automatically a nut." Well, just the opposite was the case. It was like you could suspend all these frightening beliefs you had and just say, "Wow! Have you ever seen anything like this?" There was this great spirit of "together we will manage to get over this one." Nobody was nasty to anyone. People were deferential, patting each other on the back. There were a lot of "Where were you" horror stories passed among strangers. But I remember no sense of fear.

Finally I went to Port Authority and decided I would head for Jersey, which wasn't easy. It was about four A.M. I don't remember how I got to the paper, but I arrived at six and I finished writing for the eleven A.M. deadline. I wrote an eight-column-long story that was the whole front page of the paper I worked for. It was the only first-person story I had ever done, and the piece was overwritten, with a lot of imitation Tom Wolfe in it. All kinds of exclamation points. It was very embarrassing, and at the same time it was good enough to win a prize. The lead was some trite thing about electricity and Con Ed: you know, "Dig we must." The end of the piece came from my notes, scrawled aboard a Port Authority bus as we came out of the tunnel in Jersey with blacked-out New York behind us; boom—"Weehawken, City of Light."

In addition to writing about rock music for the Washington Post, *Carl Bernstein covered the Watergate affair for that paper. He began his career in journalism at the age of sixteen as a copyboy with the* Washington Star, *and in 1965 he joined the staff of the Elizabeth, New Jersey,* Daily Journal *as a reporter. He went to the* Washington Post's *metropolitan staff the next year. Bernstein coauthored* All the President's Men *and* The Final Days, *and is at work on a book about the witch hunts of the cold-war era.★ (Linda Wheeler, courtesy Simon & Schuster)*

153

LARRY NEAL
The Assassination of Malcolm X

What I liked most about Malcolm was his sense of poetry, his speech rhythms, and his cadences that seemed to spring from the universe of black music. Because I was not reared in the black church I was something of an anomaly among Northern blacks. I did not have ready access to the rhetorical strategies of Martin Luther King. My ears were more attuned to the music of urban black America—that blues idiom music called jazz. Malcolm was like that music. He reminded many of us of the music of Charlie Parker and John Coltrane—a music that was a central force in the emerging ethos of the black artistic consciousness. Malcolm was in the tough tradition of the urban street speaker. But there was a distinct art in his speeches, an interior logic that was highly compelling and resonant.

I was a political activist, in love with Ahada, who was also a political activist. We belonged to an organization that supported Malcolm after his break with the Black Muslims. The split began with Malcolm's statement that the Kennedy assassination was an example of "chickens coming home to roost." At the time he asserted that the sins of white America had caused Allah to visit this calamity of the assassination on the country. But it was such a startling statement, made while the nation was still in mourning, that the Honorable Elijah Muhammad put Malcolm on probation. He was forbidden to do any public speaking for three months. In itself, this was quite a startling development because Malcolm was very popular in the Afro-American community at large.

Meanwhile, the Muslims were undergoing an internal struggle over the question of political activism. The Muslims generally existed outside of the civil rights struggle. They were strongly opposed to integration. They did not support any political movements outside of their structure. Malcolm, on the other hand, often addressed himself to struggles of the civil rights workers, particularly the so-called militant wing of the movement. He found himself drifting closer and closer to its nationalistic elements. He found himself speaking more and more about the murders and the beatings that some of the young organizers were experiencing in the South and in the urban communities of the North. He wanted the Nation of Islam to become more involved in the political struggle as activists, and not just as enlightened commentators on the sidelines.

Sunday, February 21, 1965, was the weirdest kind of February day I've ever seen. It was so exceptionally warm that it was almost sultry. It felt more like late April than the middle of winter. I lived on 105th Street off Central Park West then; so the three of us—me, Ahada, and her twelve-year-old daughter, Amina—headed for the IND Eighth Avenue local, which would take us to the stop at 165th Street, where Broadway and St. Nicholas intersect. The Audubon Ballroom was opposite a small park. We carried bundles of our newspaper, *Black America*, to sell at the rally where Malcolm was speaking. We were a little late, which was bad. It meant that we'd missed the opportunity to sell the paper to the crowd that usually milled outside the auditorium before the rally. It was strange and eerie when we emerged from the subway at the park. There were no policemen anywhere. We made our way up the stairs of the ballroom, and no one searched us at the door. That too was surprising. Inside, we quickly slid into one of the booths that surrounded the parameters of the dance floor. The meeting hadn't quite started.

It was the kind of Sunday that made churchgoing people put on their finest. There were flowered hats of all colors and descriptions. There were children too, a lot of children like Amina. Some of the women wore African head wraps, called gélés. There was something churchlike about the whole ambiance, but there wasn't any organ music to entertain this congregation as it fidgeted through a speech by Brother Benjamin X.

We all knew that there had been several attempts on Malcolm's life. A premonition of impending

Opposite page: Malcolm X in 1964 (Bob Adelman).

violence passed over me. The guards moved into place. I remember thinking: If it's gonna happen, it's gonna happen now. Malcolm X stood at the podium, ready to speak. He gave the Muslim greeting, "*As-salaam 'alaykum,* brothers and sisters." The audience replied, "*'alaykum as-salaam.*" And then there was a commotion, a disturbance, and Malcolm stepped from behind the podium and said, "Peace, be cool, brother—" I saw one of the security guards move towards the disturbance. Things were happening fast now.

And I thought, It would happen now, in front of all his potential followers, and in full view of the people who loved him. Then it came. The strongest possible message, direct. The blast hit him and he fell backwards. His arms flung outward from the impact of the bullets hitting him square in the chest. Then there was the rumbling of scuffling feet and chairs were overturned. Shouting and screams came from the women and children. It seemed like the shots were coming from all over the ballroom. Amina bolted out of the seat beside us. Ahada managed to catch the child before she was trampled by the mob. A gunman ran by us, shooting and hurdling over chairs in his way. The man was still firing as he ran out of the door. He was being chased by several of Malcolm's men, and he had been wounded in the thigh. Another assassin left by the side door, waving his gun, daring anyone to follow him.

There were about three seconds of silence then. Hats and bags lay strewn about the floor along with overturned chairs. Malcolm was dead on the stage. And through the intense sunlight, there crept a loud moan as men and women wept with abandon. This was a different kind of music now.

*L*arry Neal taught creative writing and literature at Yale University, Wesleyan University, and most recently, Williams College. He is the author of two volumes of poetry, Black Boogaloo and Hoodoo Hollerin Bebop Ghosts, *and his essays have appeared in* Partisan Review, Arts in Society, *the* New York Times *and* Black World. *Neal is presently the executive director of the D.C. Commission on the Arts and Humanities in Washington, and is at work on a collection of essays on black culture in the Sixties. (James Hinton, courtesy William Morrow and Company)*

*O*pposite page: Malcolm X's body, shrouded in traditional Moslem burial dress and protected by glass, on view in Harlem (Bob Adelman).

STANLEY CROUCH
When Watts Burned

It burst like a Mexican piñata stuffed full of statistics about economics, racism and frustration. Some said that it was a set-up, that the men who exhorted crowds on the streets in those first days and nights were not from Watts, but were strangers working for some violent cause—Marxists, or the ubiquitous CIA. I think it had more to do with younger blacks who were exchanging the Southern patience and diligence of Martin Luther King for the braggadocio of Malcolm X, made attractive by the Muslims' self-reliance program.

It also said something about the concepts of manhood, self-defense and "justifiable revenge" that dominated much more television time than did the real suffering of the civil rights workers. Every tactic of King's was contradicted by weekly war films, swashbucklers, Westerns, and detective shows. *Men* did not allow women and children to be beaten, hosed, cattle-prodded or blown up in Sunday school. Nonviolence, both as tactic and philosophy, was outvoted.

For all that, even though I was a member of the community and had seen many a confrontation between community people and police, I was not prepared for what I saw in these days. Sure, I had seen my street filled before with gang members beating each other over the head with tire irons, chains, bottles. But it was almost always possible for two police cars to break the thing up. And a year before the *big* riot, I had seen a smaller one take place at Jefferson High School when a pillhead had been arrested, and his sister, who had been trying to intervene, was pushed away. Bricks and bottles knocked down many police officers that day—but three drawn guns brought an end to it.

I had also read LeRoi Jones and James Baldwin, had felt enraged, but considered most of their threats no

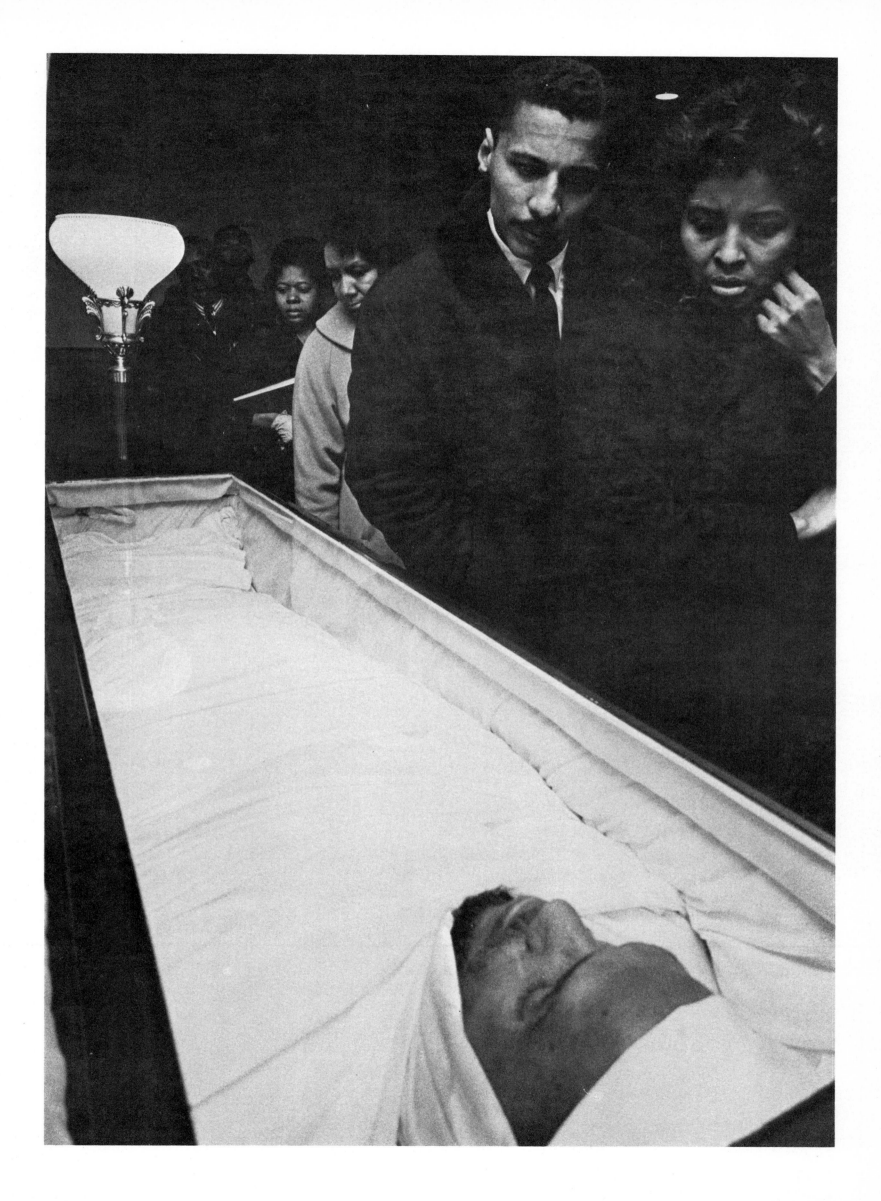

more than romantic literature, or at best, impotent fist-waving. Then, too, barbershops were always full of "would've, could've and should've" conversations about violent reactions to the racial tensions of the period.

I was hearing all of this, at nineteen, while writing speeches for an important person in Los Angeles's very nearly worthless poverty program. Since this person was an *expert* on the community, I was sent out there to find out what the disturbance was about in case the official ever had to speak authoritatively from a wellspring of hired information. Another street disturbance, I thought. Of course, I was wrong.

Watts,
after the riots
(Globe Photos).

I never saw the very important woman who finally sparked it all. She was actually seen by very few, but for a moment she was every black woman victim of white racism. She was part of a crowd that gathered to watch the arrest of a black man. As the scene got heated, the story goes, she was singled out by the police and physically abused. But momentum swept away symbols, and she was soon forgotten as windows shattered under the weight of hurled bricks, tire irons and feet.

People were in the street that night, Wednesday, August 11, talking rebellious talk, throwing bottles, milling around the projects on Imperial Highway, a six-lane artery that ran east toward the white suburbs and west toward the Harbor Freeway, passing the borders of Watts.

They were still there the next day, and by that night they had started tearing things up. The next day, Friday the 13th, the crowds were bigger, covering the sidewalks of 103rd Street, a strip of stores that sold overpriced second-rate merchandise.

The police were obviously frightened—these black people did not avert their eyes, did not tremble and stutter, but stared into their white faces with a confident cynicism, a stoic rebelliousness, even a dangerous mischief. This was unusual for Los Angeles blacks, who long before had literally been whipped into shape by Chief Parker's thin blue line, a police force known in the community for shooting or clubbing first and asking questions later. No one was afraid of them now, and no one would follow the bullhorn orders to disperse. The police did not understand.

The store owners did. They left for home. Windows were smashed and goods snatched. A few arrests were made and bottles bounced off the windows of police cars. The police made a show of force, a slow-moving line of fifteen or twenty police cars, provoking more bottles and more bricks. The police pulled out and the surge began in full force, taking 103rd Street before leaping like the proverbial wildfire over the whole black community.

I had never seen anything like it before. It was a bloody carnival, a great celebration. Warring street gangs that had been shooting each other for the past two years were drunk in the park, laughing at overturned cars, stoning or stabbing random whites who mistakenly drove through the area, jubilantly shouting how "all the brothers are *together*." Men stood in front of stores with their arms full of dreams—new suits, appliances, hats. The sky was full of smoke and there was occasional gunfire. Well-known local winos reached for Johnnie Walker Black and Harvey's Bristol Cream, leaving the cheaper stuff to feed the flames. The atmosphere at first was festive. Then on Saturday the National Guard went into action. With their arrival, the blood really began to flow. Within two days they had cordoned off the whole community.

Rumors sparked like random lightning about women and children being shot, and about subsequent cover-ups. Most of all, there was a feeling of occupation as the Jeeps rolled down the streets and the machine guns glinted in the sun, bayonets offering ugly invitations. Romantics thought the riot would take the state. But through the smoke I saw an older black woman emerge from a display window from which she had just stolen a new domestic worker's uniform. To me, she seemed to say what it was really all about.

Stanley Crouch was active in Los Angeles's
poverty program from 1965 to 1968. As a playwright
and an actor he was a member of the Watts Repertory Company,
and in 1968 he began teaching American literature and the
history of jazz at the Claremont Colleges. A musician who works
as a drummer and band leader in New York City, Mr. Crouch is
currently writing a book about jazz, Outlaws and Gladiators.
He is a frequent contributor to Downbeat,
Essence, Players, The Village Voice and
The New York Times Magazine.

Opposite page: taking the riot
to the stores—August 13th and 14th in the
commercial district of Watts (top four
photos: Wide World Photos; bottom: UPI).

ALLEN GINSBERG
Coming to Terms with the Hell's Angels

I think Peter Orlovsky and I came to San Francisco some time early in mid-'65. And the Haight-Ashbury cycle was forming, which was—incidentally—similar to the North Beach cycle: a lot of young kids coming in and creating a culture and prosperity coming with them. At that time Haight-Ashbury was just rising and becoming more charming. Kesey was around . . . and Neal Cassady was in town visiting at my house. Peter Orlovsky was there, I was there with a Buddhist girlfriend, and a young fifteen-year-old boy Buddhist acid-head who was illustrating *The Tibetan Book of the Dead* on a 150-foot scroll. Dylan was about to come to town before Christmas to give concerts at Berkeley.

Around October there was the beginning of a series of demonstrations at Berkeley, following the Free Speech Movement. There was an air of expectation and apocalyptic demand, which was quite beautiful and at the same time unrealistic. I remember this one kid kept climbing in the window of my poetry class demanding a revolution. He was demanding that I lead an immediate revolution right then and there, and he

The brothers Orlovsky, Julius and Peter, the Band's Robbie Robertson, in shades, and Bob Dylan come together in San Francisco (© Larry Keenan, Jr.).

wasn't able to define it.

The first demonstration that I remember taking place was a march from the Berkeley campus through the black district of Oakland to downtown Oakland, I guess. And I was on that daytime march. And we were maybe four or five rows from the front lines. The police stopped us from entering at the Oakland border. And so everybody sat down on the street and a sound truck was put in place and there were some speeches; at that point a fellow named Tiny—one of the Hell's Angels, who'd been behind the police lines on the Oakland side—and about seven Angels rushed out from behind Oakland police lines and tore down the big "Peace in Vietnam" banner that was being held up in front of the march, and ran over to the sound truck and cut the wires; nobody could make any speeches to be heard under the vast sky. Then there was a little scuffling with police and one of the Angels broke his leg. I'm not sure here.

Now, the reason that we were going to march through Oakland was that there were so many disadvantaged blacks—it was at the height of the black movement and we thought we could pick up a lot of marchers, particularly among poor and blacks who *were* against the war.

That's why we were stopped at the border by a straight line of what looked to us as storm troopers, the Oakland police. They were standing out there, with, I think, tear-gas masks—yeah, they had guns with them, though not drawn and pointed at us.

The October march was blocked, frustrated, so there was still the need to carry it through in a democratic fashion and "exercise Privileges"—which meant organizing another march for November. So there was a mass meeting to decide on the policy for the next march. One guy got up and said that the appearance of the Hell's Angels was parallel to the appearance of the Brown Shirt storm troopers in Germany who broke up Left democratic marches and demonstrations. He said that all the young men should march with long sticks and black and white armbands.

I printed up a handbill entitled "How to Make a March/Spectacle," which proposed a march as "Theater." It wasn't just a political march where people were supposed to run and march angry, shouting slogans; it could be seen as theater, as almost all political activity was. And given the situation, the best kind of theater would manifest the Peace that we were protesting. Pro-test being "pro-attestation," testimony *in favor* of something. So if we were going to be a peace-protest march, then we should have to be peaceful, and being peaceful took skillful means under such anxious circumstances.

My handbill outlined the possible "Acts," suggesting that the march should be like an old-fashioned parade with floats and clowns, with grandmothers carrying flowers, babies in their arms, followed by all the girls and maidens dressed up in pretty costumes, followed by a corps of trained fairies to rush up and pull down the Hell's Angels' pants and blow them on the spot if they gave any trouble, followed by a big float showing Lyndon Johnson with his pants down or something, naked virgins and beautiful boys advertising peace with flower garlands, big papier-mâché caricatures of the war, floats which would dramatize the Issues: a half-naked Vietnamese girl attacked by American soldiers all dressed up in robotic battle gear; airplanes, gaily painted dummy bombs—make a Max Reinhardt spectacle, Fritz Lang's *Metropolis*-inspired perhaps— Charlie Chaplin! Have someone disguised as W. C. Fields marching in the March, people dressed up as George Washington, and incense sticks in everybody's hands, harmonicas and guitars and funny poetic signs. Poetry March! I think probably the majority favored that attitude, a minority was noisy, at the end they voted a modified form of "manifestation": invite everybody to a community march.

Ginsberg, in the foreground with an open book, during the Berkeley to Oakland march . . .

Also, before the march there was another grand meeting with the Hell's Angels. It was at Sonny Barger's house. Now, the Angels'd threatened to come out and beat up the marchers if they marched. Kesey made a date to have a party at Barger's house and also discuss political social community developments with the Berkeley student movement. And so we, let's see, Cassady, myself, Kesey and several of Kesey's Prankster friends gathered together with about twenty Hell's Angels at Barger's house with his wife, in Oakland, and all dropped acid—except me. I was having bad trips and I didn't want to lay my bad trip on myself or anyone, not under those circumstances. I was scared, but they were all gung-ho for it. I brought along my harmonium and everybody was in a relatively excited state. The house interior was like some strange giant puppet theater, the Pranksters in the strange Prankster costumes and Angels in their Angel costumes. We did finally get into a discussion of what to do about the march and I was trying to discourage Barger from attacking; so was Kesey, very manfully, trying to talk sense to Barger. He told Barger that it wasn't really a communist plot, the main thing that he kept telling him was that it wasn't *just* communists. The Angels' argument was we gotta fight 'em here or there. Our argument was we don't have to fight them anywhere; why fight at all? We went over there—Americans invaded there, they hadn't invaded us. There's no point in picking a fight on their territory or turf.

And it was beginning to get a little acrimonious because it was somewhat blocked, although I think Kesey was making sense to them. He was succeeding, but there was still a great deal of resistance. So I pulled out my harmonium and began chanting the Maha Prajnaparamita Sutra, which is a text basic to both Tibetan and Zen Buddhism ("Highest Perfect Wisdom" Sutra).

. . . that ended in a confrontation with the Hell's Angels (both Jeffrey Blankfort).

So I started chanting the Prajnaparamita Sutra, which was not an argument, simply a tone of voice from the abdomen. I kept up this monosyllabic deep-voiced monochordal chant for a few minutes, and pretty soon Tiny joined us. I was sitting on the floor playing my harmonium and chanting, and Tiny joined me and began going, "Om, om, zoom, zoom, zoom, om." Pretty soon we had a gang of about twenty people and then Neal and I think Kesey joined in—pretty soon the whole room was chanting. It brought the whole scene down from the argument to some kind of common tone—because they were desperate too. They were just arguing because they were desperate; they didn't know what else to do except argue and maintain their righteous wrath. It settled everybody's breath there in a neutral territory where there was neither attack nor defense.

I was absolutely astounded, I knew it was history being made. It was the first time in a tense, tight situation that I relied totally on pure mantric vocalization, breath-chant, to alleviate my own paranoia and anxiety, resolve it through breathing out long breaths. Well, the upshot was that several days later the Angels issued their Newspaper Edict, saying that it would *demean* them to attack the filthy marchers, they wouldn't touch 'em with a ten-foot pole, dirty communists. They sent a telegram to Lyndon Johnson offering to fight against the commies in Vietnam and offering themselves as G-O-R-I-L-L-A soldiers, they spelled it in the telegram, printed in the S.F. *Examiner*—it was funny because the last publicity image the conservative, middle-class prowar right wing wanted was the Hell's Angels as a bunch of gorilla allies: it showed up the bestial nature of the war, to begin with. Also it resolved the temporary march situation and it also saved face for the Angels! Their cover story was that the marchers were too icky to attack. That "happy ending" came mostly from Ken Kesey's statesmanship and his common sense, because he'd been the one enlightened person on the scene—he wasn't on the left or right. Instead of banning and denouncing the "outlaw" Angels, he socialized with them and let a little light into their scene.

It was December then, and Dylan came to town for his West Coast tour. I saw a lot of him, and he gave me thirty or forty tickets for opening night. A fantastic assemblage occupied the first few rows of Dylan's concert: a dozen poets, myself, Peter, Ferlinghetti, Neal, and I think Kesey, Michael McClure; several Buddhists; a whole corps of Hell's Angels, led by Sonny Barger, Freewheelin' Frank and Tiny; and then came Jerry Rubin with a bunch of peace protestors. Fantastic.

Afterwards, I took Barger, McClure and several Angels to Dylan's dressing room. Barger pulled a joint out of a cellophane bag of forty to offer Dylan, but Dylan wouldn't mess with it. Then he got into a very funny conversation with Barger, saying something like "Look, you guys got something to say, don't you? You want to talk to the people, saying something to the nation? Well, what's your act? Why don't you come to New York and we'll put you on at Carnegie Hall. But you gotta get your show together, get your shit together. Do you have any songs? Can you recite poetry? Can you talk? If you want to extend yourselves, you can't make it by hanging around Oakland beating up on your own image."

They were stunned or stoned, but at the same time they realized that they had nothing to say, or else if they did, they hadn't found the right theater. And we'd had the same realization: our march had to get its theater together, just as the police and the government did. I think that was the beginning of our realization that national politics was theater on a vast scale, with scripts, timing, sound systems. Whose theater would attract the most customers, whose was a theater of ideas that could be gotten across?

Dylan was in town during the debates about the march, so I told Dylan about this, you know, all the scenes I'd seen and what was going on, and he thought; then he said Jerry Rubin had sent a message to him, would he join the march, lead the march? He wanted Dylan to lead the march, and they were still arguing whether it would be an angry chain march or what.

So Dylan said, okay—paraphrase—"Except we ought to have it in San Francisco right on Nob Hill where I have my concert, and I'll get a whole bunch of trucks and picket signs—some of the signs will be bland and some of them have lemons painted on them and some of them are watermelon pictures, bananas, others will have the word Orange or Automobile or the words Venetian Blind, I'll pay for the trucks and I'll get it all together and I'll be there, and we'll have a little march for the peace demonstration. What they're doing is too obvious, it's a bad show, chickenshit poetry, they don't know what the kids want, who's their public?" His image was undercurrent, underground, unconscious in people . . . something a little more mysterious, poetic, a little more Dada, more where people's hearts and heads actually were rather than where they "should be" according to some ideological angry theory.

So I reported Dylan's ideas back to Jerry Rubin and the Vietnam Day Committee marchers, and they didn't act on it, they didn't realize what was being offered them on a silver platter. I think Dylan offered it somewhat ironically, but I think he would have gone through with it. I think he was *interested*, he wanted to do *something*, but the terms of the march were too negative, not good enough theater, not even effective as propaganda, it never would have penetrated through to the young kids who didn't want to get involved in a crazed anger march.

And that always was the trouble with the marchers, before and after. There was too much anger marching, we'll come to more sublime calm theater in the next decade.

Allen Ginsberg is codirector of the Naropa Institute's Jack Kerouac School of Disembodied Poetics, and a member of the American Institute of Arts and Letters. In 1976, he traveled with Bob Dylan's Rolling Thunder Revue and he began an album, First Blues, *produced by John Hammond, Sr., which was finished in 1977. Ginsberg's latest books are* Mind Breaths: Poems 1972-1977 *and* Journals: Early Fifties-Early Sixties.★ *(Baron Wolman)*

Opposite page: Robertson, Michael McClure, Dylan and Ginsberg meet during Dylan's 1965 West Coast tour (© Jim Marshall). Page 164; San Francisco Hell's Angels—outlaw theater (© Gerhard E. Gscheidle).

1966

CALENDAR

January: 1 "Sounds of Silence" is number one single; Health warnings appear on cigarette packs; 8 Rubber Soul vaults into LP lead; 11 Draft controversy arises over reclassification of student demonstrators to 1-A; 13 Batman comes to TV; 17 Cabinet's first black is HUD Secretary Robert Weaver; 21-22 Trips Festival brings San Francisco hippies together; 31 U.S. resumes bombing in Vietnam.

February: 1 LSD comes under federal regulation; 2 208 die in record East Coast blizzards; 10 First draft-card burning conviction; 14 In Cold Blood tops nonfiction list; 19 "Lightnin' Strikes" at top of chart while Stevie Wonder's "Uptight" climbs.

March: 2 U.S. acknowledges the loss of one hydrogen bomb in B-52 crash off Spanish coast; 5 "The Ballad of the Green Berets" is top single; 9 General Motors admits harassing Ralph Nader following publication of Unsafe at Any Speed last year; 12 If You Can Believe Your Eyes and Ears brings the Mamas and the Papas to the LP chart; 18 Scott Paper offers a $1.00 paper dress; 21 Supreme Court rules Fanny Hill not obscene; 25-27 Antiwar International Days of Protest; 28 The Avengers becomes TV regular.

April: 8 Time magazine cover asks "Is God Dead?"; 14 Federal government becomes sole pharmaceutical distributor of LSD; 350 people buy Washington Post ad declaring their refusal to pay taxes to support the war; 18 Best-picture Oscar goes to The Sound of Music; Masters and Johnson shatter sexual myths with Human Sexual Response; 21 U.S. combat toll in Vietnam reaches 3,047.

May: 7 "Gloria" reaches Top Ten; 8 CBS broadcasts Death of a Salesman; 14 Black power advocate Stokely Carmichael is elected head of SNCC; 28 Ray Charles enters chart with "Let's Go Get Stoned."

June: 2 Unmanned Surveyor I successfully lands on moon; 6 Sniper wounds James Meredith on Mississippi march; 12 Minimum wage is raised to $1.40; 13 Supreme Court rules in Miranda case that suspects must be informed of their rights; 29 U.S. bombing raids reach Hanoi and Haiphong.

July: 2 The Fugs enter LP chart; 12-15 Chicago blacks riot; 14

Murder of eight Chicago student nurses; 15-22 Brooklyn blacks riot; 17 Runner Jim Ryun regains mile world record for U.S.; 18 House questions Justice Douglas' morals; Cleveland blacks riot; 25 Chinese newscasts boast of Chairman Mao's fitness after Yangtze swim; 28-29 Baltimore erupts; 29 Bob Dylan in motorcycle accident as Blonde on Blonde begins LP chart climb.

August: 1 Texas sniper Charles Whitman kills 14; 5 John Lennon's "We're more popular than Jesus" statement creates furor; 6 Luci Baines Johnson marries Patrick Nugent; 13 "Summer in the City" replaces "Wild Thing" as leading single; 18 Chinese youth forms Red Guard to erase Western influences in China; 29 San Francisco concert marks last live appearance of Beatles.

September: 3 "Sunshine Superman" is leading single with "Bus Stop" climbing; 4 U. of Pennsylvania is first college to drop classified government research; 8 Star Trek's TV debut; 12 The Monkees invade TV; 16 New Metropolitan Opera House at Lincoln Center opens; 19 Timothy Leary proclaims LSD the sacrament of his new religion; 20 George Harrison goes to India; 21 Treasury Dept. reports Vietnam War costs $4.2 billion a month.

October: 5 Near nuclear disaster at Enrico Fermi reactor; 8 Butterfield Blues Band's East-West enters LP chart; 15 U.S. troops exceed regular Vietnamese forces at 320,000; 17 Housewives boycott supermarket high prices; 29 "96 Tears" leads chart with "Walk Away Renee" fifth; 31 Rush to Judgment is top nonfiction seller.

November: 1 Abu-Simbel temple is saved from Egypt's Aswan Dam; Kennedys give JFK death photos to National Archives; 4 Heavy floods damage Florence art treasures; 8 California elects Reagan governor; 12 Parsley, Sage, Rosemary and Thyme climbs LP chart; 21 Johns Hopkins reports first sex change operations in American hospital.

December: 2 First Friday Roman Catholics can eat meat; 5 Supreme Court orders Georgia legislature to seat Julian Bond; 10 "Good Vibrations" and "Winchester Cathedral" battle for chart lead; 15 Walt Disney dies; 22 U.S. toll in Vietnam reaches 6,407.

Top: Paper-dressed Ms. Hope Ruff at a party with Andy Warhol (John Cameola/Globe Photos). Bottom: Ralph Nader and the Washington, D.C., beltway (Wide World Photos). Opposite page: striking farmworkers marching during the 1966 Delano to Sacramento UFW pilgrimage in California (John A. Kouns).

STEWART BRAND
Why Haven't We Seen the Whole Earth?

It was one month after the Trips Festival at Longshoremen's Hall when the "whole earth" in *The Whole Earth Catalog* came to me with the help of one hundred micrograms of lysergic acid diethylamide. I was sitting on a gravelly roof in San Francisco's North Beach. It was February 1966. Ken Kesey and the Merry Pranksters were waning toward Mexico. I was twenty-eight.

In those days, the standard response to boredom and uncertainty was LSD followed by grandiose scheming. So there I sat, wrapped in a blanket in the chill afternoon winter sun, trembling with cold and inchoate emotion, gazing at the San Francisco skyline, waiting for my vision.

The whole earth on the back cover of the first catalog, 1968.

The buildings were not parallel—because the earth curved under them, and me, and all of us; it closed on itself. I remembered that Buckminster Fuller had been harping on this at a recent lecture—that people perceived the earth as flat and infinite, and that that was the root of all their misbehavior. Now from my altitude of three stories and one hundred mikes, I could *see* that it was curved, think it, and finally feel it.

But how to broadcast it? It had to be broadcast, this fundamental point of leverage on the world's ills. I herded my trembling thoughts together as the winds blew and time passed. A photograph would do it—a color photograph from space of the earth. There it would be for all to see, the earth complete, tiny, adrift, and no one would ever perceive things the same way.

But how to accomplish this? How could I induce NASA or the Russians to finally turn the cameras backwards? We could make a button! A button with the demand "Take a photograph of the entire earth." No, it had to be made a question. Use the great American resource of paranoia . . . "Why haven't they made a photograph of the entire earth?" There was something wrong with "entire." Something wrong with "they."

"Why haven't we seen a photograph of the Whole Earth yet?" Ah. That was it.

Brand, the button salesman (reprinted by permission of the San Francisco Chronicle).

The next day I ordered the printing of several hundred buttons and posters. While they were being made I spent a couple of hours in the San Francisco library looking up the names and addresses of all the relevant NASA officials, the members of Congress *and* their secretaries, Soviet scientists and diplomats, UN officials, Marshall McLuhan and Buckminster Fuller.

When the buttons were ready I sent them off. Then I prepared a Day-Glo sandwich board with a little sales shelf on the front, decked myself out in a white jump suit, boots and costume top hat with crystal heart and flower, and went to make my debut at the Sather Gate of the University of California in Berkeley, selling my buttons for twenty-five cents.

Lois Jennings, a newly arrived Ottawa Indian lady that I later married, helped me override the stage fright. It went perfectly. The dean's office threw me off the campus, the *San Francisco Chronicle* reported it, and I had my broadcast.

It was so enjoyable, conducting street-clown seminars on space and civilization, that I kept returning to Cal. Then I branched out to Stanford. And then to Columbia, Harvard, MIT. "Who the hell's that?" asked an MIT dean, watching hordes of his students buying my buttons. "That's my brother," said my brother Pete, an MIT instructor.

Stewart Brand, 1969 (Baron Wolman).

In the fall of 1967, the first really convincing photos began to appear, culminating in the beautiful Apollo 8 color photo with the moon in the foreground.

Years later, I was talking to a group about Indians when one of the kid's fathers suddenly burst out: "You're the guy!"

"What?" said I.

"I investigated you. I was doing that sort of work for NASA in 1966. They wanted to know if you constituted a threat to the United States government. I checked you out. You seemed all right, so I wrote them that this was California, where people took strange notions, and that you were acting alone and probably constituted no great threat. I signed my name, Captain So-and-so, and then I remember I added a postscript: 'P.S. By the way—why *haven't* we seen a photograph of the whole earth yet?'"

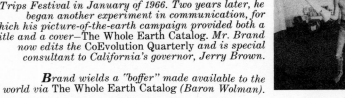

Stewart Brand organized the San Francisco Trips Festival in January of 1966. Two years later, he began another experiment in communication, for which his picture-of-the-earth campaign provided both a title and a cover—The Whole Earth Catalog. Mr. Brand now edits the CoEvolution Quarterly and is special consultant to California's governor, Jerry Brown.

Brand wields a "boffer" made available to the world via The Whole Earth Catalog (Baron Wolman).

JERRY RUBIN
A Yippie Goes to Washington

In Berkeley, rumors of subpoenas to the House Committee on Un-American Activities began to surface at the beginning of August. A year earlier, a group of students, professors and dropouts called the Vietnam Day Committee had shocked the nation by blocking troop trains carrying soldiers to the Oakland Army Terminal. We did everything possible to make life miserable for Lyndon Baines Johnson and his war. We organized teach-ins, mass marches and draft-card burnings. When General Maxwell Taylor came to town, we greeted him by surrounding his limousine with barbed wire. Berkeley was a hotbed of antiwar activity, and the Congress wanted it cooled.

HUAC intended to scare everybody to death with the subpoenas—it was a tactic that had worked well against "Communists" in the Fifties. But what passed as a trauma in most places became an honor in Berkeley. Everyone was hoping they would get a subpoena, including me, and finally, it arrived. I was thrilled. I made the rounds of the newspapers and radio and television stations denouncing HUAC as a witch-hunter.

The people who got subpoenas were heroes. Those who didn't had "subpoenas envy." Everyone wanted one, because they flew us to Washington, put us up in a hotel, and all we had to do was defend our beliefs.

I had to decide how to handle the hearings. I knew that the best strategy would be to countershock the committee with my own theater—to take the initiative away from HUAC. So I decided to go to the hearings as an American Revolutionary War soldier, complete with blue cutaway coat with lots of brass buttons, knee breeches, buckle shoes and a tricornered hat.

Most of the serious people on the Left in Berkeley were against it. They thought I should be rational and intellectual in my opposition to HUAC, not theatrical. But I had to trust my own media instincts. The only way to hurt HUAC was to zap them—you couldn't outreason them in their own arena of irrationality. HUAC's intention in investigating antiwar activity was to gather evidence to support pending legislation designed to declare actions like blocking troop trains illegal and punishable by up to twenty years in prison and a $20,000 fine.

Rubin in disguise in Berkeley —this time as a Viet Cong guerrilla (© Alan Copeland).

I felt that to take the committee seriously would be devastating—we had to attack its very legitimacy. My action was addressed to a specific audience. I was speaking to young people across the nation, and I knew my uniform would communicate to them that you didn't have to be scared, that you could turn your fear into courage. I wanted the image of me in costume at the hearings to inspire more outrageous antiwar actions.

In Washington, the night before the hearings, I freaked out. No one had ever done what I was planning to do before. I was going to make a national asshole out of myself by wearing a costume to a congressional hearing. Congressional hearings were respectable, even sacred. People were going to laugh at me. At the last minute I thought I might not do it. I couldn't sleep. I was really sweating. I thought, "What am I doing? Am I crazy?" But the next day, in the sweltering heat of a Washington August, I thought, "To hell with it. I'm going to do it. What do I have to lose?"

The hearings opened on August 16th. I arrived in my outfit and the guards were so shocked they wouldn't let me in at first. I kept screaming, "But I'm a subpoenaed witness." The U.S. marshals and the D.C. police blocked me at the door. Beverly Axelrod, my lawyer, yelled, "I'm an attorney for the witness and the police won't let us in," and when Joe Pool, the committee chairman, finally admitted us, the press immediately turned toward us. There I was, dressed in a Revolutionary War uniform, accused of treason.

As soon as I got to the hearing room, I knew that I'd done the right thing. What HUAC didn't understand was that what worked in busting "Communists" in the Fifties wouldn't work any more. They thought they could just frighten everyone into submission. But they were dealing with a different situation now. I was from a counterculture. I wasn't trying to keep a job or protect my own economic interests. I was a representative of the fact that there were two cultures at war, with different values.

The hearings became a circus. Progressive Labor people, who had been subpoenaed in large numbers, filibustered by giving unsolicited lectures on racist/fascist America, and threatened to vomit all over the committee's table. Marshals used physical violence in arresting people and thus desecrated the congressional hearing room. One of our lawyers, Arthur Kinoy, argued strenuously with Pool, who shook his finger at him and told him to sit down. When Kinoy refused, he was put in a hammer lock and removed from the room by three U.S. marshals.

The hearings went on for four foolish days, and finally were abruptly canceled. I jumped up and screamed, "I haven't had a chance to testify, I want to testify!" As I was screaming, I was grabbed by two large marshals and shoved into the elevator, losing my tricornered hat in the process. The hearings were clearly a victory for the antiwar movement, and the beginning of the end for HUAC. They taught me the power of the media to instantaneously transform national consciousness. And even though I didn't know it at the time, for me it was the start of "Yippie"—guerrilla theater media politics.

HUAC subpoenaed Jerry Rubin in 1966 because of his activities as cochairman, cofounder and active member of the Vietnam Day committee. He was arrested, jailed and fined for disorderly conduct at the end of the '66 hearings. A year later, he and Abbie Hoffman created the Youth International Party (Yippie), which played a major role in the demonstrations at the Democratic Convention in Chicago in the summer of 1968. A year later, Rubin was one of the eight defendants in the infamous Chicago conspiracy trial. He is the author of four books; his latest, Growing (Up) at Thirty-seven, was published in 1976. Rubin is now lecturing and writing, and living in New York City.★

Beverly Axelrod defends Jerry Rubin at the 1966 HUAC hearings (Wide World Photos).

171

PAUL KRASSNER
Lenny Bruce, Lawyer

"The role of a comedian," Lenny Bruce once told me, "is to make the audience laugh at a minimum of once every fifteen seconds on the average, or let's be liberal and say one laugh every twenty-five seconds."

Years later, he acknowledged that he was changing.

"I'm not a comedian," he explained. "I'm Lenny Bruce."

One night, a year or so before he died, Lenny and I sat in the living room of his home in Hollywood, fooling around with a tape recorder.

"I will confess to some experiences that I've had," he fantasized. "Forbidden sights I have seen. The most beautiful body I've ever seen was at a party in 1954. I was in the bedroom getting the coats. The powder-room door had been left intentionally ajar, and I viewed the most perfect bosom peeking out from the man-tailored blouse above a tweed pegged skirt.

" 'You like what you see? They *are* nice, aren't they?' she said, caressing the area near her medallion. 'Yes, they are very nice.' 'Would you like to touch them?' 'I'm—I'm—' 'You're shocked,' she said, 'aren't you?' Indeed I was. Eleanor Roosevelt had the prettiest tits I had ever seen or dreamed that I had seen.

" 'I've got the nicest tits that have ever been in this White House, but because of protocol we're not allowed to wear bathing suits, you know. I get a million offers for pictures, but being saddled with the Girl Scout coordinators has left me with only a blind item in a gossip column: 'What Capitol Hill biggy's wife has a pair of lollies that are setting the Washington-go-round a-twitter?' "

Lenny Bruce's problem was that he wanted to talk on stage with the same freedom he exercised in his life. This harmless little bit of incongruity about Eleanor Roosevelt showed up in his act from time to time. Murray Kempton, whose criticism was usually of a more political nature, said it reminded him of *A Child's Christmas in Wales* by Dylan Thomas. Poetry or not, it certainly didn't fall within the definition of "hardcore" pornography that the Supreme Court ruled was not protected by the First Amendment.

Nevertheless, Lenny was arrested in a Greenwich Village coffeehouse called the Cafe Au Go Go for giving an indecent performance. At the top of the complaint was "Eleanor Roosevelt and her display of tits." He was found guilty, two to one, by a three-judge panel. Between the guilty verdict and the sentencing, he fired his lawyer and decided to handle the case himself. He was superb at the trial. He had done his legal homework and had discovered that in 1931 then-governor Franklin Delano Roosevelt had signed an amendment to the New York obscenity law which would have excluded from arrest: stagehands, spectators, musicians, and—here was the fulcrum of his defense—actors. Actors! Lenny the Lawyer said, "Ignoring the mandate of Franklin D. Roosevelt is a great deal more offensive than saying Eleanor has lovely nay-nays."

Still, Lenny was sentenced to four months in the workhouse.

"Where can I appeal?" he asked.

"The court cannot act as counsel," replied the judge.

In the press room of the criminal courts building in New York, radio and TV reporters interviewed Lenny. NBC's Gabe Pressman asked him, "Do you believe in obscenity?"

"What do you mean?" replied Lenny. "Do I believe we should pray for obscenity?"

As we were walking into the lobby, a man came up and said, "Listen, I have some stag films and party records that you might be interested in . . ." Lenny and I went for some pizza instead. Then we headed for his hotel room where, to help unwind from the day's tension, he played some old tapes, ranging from faith healer A. A. Allen to patriotic World War II songs:

Goodbye, Mama
I'm off to Yokahama

172

The Land of Yama-Yama

"That's my favorite line," said Lenny, and he played it over again.

He hadn't been able to get work in six months. Club owners were afraid to book him. He almost got an engagement in Philadelphia—where he was once arrested on a trumped-up narcotics charge and then cleared—but the deal fell through; the district attorney wanted him to show up a couple of days early to see if there was morphine in his system and to present his material in advance.

About this time, we drove to Atlantic City and passed signs along the way that read CRIMINALS MUST REGISTER.

"Criminals must register," Lenny mused. "Does that mean, in the middle of a holdup, you have to go to the courthouse and register? Or does it mean that you *once* committed a criminal act? Somebody goes to jail, and after fifteen years' incarceration you make sure you get them back in as soon as you can by shaming anyone on TV who would forgive them, accept them or give them employment. 'The Unions knowingly hire ex-convicts.' "

Now it had come to pass: Lenny Bruce MUST REGISTER.

Lenny went before the court of appeals seeking an injunction that would prevent district attorneys from arresting him in the future. This three-judge panel was headed by Thurgood Marshall, formerly chief counsel for the National Association for the Advancement of Colored People.

Lenny pleaded that he was like a carpenter whose tools were being taken away. He compared the denial of his rights to "a nigger who wants to use a toilet in Alabama."

Said Judge Marshall: "You're not a Negro, Mr. Bruce."

"Unfortunately not, Your Honor," replied Lenny to the black magistrate. His request was denied.

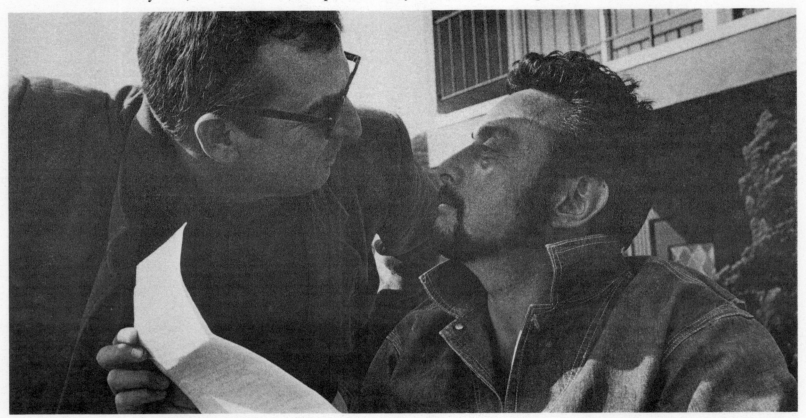

Lenny Bruce died August 3, 1966. They buried him in a Jewish cemetery on the West Coast, and when his friends wanted to have a picnic on his plot that day, the owner closed the premises, asking Lenny's mother, "Who's gonna clean up?"

Paul Krassner, founder and editor of
The Realist, *edited Lenny Bruce's autobiography,*
How to Talk Dirty and Influence People. *He
is presently working the college circuit
as a stand-up satirist. (© Paul Kagan)*

*This page, top: Lenny at home a
year before he died, and above, with
Terry Southern (B. Claxton/Globe Photos).
Opposite page: Bruce in a New York hotel
in 1964 (Wally Huntington/Globe Photos).*

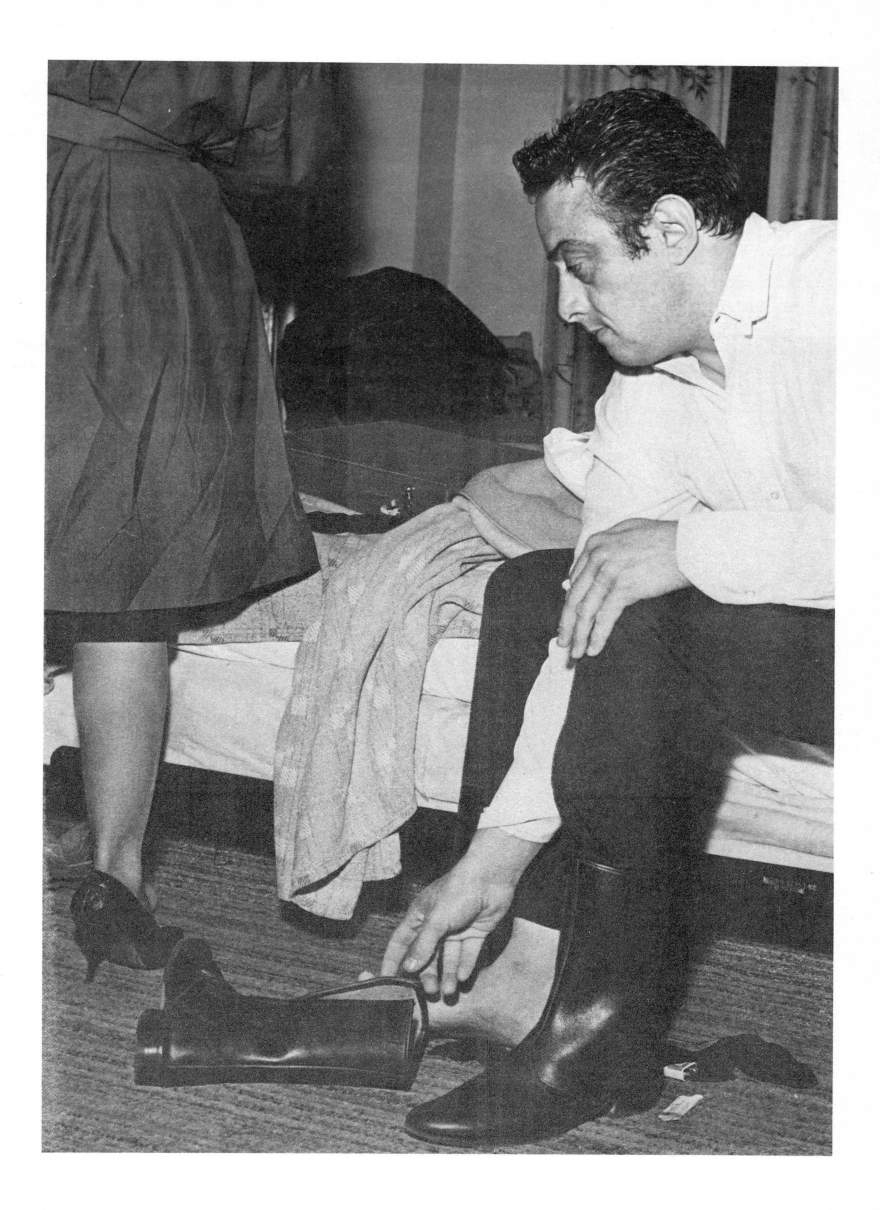

Mississippi

The Meredith March through Mississippi began June 6, 1966, as a private protest for James Meredith and four friends. On the second day, near Hernando, Mississippi, Meredith was wounded by a sniper, and his personal odyssey was transformed into a mass demonstration—a "march against fear." On June 8, twenty people started walking from the place where Meredith was shot, and for three weeks the marchers traveled 200 miles through Mississippi. By the time they reached Jackson, their destination, they were fifteen thousand strong.

Coming into Jackson. Left to right, Juanita and Ralph Abernathy, Coretta and Martin Luther King, Floyd McKissick of CORE and Stokely Carmichael of SNCC, walk together. Throughout the march the emerging "black power" stance of SNCC and CORE threatened to divide the civil rights movement (Bob Fitch/Black Star).

Opposite page: the boys on the back of the truck—the Meredith March press corps (Bob Fitch/Black Star). Overleaf: Mississippi blacks answer Meredith's attacker (Bob Fitch/Black Star).

GERALD W. GETTY
A Defense for Richard Speck

The murders happened on the night of July 13th. I was on my way home from a fishing trip when I heard the news on the radio: eight nurses had been strangled and their throats slashed in a townhouse in Chicago. One nurse had survived by hiding under the bed. I was Cook County public defender at the time, so I couldn't help wondering if I would be involved.

The police sought a suspect named Richard Speck. Neighbors claimed to have seen a heavily tattooed man matching his description in the area, and the newspapers and radio carried nothing else during those hot Chicago days. Three days later, when a tattooed man appeared at Cook County Hospital in an ambulance, a doctor took a look at him and immediately called the police. It was Richard Speck. After seeing his picture in the paper, he had slashed his wrists. He was soon taken to the hospital section of the Cook County Jail.

I was appointed to represent him that day, and a week later met him for the first time. He was a tall, gangly individual with a pockmarked complexion, very ill from loss of blood and with a frightened look. I told him that I'd spoken with his brother-in-law and sister who lived in Chicago, and that he was not to talk to anybody, including me. I figured the place was bugged, and he was in no condition to talk anyway.

About a week later, he was released from the hospital section of the jail, and we talked again at length about his background and whereabouts at the time of the murders.

Speck had come to Chicago from his home in Dallas, bent on getting a job on a ship. After staying with his sister, he applied at the seaman's union hall on the 12th of July. He got an assignment, but was out of luck: the man he was supposed to replace showed up anyway. There is some evidence he slept in an unfinished house that night, washed up in a gasoline station the next morning, and returned to the seaman's hall. His sister brought him some money and he got a room in a hotel, the Shipyard Inn. Then somewhere between 12:30 and 1:30 P.M. he went into a tavern where he met three Canadian sailors. He drank with them until around 8:00, they came back to his room, and the last thing he remembered was mainlining a narcotic with them. He had never taken one before, though he had used uppers and downers. That was 8:30 or 9:00. He remembered nothing after that.

Richard Speck (UPI).

It was 11:00 P.M., the surviving nurse said, when a man came to her bedroom door with a pistol. He herded the nine nurses into a south bedroom and tied them up. Around 12:30 he took the girls out of the room, one by one, and then killed them.

Speck told me it was a terrible thing that all those girls were killed, and I came to the point. Did you have anything to do with it? He said, "Mr. Getty, if I had anything to do with it, I don't remember it."

We discovered two of the best alibi witnesses a defense lawyer ever had. Two days after Speck's apprehension, a couple named Mr. and Mrs. Dufrayer, who worked in a restaurant a couple miles from the occurrence, called the state's investigators to say that they'd recognized the suspect in the papers as the man who had had a hamburger and some whiskey at the restaurant between 11:45 and 12:30 July 13th. The state never turned that statement over to the defense. We discovered them six months later when their names were added to a list of the state's witnesses. The police investigators tried several times to get them to change their testimony, but they never succeeded. As it turned out, it didn't make any difference.

The trial began in February in Peoria. I wanted to transfer the trial to another county where the publicity might be less adverse, but they gave me Peoria. Any county in the state probably would have been the same.

We pleaded not guilty. The surviving nurse gave eyewitness testimony, but I think her testimony weakened under cross-examination. She couldn't remember any of the assailant's distinguishing features. In a taped police interview she had remarked, "All Americans have the same faces." There was no light that night for identification—the most light probably came from the hallway when a door opened.

Corazon Amurao, the survivor and "perfect eyewitness" (UPI).

Speck had long, combed-back hair and a severely pockmarked face, but the original police-artist drawing of the suspect showed a crew cut and no pockmarks. In addition, she identified him in his hospital room, not in a police lineup. This could have tainted her identification.

There were three smudged prints on the back of the bedroom door. The experts identified them as Speck's. One print had ten points of similarity to Speck's, the others seventeen, but they were smudged. Those smudges could have hidden points of dissimilarity; the experts testified that if even one point of dissimilarity was found, the prints would have been thrown out. Twenty-nine other fingerprints and two palm prints were also found. They didn't belong to Speck or to any other known persons who had entered that house. Who else was in that house that night?

We took six weeks to pick a jury. Speck and I talked a lot about the death penalty. He felt all the time we spent trying to select jurors, we were merely picking people to authorize a killing. I had many people tell me that they couldn't serve on the jury because if they ever found him not guilty, they wouldn't be able to go home because of what people in the neighborhood would say.

He always referred to me as his only friend, and he would not go into the courtroom unless he could look out and see me there. Otherwise, the marshals would have a terrible problem on their hands. When he was a child, he couldn't go up and recite in class—he had that reticence, a bashfulness, that inability to face people. I think he did have something wrong with him mentally. He had had a fever of 106 degrees as a child, and I think it damaged his brain. He could never cope with the outside world. If he got a job, and got paid, he'd blow the money that very day. He couldn't take care of himself properly. The rest of his family were good, law-abiding, hard-working business people, mortified, naturally, about what had happened.

We spent six weeks picking a jury and two weeks in trial. And the jurors arrived at a verdict in forty-nine minutes. Guilty. I polled them. What else can you do? I asked their verdicts individually. Guilty. Richard turned to me and said I'd done a good job, I'd done my best. But adverse publicity, people crying for his death, a nice little lady dressed in white and built up as a perfect eyewitness, and smudged prints—he knew it was coming. That's what he said.

Gerald W. Getty represented over four hundred accused murderers during his twenty-nine-year career with the Cook County public defender's office. Richard Speck was his only client to receive the death penalty, and his sentence was later changed to life in prison. Getty pubished Public Defender, *about his life in court, and in 1972 he left his position as head of the defender's office to establish his own law firm.*★

Above, left: the eight student nurses, and right, the convicted murderer (UPI).

TEENIE WEENIE DEANIE
The Maestro of LSD

Owsley and I had all the raw chemicals and new equipment packed in footlockers loaded in the Studebaker pickup, and we were ready to begin the *Mission: Impossible* journey from Berkeley to the secret LSD laboratory. Only I didn't know where it was, and when I asked, Owsley just laughed.

"You'll have to wait and see. Meanwhile, try some of my new drug of the future—STP—and then we'll get rolling. Got lots to finish up in the city."

We both took a white pill, my first STP, and left his small palace in the Berkeley flatlands.

"Before we fly away, I want to visit some chicks in North Beach," Owsley said, a very typical Owsley event. He was the famous "Mr. Big" in the S.F. scene, and he used his fame and exotic drugs to entice the pretty, young female trippers whenever he got the chance. He seemed quite fond of himself and his position in the emerging acid world of 1967. My memories include Owsley standing in front of mirrors with his hair in curlers, the first man I met to use the now-common blow dryer. I was going to be his new lab assistant.

Midnight, and skillfully manning the controls of the pickup, we hit North Beach completely gassed, giggling and wired out of our skulls—nonstop talk exploding with psychedelic insight. What we were doing was making an official Owsley exit from San Francisco, and after a two-hour stopover, we headed off for the Grateful Dead house on Ashbury, with many phone calls along the way to let people know Owsley was off on another sacred mission.

We pulled up in front of the Dead house at 4 A.M., in a truck loaded with enough drugs to produce pounds of acid. My STP high just beginning to peak, I recognized a familiar face across the street, under the mercury vapor lamp.

"Hey, Owsley, there's Cassady. Hey, Neal, what's happening?"

Neal was standing backed up against a parked car, with a transistor radio held up to one ear, and his sledge hammer bouncing around in his other hand.

"Dean, well, you understand, I am standing here on the chance that, well, you see, I know . . ." and we three walked inside the Dead house, Neal and I rapping at top speed about God and the universe. It was the second time in months of being around Cassady that I could follow his conversation; the STP was keeping me at a pace equal to Neal's and it was pure pleasure to be there with him and his vision. Sunrise came and went, and still we were sharing the psychedelic mind; only, Owsley appeared not to be getting the attention he always demanded in a group. He just sat there and listened, and finally made a typical power move, giving me, his new employee, an order.

"Let's go."

So we drove to the airport, shipped the trunks to Denver, and put ourselves on a plane to L.A. We were taking a roundabout flight, somehow trying to figure out if The Man was following us. And if he wasn't, he sure was a fool, because by that morning we were two spaced-out, drugged weirdos, peeking over our shoulders while trying to look cool. Not Too Obvious.

By the time we hit the Continental waiting lounge in the L.A. airport, with a three-hour wait for the flight to Denver, we must have been quite a sight . . . completely stoned on a variety of drugs, and both of us very strangely dressed. Owsley had long black hair, too-hip sunglasses, a black leather vest over a Prince Valiant–style puffy shirt. A huge bear claw hung around his neck. He was standing on high-heeled pointy-toed boots and oozed the smell of patchouli oil. He also had a few hits of illegal acid in his vest pocket. I had

adopted the New York Puerto Rican Polk Street fag velvety look, and my super-mod overcoat had a secret stash for my favorite drug, "Ice Pack" grass. We decided to try and sleep before the flight.

Owsley crashed on the floor, and I moved three rows away from him, trying not to appear connected with the crazy on the rug, but it was obvious to anyone who looked that there were two hairy freaks in the waiting lounge, and they knew each other.

The flight was finally announced, and we deliberately waited to board the plane until the last moment. As we approached the gate, two plain-clothes cops demanded that we follow them into a special screening room.

"Hey, man, we're going to miss the plane. What's going on?"

They searched us for weapons, and somehow missed the drugs the first time around, but decided that we were *too* different to just let go.

"Let's run a check through headquarters. Let me see your driver's licenses." I just about shit in my pants. I knew that Owsley had a record in L.A. County and was notorious as a suspected illegal chemist, and that the next search would get us busted. My career as a rich, LSD flower hippy was swiftly coming to an end. My name went in first; I was clean, so nothing came back about me.

"Final boarding call for Denver" over the PA system, and "Hey, Officer, we can't miss this flight, our jobs depend on it."

So while one cop spelled Owsley's name on the phone, the other cop relented and let us board the plane. This reassured Owsley that he was still invincible, and he decided to keep the acid he was carrying. I was sure they would pop us at the Denver airport, and smoked up my grass in the toilet. But nothing happened in Denver.

After two taxi rides, and many blocks of walking to elude any followers, we finally ended up in a very respectable neighborhood at the door of a typical residential brick house, in an older, settled part of town, where only God knows how many LSD and STP and DMT trips were being produced in the basement. Descending the basement stairs was like entering a psychedelic spaceship. The walls were covered with machinery and bubbling flasks, coiled glass tubes dripping potential weirdness from container to container, floor to ceiling. Huge glass cauldrons surrounded with dry ice covered the floor, oozing white clouds of spacey vapors into the room. "Very serious business" flashed through my brain.

"What should we call it this time?" Owsley asked. He explained to me that pure acid was a white crystal mixed with a chalky paste, and that until recently he'd always left the paste its natural color. "Now we change the color to fool The Man," he explained. "All we do is add some food coloring to the paste and we have whatever we want." The most recent product to hit the market was Purple Passion, but the drug of choice on the San Francisco Scene was White Lightning, Owsley's most famous creation. That weekend we synthesized it by the ounce.

Teenie Weenie Deanie is currently writing a book on his adventures in the Bay Area during the psychedelic Sixties. (courtesy of the author)

1967

CALENDAR

January: 3 *Jack Ruby dies in Dallas;* **5** *Gordie Howe is first hockey player to score 700 goals;* **15** *NFL wins the first Super Bowl; Rolling Stones sing censored version of "Let's Spend the Night Together" on Ed Sullivan;* **16** *Mrs. Wallace succeeds her husband as Alabama governor;* **21** *Mao orders Army intervention in student/worker clashes as Cultural Revolution expands.*

February: 4 *"For What It's Worth" and "Sock It To Me— Baby" are new singles;* **11** *Mothers of Invention's* Freak Out *makes chart;* **14** *State Dept. admits CIA funded NSA;* **22** *Broadway premiere of* Mac-Bird!

March: 1 *Congress excludes Representative Adam Clayton Powell for misuse of funds; Publication of* The Medium is the Massage; **6** *Stalin's daughter defects from Russia;* **7** *Teamster president Hoffa finally goes to jail for jury tampering and pension-fund fraud;* **16** *First reports of genetic damage from LSD use;* **25** *"Happy Together" leads singles chart while new LP entries include* Surrealistic Pillow *and* The Doors; **29** *David Brinkley refuses to cross picket lines of TV network strike.*

April: 4 *FDA announces plans to study effects of smoking dried banana peel;* **5** *First Gray Line tour through Haight-Ashbury;* **7** *Publication of* Death of a President *despite Jackie's court suit;* **15** *Spring Mobe's New York demonstration draws 100,000;* Vogue *spread captures Twiggy's influence on fashion;* **24** *Daylight Savings Time begins nationwide;* **28** *Muhammad Ali is stripped of boxing title for refusing Army induction.*

May: 3 *U.S. publication of Ho Chi Minh on Revolution;* **6** *Grateful Dead enters chart;* **11** *One Jackson State student dies in rioting;* **13** *70,000 parade in New York in support of military;* Fresh Cream *is new LP entry;* **20** *"Groovin'" becomes number one;* **23** *U.S. admits its jets violated Chinese air space.*

June: 3 *Aretha Franklin dominates charts with* I Never Loved a Man *and "Respect";* **4** Mission: Impossible *wins its first Emmy;* **5-10** *Israel invades U.A.R., Syria and Jordan;* **10** *Country Joe and the Fish enter LP chart;* **16** *Attorney General Ramsey Clark*

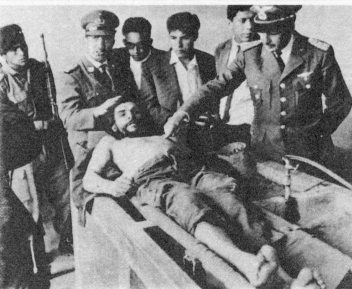

Top: the Glassboro summit—Kosygin, left, with an interpreter and LBJ (Richard Knapp/Photo Trends). Center, left: Twiggy emerging (Photo Trends); right: Adam Clayton Powell in Bimini (Bob East/Photo Trends). Bottom: Bolivian military officers display the body of Che Guevara (UPI). Opposite page: Black Panther Bobby Seale's message on a poster in New York City (Charles Gatewood).

restricts wiretapping; Monterey Pop Festival opens; **19** *Paul McCartney admits taking LSD;* **23-25** *LBJ and Kosygin confer at Glassboro, N.J.;* **28** *Mick Jagger and Keith Richard spend the night in jail after drug arrest.*

July: 1 Sgt. Pepper *moves into number one LP slot;* **11** *Newark riot leaves 26 dead as long hot summer heats up;* **15** *First mailing of Master Charge credit cards;* **24** *Federal troops sent into Detroit as 43 die in rioting;* **29** *"Light My Fire" and "Whiter Shade of Pale" battle for chart lead;* **31** *Galbraith's* The New Industrial State *heads nonfiction list.*

August: 13 Bonnie and Clyde *premieres;* **26** *"Ode to Billie Joe" takes over singles lead as* Are You Experienced *and Bee Gees' 1st enter LP chart;* **27** *Beatles hear of Brian Epstein's death while on retreat with the Maharishi;* **29** The Fugitive *catches the one-armed man.*

September: 7 *U.S. troops in Vietnam number 464,000;* **10** *Billie Jean King adds triple win at Forest Hills to her July sweep at Wimbledon;* **16** *Vanilla Fudge on chart;* **23** *"The Letter" claims singles lead;* **30** *LBJ okays $20 billion for Vietnam military actions in fiscal 1968.*

October: 3 *Woody Guthrie dies at 55;* **5** *Vietnam combat has claimed 13,643 Americans, with 756 missing;* **6** *San Franciscans stage "Hippie Funeral";* **10** *Bolivia confirms guerrilla leader Che Guevara killed there;* **19** *Liberation News Service sets up underground wire service;* **21-22** *Antiwar marchers storm the Pentagon.*

November: 1 *Paul Newman is* Cool Hand Luke; **4** Strange Days *enters chart;* **7** *Cleveland and Gary elect black mayors;* **9** *First issue of* Rolling Stone *magazine;* **11** *Linda Ronstadt enters chart with "Different Drum";* **20** *U.S. Census clock passes 200,000,000 mark;* **21** *Yoko Ono miscarries with newly divorced John Lennon at her side; LBJ signs Air Quality Act;* **27** The Confessions of Nat Turner *is best-selling novel.*

December: 3 *First successful heart transplant;* **9** *Lynda Bird's White House wedding;* Disraeli Gears *enters chart;* **10** *Otis Redding dies in plane crash;* **21** *Dustin Hoffman is* The Graduate.

If we worry about what's going to happen to us, we couldn't accomplish anything....Justice is gonna come when the mass of people rise up and see justice done....The more they try to come down on us, the more we'll expose them for what they are......

PIGS

CHARLES PERRY
The Gathering of the Tribes

Our car slid along the sunny freeway like a big pat of butter on a hot plate. I remember Bill saying, as he relit the joint we'd put out when we went through the Bay Bridge tollbooth, "If there were a big gong"—deep toke and meditative pause—"a big fucking gong in the sky . . . "—he outlined a vast shape with inspired hands—"and every time somebody took a hit of acid this morning"—he exhaled—"it went *bong!*"

Whoosh. The image was stunning.

"Bong!" "Bong bong bong!" The car erupted with exclamations of cellular insight.

It really did seem there were cosmic reverberations from all the LSD being dropped on January 14, 1967, the morning of the San Francisco Human Be-In. We could sense thousands of cars homing in from all directions of the great golden appleskin of Earth. Even now crowds of walkers were in procession from the Haight-Ashbury, doubtless taking the most natural route, oblivious to established walkways; some probably going through trees or walking on water. The tiniest tendrils of greenery in Golden Gate Park had to be rotating in the direction of the Polo Field.

We had to be there. My friends and I had being doing acid for four or five years and wondering where our visions of love and serenity could fit into a world where the big facts were things like race war, the Bomb and the endless, crazy war in Vietnam.

Now there was to be this big meeting in the park in order to . . . well, who knew why. To be there. To be all of us stoned together. "A gathering of the tribes," it was called. Something would come of it.

We also had to be there because we were living in Berkeley. Like most of the people we knew there, folkies and artists and dropouts from the radical-politics scene, we were inclined to go on peace marches and pay some attention to the spokesmen of the Berkeley Left. But there was a dangerous narrowness about them, becoming more obvious as Berkeley became more narcissistic. Ever since the Free Speech Movement, which brought a great blast of media attention, the politicos had come to think of fame as their natural right.

But now the Haight was making the same claim, and that was a pisser. Berkeley distrusted rock and roll—throughout the McCarthy years rock had been the enemy and folk music was the true revolutionary music: pure, uncommercial, a little academic, a small pond not too overcrowded with the right-size frogs. It distrusted drugs, though it had signed along on the sexual-freedom movement, which opened the door to every form of hedonism. But most of all, the Berkeley politicos despised the Haight's lack of politics and resented the fact that these nobodies, who didn't even have a position on the Port Chicago vigil, for Chrissake, had stolen their thunder as young rebels and were cutting into their recruiting among younger college students.

The Be-In was intended, in some people's minds at least, to heal that conflict. That was the meaning of the subtitle "A Gathering of the Tribes." It sounded like a bright idea to us, and probably to those like us who weren't exclusive members of one tribe or the other.

When we got to the Polo Field, there were indeed thousands of cars inching toward the Be-In. They were parked on lawns, in bushes, three-deep at intersections, a lot of them at pretty stoned angles. They said later that sixty-nine cars got ticketed that day. We found a parking place six blocks away.

The closer we got to the Polo Field, the more we saw; tributaries of walkers flowing into larger and larger streams. There were lots of smiles, the unique Be-In smile, at once conspiratorial, caressing, aston-

Lawrence Ferlinghetti in floppy hat and beads at the Human Be-In, above (© Lisa Law). Opposite page: Country Joe McDonald (Gerhard E. Gescheidle).

ished and beaming with stoned-out optimism. We'd left automobiles out in the streets, along with middle-aged hostiles, General Westmoreland and the whole dead-end culture. Here in the bosom of nature were people our age in simple cheap clothes, jeans and Goodwill cast-offs, with little acid-head adornments and emblems of the faith. Paisley patches. The absurd buttons of the time, reading "Freak Freely" or "LSD Did This to Me" and the like. Beads, feathers, robes—simple things that suggested the bounty of nature rather than the regimentation of technology. The whole psychedelic sensorium—painted faces, bells, incense.

Lenore Kandel, evangelist of psychedelic sexuality (© Paul Kagan).

It was a giddy high. Except the puzzling thought: what were we doing here? Was this a political demonstration? A religious gathering? A party? Or maybe—when all else fails, merely register what you see—some kind of pilgrimage through this endless stretch of dusty shrubbery? . . . But in a sense, all life is a pilgrimage, isn't it . . . so it was just life . . . only, my God, look at the crowd here in the Polo Field, it's life *with a lot of people*. That's it, *life with a lot of people*. We were Being-In. A lot of stoned people were wandering around blowing their minds on how many others were there. It was like awakening to find you'd been reborn and this was your new family.

On a low stage, barely visible to most of the crowd, a series of speakers were apparently trying to remind us what we were there for. The PA system wasn't very good and it was hard to make out what was being said. When we squeezed our way up front we found it was only some middle-aged creep named Timothy Leary telling us—us!—to turn on, tune in and drop out. Absurd. At one point the Grateful Dead played and some of us danced. It was strange to do our flopping, formless, freak-freely dancing in the pale hazy afternoon sun. There was not the mysterious resonance of nighttime, when the strobe lights gave each instant of dance a framed, separate pose unrelated to the others, like scenes from some unknown myth.

Jefferson Airplane sang "Let's Get Together." Okay, that's what we were there for. Everybody sang along. A chant went up: "We Are All One." We chanted along with Gary Snyder the mantra of Maitreya, the coming Buddha of Love; we chanted along with Allen Ginsberg the mantra of Shiva, the god of dynamite hashish. We sat, we smoked, we roamed.

People were giving each other things. The Diggers were giving away turkey sandwiches and hamburgers. People were passing out incense and feathers and slightly grimy slices of apple. There was a good chance of taking acid in anything you ate, but how could you refuse? I was giving away poems. I had written this poem on a hundred little colored pieces of paper: I kiss you

shamelessly
on the navel
"Eek!" "I kiss
you shame
lessly on the
navel!" Eek.

Left: Allen Ginsberg's friend Maretta, Danny Rifkin, co-manager of the Grateful Dead, and poet Gary Snyder Being-In (© Paul Kagan). Opposite page: Ginsberg dances as the tribes gather (© Lisa Law).

Some people smiled, some knitted their brows. Up around the generator for the PA system, which was being guarded by Hell's Angels, I handed one to a tall, cadaverous Angel I knew. He was leaning on a railing, blowing his mind on the crowd. I stuck the navel poem in front of his eyes, and he read it. Then he probably laughed, though in earthly terms it looked more like his knees gave way and he crumpled to the ground. Maybe it was because his name was Gut.

The sun rolled slowly through the sky. More speakers, more bands, more faces in the crowd. So many people to be, as in the Donovan song. Such a big unspoken secret we shared. So many dogs wandering around.

The biggest moment came from the sky. A parachutist! We ran over to the empty part of the field where he landed, but he seemed to have disappeared. Probably packed up and slipped away, having done his thing. But the hippie rumor grapevine quickly made it into a miraculous disappearance, just as it was sure the parachutist was Owsley, the LSD chemist.

The press would go bananas in the next days trying to figure out what this event was about. It would become one of the grand mythic elements of the Haight mystique, along with indiscriminate love and the anonymity of the Diggers—the notion of a meeting without any purpose other than to be. Together.

Though politicization of the hippies didn't seem to occur, the Be-In gave everybody the idea of a potentially independent community, even a political force, a new minority group. The attendance was estimated at between 10,000 and 20,000, but the exact figure seemed incredibly irrelevant. I went back to the Polo Field a couple of days later and tried to figure out how so many people had gotten into such a small place—and we hadn't even filled the field. A regularly scheduled rugby game had taken place at the same time at the west end of the field: Olympic Club vs. Oregon State University, 23–3. That was the only quantifiable thing that took place there that day. I wished there had been a big gong in the sky.

At the time of the Human Be-In, Charles Perry was employed as an animal caretaker and dealt a pretty good grade of weed. He quit his job in August 1967 to devote full time to his duties as lead oboist for the Tampai Gyentsen (Banner of the Faith) Tibetan Orchestra. Early in 1968 he started working for Rolling Stone *magazine, where he is now an associate editor. He is currently writing the history of the Haight-Ashbury.*

Charles Perry, center, and his oboe in Los Angeles, 1967 (courtesy Charles Perry).

ELDRIDGE CLEAVER
Meeting the Black Panthers

My life in early 1967 was spent working toward February 21st, the anniversary of the assassination of Malcolm X. The Nation of Islam had split into the followers of Malcolm's teaching and the followers of Elijah Muhammad's. We who followed Malcolm evolved into various kinds of black nationalists. By the time I was released from prison in December 1966, we had developed a program at Soledad to continue his work. My thing was to come to the Bay Area and organize a San Francisco branch of the Organization of Afro-American Unity.

By January the first, I had rented a house in San Francisco and pulled some people together. We called it the Black House, and it had a huge living room that was used for meetings, black power dances and speakers. Since we had public meetings there, the matter of security arose. I met with a few other people and said, "We need guns," and one of the guys said, "Man, you should be across the Bay, over there in Oakland with Bobby Seale." I asked him, "Who is Bobby Seale?" and at first he wouldn't say anything. Then I pressed him, and he said, "Well, he's over in Oakland; he's organizing some brothers around guns."

Meantime, Malcolm X's wife, Betty, had been invited to come to San Francisco to mark the anniversary of his death, and to give her blessings to the new branch. Malcolm was a devil, by decree of Elijah Muhammad, and the Muslims were strong in S.F. This was the first public meeting honoring Malcolm since he had been killed, and there was a lot of paranoia that Betty would be assassinated. The logistics of going to the airport to meet her, protecting her while she was here and getting her safely back on the plane had to be worked out.

The Panthers came to a planning meeting about the security question. They were in uniforms and brought guns. Black pants, black leather jackets, black berets, powder-blue shirts, black shiny shoes and pretty guns—shotguns, carbines, pistols in holsters. It was the first time I'd ever seen them, and it was unbelievable because it was perfect. They were organized and armed, and it made sense. Other radicals used the Cuban image—we had a lot of Che Guevaras with beards, fatigues and cowboy boots, but the image I had of how to function with guns in the city was the Mafia. They'd had armies in cities for decades, and had

Huey Newton, co-founder with Bobby Seale of the Black Panther Party, in an Alameda, California, jail in 1968 awaiting trial on charges stemming from a shoot-out with police (Howard Bingham).

blended in with the environment. So did the Panthers.

But they were overtly honest and open. If you walk around with a holster, it means that you're not trying to conceal the weapon, that you know you have a right to carry it.

The day Betty arrived at the San Francisco airport, Huey Newton and some other cats with guns went there to meet her. The program was for them to bring Betty directly from the airport to the offices of *Ramparts* magazine (where I was an editor) at the foot of Broadway in San Francisco. Going to a pad would have guaranteed a shoot-out.

When they arrived at *Ramparts,* cops and reporters and TV crews converged en masse, and there was a huge traffic jam outside. A captain climbed up the stairs and asked, "Who's in charge here?" Warren Hinkle, the editor, said, "I guess I am." Here were all these cats with guns and he said, "Everything's okay. There's no problem here." It was private property, so the police went outside and waited.

Eventually we had to go. Huey sent everybody out in groups, and, with Bobby, went last. There were about a dozen Panthers besides the two of them. Huey had a 12-gauge shotgun and Bobby had a .45.

They walked out onto Broadway, and suddenly Huey took an envelope and covered the lens of a TV camera. The guy with the camera hit his hand, and Huey told a cop, "Arrest this man, he accosted me." And the cop said, "If we arrest anybody, it's going to be you." Huey talked about his constitutional rights, then held up the envelope again, and when the guy hit his hand once more, he pushed him down the hill.

Eldridge Cleaver, left, visits Newton in jail, summer 1968 (Jeffrey Blankfort).

The cops went—like that! One cop stepped forward—he was really freaked out, growling; another cop was telling him, "Joe, Joe, come back, Joe." Huey asked that cat, "Man you gonna draw it? Go ahead and draw it, you big fat motherfucking pig." Everybody was just dumfounded. The cops weren't even chasing us. I thought I might have an orgasm. It was a fantastic and exhilarating moment.

Maybe because I was a parolee, I had felt that you were vulnerable if you had a gun, but these people had a concept that was based on the Constitution—that the people had a right to bear arms. Huey and Bobby had listened to Malcolm when he called for armed defense teams throughout the United States to deal with those who brutalized the black community.

The rest of the weekend was just as unbelievable. There was a rally that started with a march in Hunter's Point to the spot where a black kid had been killed. Then there was a march to the Bayview Community Center. It was the convening of a free assembly by forces in the community that had never before come together. It was organized by people other than Black Democrats or preachers. The grass-roots element which had exploded in Watts finally had the elements of stability and continuity.

Betty talked about what Malcolm believed, and combated some of the lies that had been told about him—it was really kind of a defensive speech—but everybody was in harmony with Malcolm. And the Black Panther Party was in control of the heaviest moment, because they were dealing with security.

After that weekend, I took an opportunity to leave California to do a story on Stokely Carmichael for *Ramparts* and to think about all this. As soon as I came back, I joined the Party.

My goal was the organization of a machinery to create a consensus, to organize people in a diaspora, without a land of their own. The model in my head was Herzl's World Zionist Organization—I had studied its history in prison.

But it wasn't just a question of a homeland. Were we to stay here? Go to Africa? Burn the mother down? At this stage we didn't have to have the final solution.

After nine years in prison, where he wrote Soul On Ice, *Eldridge Cleaver joined the Black Panther Party in spring 1967 to become its Minister of Information. In April 1968, two days after the assassination of Martin Luther King, he was wounded by the police in a gun battle that left Panther Bobby Hutton dead at age seventeen. Ordered to return to prison on a parole violation, Cleaver left the United States in November 1968, afraid for his life if he returned to jail. He remained in exile until November 1975, when he returned to stand trial on assault charges stemming from the 1968 incident.★(Jeffrey Blankfort)*

Opposite page, clockwise from top: a "Free Huey" rally in Oakland, 1968; Bobby Seale at a demonstration for Newton at the Alameda courthouse (both Jeffrey Blankfort); Seale pins a Huey Newton button on slain Panther, Bobby Hutton, April 1968 (Lonnie Wilson/Photo Trends); Bill Brent speaking at a rally following the Hutton funeral (Jeffrey Blankfort). Overleaf: the Oakland Panthers in Bobby Hutton Park (Jeffrey Blankfort).

MUHAMMAD ALI
The People's Champ

I'm sweating. I look around. It seems like everyone in the entire Houston induction center has crept into the room. For months I've drilled myself for this moment, but I still feel nervous. I hope no one notices my shoulders tremble.

My mind races back to the day when I was sitting on a bench at my first Golden Gloves competition, waiting for my turn to go into the ring. I was amazed at how big Chicago was compared to Louisville, and the prospect of facing unknown opponents from strange places overwhelmed me. An old battered-faced ex-pug called Punch Drunk Don was sweeping the floor behind me, and he noticed my knees knocking. He leaned down over my left ear and whispered, "Son, always confront the thing you fear."

But what do I fear now? Is it what I'll lose if they take my title? If I'm jailed or barred from the ring? Is it fear of losing the good, plush, glamorous life of a World Champion? . . .

 Why am I resisting? My religion, of course, but what a politician told me in Chicago is true. I won't be barred from the Nation of Islam if I go into the Army. "Who are you to judge?" he had asked. All my life I've watched White America do the judging. But who is to judge now? Who is to say if this step I'm about to be asked to take is right or wrong? If not me, who else? I recall the words of the Messenger: "If you feel what you have decided to do is right, then be a man and stand up for it. . . . Declare the truth and die for it."

The lieutenant has finished with the man on my left and everybody seems to brace himself. The room is still and the lieutenant looks at me intently. He knows that his general, his mayor and everybody in the Houston induction center is waiting for this moment. He draws himself up straight and tall.

Something is happening to me. It's as if my blood is changing. I feel fear draining from my body and a rush of anger taking its place.

I hear the politician again: "Who are you to judge?" But who is this white man, no older than me, appointed by another white man, all the way down from the white man in the White House? Who is he to tell me to go to Asia, Africa or anywhere else in the world to fight people who never threw a rock at me or America? Who is this descendant of the slave masters to order a descendant of slaves to fight other people in their own country?

Now I am anxious for him to call me. "Hurry up!" I say to myself. I'm looking straight into his eyes. There's a ripple of movement as some of the people in the room edge closer in anticipation.

"Cassius Clay—Army!"

The room is silent. I stand straight, unmoving. Out of the corner of my eye I see one of the white boys nodding his head at me, and thin smiles flickering across the faces of some of the blacks. It's as if they are secretly happy to see someone stand up against the power that is ordering them away from their homes and families.

The lieutenant stares at me a long while, then lowers his eyes. One of the recruits snickers and he looks up abruptly, his face beet-red, and orders all the other draftees out of the room. They shuffle out quickly, leaving me standing alone.

He calls out again: "Cassius Clay! Will you please step forward and be inducted into the Armed Forces of the United States?"

All is still. He looks around helplessly. Finally, a senior officer with a notebook full of papers walks to

*Above: Ali and associates at Houston induction center (Wide World Photos).
Opposite page: the champ with one of his attorneys, Hayden Covington, filing a petition to
halt induction on the grounds that Ali is a minister (Wide World Photos).*

the podium and confers with him a few seconds before coming over to me. He appears to be in his late forties. His hair is streaked with gray and he has a very dignified manner.

"Er, Mr. Clay . . ." he begins. Then, catching himself, "Or Mr. Ali, as you prefer to be called."

"Yes, sir?"

"Would you please follow me to my office? I would like to speak privately with you for a few minutes, if you don't mind."

It's more of an order than a request, but his voice is soft and he speaks politely. I follow him to a pale-green room with pictures of Army generals on the walls. He motions me to a chair, but I prefer to stand. He pulls some papers from his notebook and suddenly drops his politeness, getting straight to the point.

"Perhaps you don't realize the gravity of the act you've just committed. Or maybe you do. But it is my duty to point out to you that if this should be your final decision, you will face criminal charges and your penalty could be five years in prison and ten thousand dollars fine. It's the same for you as it would be for any other offender in a similar case. I don't know what influenced you to act this way, but I am authorized to give you an opportunity to reconsider your position. Regulations require us to give you a second chance."

"Thank you, sir, but I don't need it."

"It is required."

I follow him back into the room. The lieutenant is still standing behind the rostrum, ready to read the induction statement.

"Mr. Cassius Clay," he begins again, "you will please step forward and be inducted into the United States Army."

Again I don't move.

"Cassius Clay—Army," he repeats. He stands in silence, as though he expects me to make a last-minute change. Finally, with hands shaking, he gives me a form to fill out. "Would you please sign this statement and give your reasons for refusing induction?" His voice is trembling.

I sign quickly and walk out into the hallway. The officer who originally ordered me to the room comes over. "Mr. Clay," he says with a tone of respect that surprises me, "I'll escort you downstairs."

When we reach the bottom of the steps, the television cameramen who had been held up by the guards focus their lights on us, while a platoon of military police scuffle to keep them behind a rope that blocks the end of the corridor.

"Muhammad," a reporter yells, "did you take the step? Are you in the Army?"

"Can we just have a minute, Champ?" another shouts. "What did you do? Can you just tell us yes or no?"

I keep walking with the officer who leads me to a room where my lawyers are waiting. "You are free to go now," he tells us. "You will be contacted later by the United States Attorney's office."

I step outside and a huge crowd of press people rush toward me, pushing and shoving each other and snapping away at me with their cameras. Writers from two French newspapers and one from London throw me a barrage of questions, but I feel too full to say anything. My lawyer Hayden Covington gives them copies of a statement I wrote for them before I left Chicago. In it I cite my ministry and my personal convictions as reasons for refusing to take the step, adding that "I strongly object to the fact that so many newspapers have given the American public and the world the impression that I have only two alternatives in taking this stand—either I go to jail or I go into the Army. There is another alternative, and that is justice."

By the time I get to the bottom of the front steps, the news breaks. Everyone is shouting and cheering. Some girls from Texas Southern run over to me, crying, "We're glad you didn't go!" A black boy shouts out, "You don't go, so I won't go!"

I feel a sense of relief and freedom. For the first time in weeks I start to relax. I remember the words of a reporter at the hotel: "How will you act?" Now it's over, and I've come through it. I feel better than when I beat the eight-to-ten odds and won the World Heavyweight Title from Liston.

"You headin' for jail. You headin' straight for jail." I turn and an old white woman is standing behind me, waving a miniature American flag. "You goin' straight to jail. You ain't no champ no more. You ain't never gonna be champ no more. You get down on your knees and beg forgiveness from God!" she shouts in a

raspy tone.

I start to answer her, but Covington pulls me inside a cab.

She comes over to my window. "My son's in Vietnam, and you no better'n he is. He's there fightin' and you here safe. I hope you rot in jail. I hope they throw away the key."

The judge who later hears my case reflects the same sentiment. I receive a maximum sentence of five years in prison and ten thousand dollars fine. The prosecuting attorney argues, "Judge, we cannot let this man get loose, because if he gets by, all black people will want to be Muslims and get out for the same reasons."

Four years later, the Supreme Court unanimously reverses that decision, 8–0, but now this is the biggest victory of my life. I've won something that's worth whatever price I have to pay. It gives me a good feeling to look at the crowd as we pull off. Seeing people smiling makes me feel that I've spoken for them as well as myself. Deep down, they didn't want the World Heavyweight Champion to give in, and in the days ahead their strength and spirit will keep me going. Even when it looks like I'll go to jail and never fight again.

"They can take away the television cameras, the bright lights, the money, and ban you from the ring," an old man tells me when I get back to Chicago, "but they can't destroy your victory. You have taken a stand for the world and now you are the people's champion."

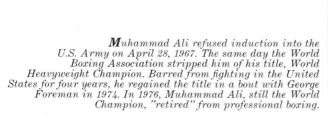

Muhammad Ali refused induction into the U.S. Army on April 28, 1967. The same day the World Boxing Association stripped him of his title, World Heavyweight Champion. Barred from fighting in the United States for four years, he regained the title in a bout with George Foreman in 1974. In 1976, Muhammad Ali, still the World Champion, "retired" from professional boxing.

Muhammad Ali being escorted from the induction center, above, and greeted by supporters after refusing to enter the U.S. Army, opposite page (Wide World Photos). Above, left: Ali after retaining his title in a European bout with Henry Cooper (Globe Photos). Left: Ali up against Atlanta Mayor Maynard Jackson, with Julian Bond as referee, at a Black Muslim benefit, 1975 (Ken Hawkins/Globe Photos).

SAM BROWN
The Student CIA

As the year began, I was a student at Harvard Divinity School, and chairman of the National Supervisory Board of the National Student Association (NSA), the organization of college student governments around the country. The supervisory board was similar to a board of directors—we were removed from the workings of the full-time staff. At our January meeting, we learned that *Ramparts* magazine would be running a story saying the NSA was funded substantially by the CIA. *Ramparts* had been given the story by a "paranoid former staffer" who was mad at everybody, we were told; there was no substance to it; it was inconsequential.

The March 1967 issue of Ramparts *containing the NSA/CIA story.*

Then, on February 13, 1967, I was in the Harvard Divinity School library, quietly pursuing some obscure German texts, when a friend came in to tell me that I had received a call from Phil Sherburne, the past president of NSA and a student at Harvard Law School. The *Ramparts* article would be reported the next morning in the *New York Times.*

Sherburne confirmed the rumors. In fact, he said, since the early Fifties the National Student Association had been partially financed by the CIA. Suddenly I was faced with the fact that all of the people whom I thought were my good friends had an entirely different agenda about which I knew nothing. People that I respected had known all along that NSA was funded by CIA fronts.

The money came through groups like the Foundation for Youth and Student Affairs—FYSA—a tax-exempt organization. We all knew that $300,000 or $400,000 a year came from FYSA, but we'd been told that their endowment originated with the Corning Glass people.

The supervisory board learned the truth about the same time the rest of the world did. None of us had the vaguest notion of what the hell could or should be done. I just got on an airplane and went to Washington the next morning, not knowing exactly why, but knowing that something had to be done.

I arrived at NSA headquarters in Washington, D.C., to find network cameras outside the building and the officers of the association either completely traumatized or without any sort of staff respect. NSA had two main branches: a large domestic staff concerned with academic freedom and educational reform, and an international affairs branch presumably involved with student activities around the world. The domestic affairs staff felt betrayed by CIA support of the international staff. The general ambiance of the international staff had been "Let's bring a lot of people to the United States so they can see us and love us," and now it turned out that most of the staff had been "witting"; aware of the covert relationship. That's a very precise word, apparently used by the CIA. People were either "witting" or "unwitting."

I hastily assembled a committee of investigation. While the news media hovered outside, staff people and former officers recounted horror stories and paranoid conspiracy theories. One was that the revelations were part of an FBI plot to discredit their rivals, the CIA. Other scenarios included skulduggery and mystery murders perpetrated to keep the CIA's involvement with foundations secret.

None of us knew enough to separate the fact from the fiction in these theories, but the dozen of us on the committee changed hearing rooms regularly because of our fear of being bugged. We walked only in groups at night, behaving as if all the tales were true and our lives were in danger. By Friday, February 17th, we had come up with the bare bones of a report.

The intent of the CIA was not so much, I think, to gather information about the activities of students at home as to find out about the activities of foreign students. The most sophisticated theory I heard for their involvement was that the CIA figured there was a very small elite class in most less-developed nations. That class was going to run these countries; the CIA liked knowing as much about those people as they could, and, more importantly, they wanted to have as many of them as possible trained in this country.

I thought that the Senate had basically failed in its oversight responsibilities. On *Meet the Press,* Senator Henry Jackson, a member of the Senate Intelligence Oversight Committee, said that the CIA/NSA affiliation was certainly legitimate because, after all, we were in the middle of a cold war. The typical defense line of past officers of NSA was that the mood of the country had been very different in the Fifties: The CIA might have overstepped its bounds, but it was considered patriotic to help them then. We couldn't judge NSA's actions in the Fifties by the standards of 1967.

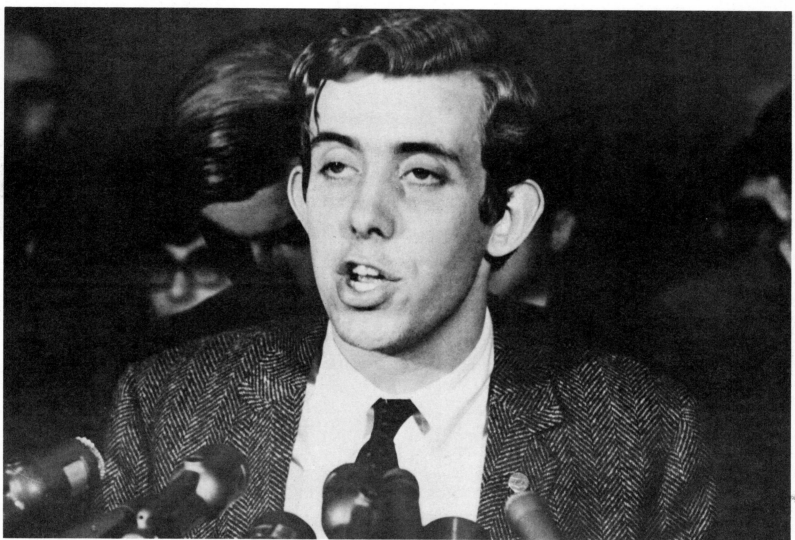

I was impressed with this argument, but at the same time could not excuse the NSA. Somebody had to stand up and say they couldn't do it any longer.

I left school that spring and traveled around the country speaking at campuses about the CIA/NSA relationship and how we had to break out of it. I felt the CIA involvement was the most fundamental threat to the stability of American society. What makes America work are the voluntary institutions, and if they're controlled by the government, we're all finished. It's an old theory; de Tocqueville said it, but I continued to believe it. I felt strongly that we had to find ways to build strong voluntary organizations which were not controlled by the government; which we were free to criticize.

And then that summer the best thing possible happened to me. I ran for president of the association and lost by two votes. As a result, I became chairman of an organization called the Alternative Candidate Task Force. Later it became known as the Dump Johnson Movement. Another story.

Sam Brown continued his opposition to President Johnson's Administration as Senator Eugene McCarthy's Volunteer Coordinator during the 1968 presidential campaign. He moved to Colorado in 1970 and two years later was instrumental in the successful fight to prevent the 1976 Olympics from being held there. Brown served as state treasurer of Colorado from 1974-1976. He now heads the federal volunteer agency, Action. (Alison Teal)
Above: Sam Brown on February 17th, confirming that the CIA obtained "sensitive information" from members of the National Student Association (Wide World Photos).

LOU ADLER
Music, Love and Promoters

I was producing and managing the Mamas and the Papas when in April, John Phillips and I were approached by promoters who had reserved June 16th, 17th and 18th at the Monterey Fairgrounds for a series of large outdoor concerts. They were hoping to bring together a lot of different facets of pop music, and they were interested in booking the services of the Mamas and the Papas and other groups, like Simon and Garfunkel and the Beach Boys.

Coincidentally, just a few months before at a gathering at Cass Elliot's house, someone—I think it was Paul McCartney—said that it was about time that rock and roll became recognized as an art form, instead of just a musical phase. Rock and roll had in fact grown up; we had experienced the Beatles and the Rolling Stones, and Dylan going electric. By the time John and I met again with the promoters and other artists, those three days at Monterey seemed like a great idea—it could be a celebration, a festival, that would show the evolution of contemporary music, and demonstrate where it might be heading.

We thought that any such festival should be nonprofit and the performers' show as much as the audience's; with the best sound system and lights, and the best working and living conditions possible. The promoters weren't geared to that thinking. Since it was a commercial venture, they were interested in producing a profit, naturally and rightfully so.

We were getting nowhere, and the idea might have died right there, but finally a group of us offered to buy the dates from them. Terry Melcher, Johnny Rivers, John Phillips, Paul Simon and I split the initial cost. Two of the three original promoters, Alan Pariser and Derek Taylor, stayed on and were instrumental in making the festival work.

We had about six to eight weeks to organize what was to become known as a pop festival; we had no guidelines. There had never been a festival quite like the one we wanted to do. And we sort of winged it. We 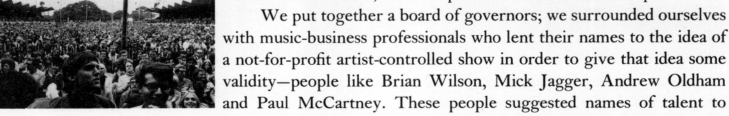 utilized our instincts, friendships and business relationships.

We put together a board of governors; we surrounded ourselves with music-business professionals who lent their names to the idea of a not-for-profit artist-controlled show in order to give that idea some validity—people like Brian Wilson, Mick Jagger, Andrew Oldham and Paul McCartney. These people suggested names of talent to make up the program of thirty or so acts that would appear during the three-day period. I think it was McCartney who suggested Jimi Hendrix; and Andrew Oldham suggested the Who. The time must have been right, for the industry rallied around the idea immediately after the publishing of free *Cash Box* and *Billboard* ads announcing the event. The offices opened in a building on Sunset Boulevard across the street from Ciro's.

The music scene in San Francisco was giant on a local level and starting to spread, so it was important for them and the festival that San Francisco be included. To San Francisco, Los Angeles represented The Business—everything that was slick. San Francisco's self-image, on the other hand, was just the opposite— everything should be free, everything that smacked of business, except, of course, their recording contracts. It didn't help that John and I had just finished recording Scott McKenzie singing "San Francisco (Be Sure to Wear Flowers in Your Hair)."

We talked to Bill Graham, who understood the needs and feelings of these performers. He had been in San Francisco from the beginning of that rock scene and was part of the life there. He had fought for and

The audience at Monterey, above, and the stars, opposite page, left to right: Mama Cass, Buddy Miles, Jimi Hendrix, Brian Jones (both © Paul Kagan).

against the musicians, understood their extremism, and knew when it would hurt them or help them. The late Ralph Gleason, who was then a music critic on the *San Francisco Chronicle,* and throughout the years and musical changes had retained great stature on the music scene, listened to our side and also offered to help bring the factions together.

John Phillips and I flew up to meet Graham and representatives of the San Francisco groups at the Fairmont Hotel. People were there from the Grateful Dead, Quicksilver Messenger Service, the Jefferson Airplane, Big Brother and the Holding Company, and a few Diggers, a group that we'd heard were feeding people and opening up free houses in the Haight.

From the very start we were two opposing forces. Although I'd come from somewhat of a street background, and John had spent a lot of time in the Village, to them we were strictly uptown hippies. Their point of view was that *everything* should be free, no matter what the cost, which we felt was impossible because of the quality of what we wanted. At one point, John and I were ready to split and forget the whole idea of using San Francisco groups. It might have ended there, but Graham and Gleason were able to put it back together.

To finance the festival we sold the future television film rights to ABC. What was shot eventually became D. A. Pennebaker's *Monterey Pop* motion picture because the network hierarchy found parts of the footage unacceptable, especially the sexuality of the Hendrix scenes.

The theme was "Music, Love and Flowers," and we expected 15,000 people. In three days, at least three times that many passed through the town of Monterey. We piped the music all over the fairgrounds and there were cultural, both pop and historic, exhibits. Volunteer doctors put together a little hospital to handle the serious drug cases, and the Diggers got their chance to give away free food.

The festival was made up of memorable highlights, but the most electrifying was Janis Joplin. Plain and simple. I can't remember another situation in which the entire industry jointly experienced the emergence of an incredible talent. She literally and in the most dramatic sense became a star immediately, and in doing so validated the San Francisco sound. Her second performance ended with "Ball and Chain," and when she left the stage she just kicked up her heels.

Festival organizer and performer, Paul Simon (Jann Wenner).

With Otis Redding, a different kind of musical discovery happened. The Beach Boys were supposed to have closed the show on Saturday night, but they backed out suddenly. We looked to Otis; I don't think he had ever played before that big an audience—especially a primarily white audience—but his manager Phil Walden never had a doubt about the outcome. When Otis came offstage, he couldn't stop moving; he was like a boxer who has just won a championship fight by a knockout, and he didn't want it to end.

I remember the last afternoon, too. A sitar concert by Ravi Shankar was scheduled. He had been signed by the previous promoters, and some of us had our doubts. He laid down a lot of rules, too, like "no smoking." But then his set began. He had the whole afternoon. A light drizzle had been falling all morning and opened into beautiful sunlight. The audience was silent and intense. Shankar later said that his performance there was one of the most positive experiences he'd ever had in concert.

Every performer said he or she felt as if he or she were getting a performance in return from the audience. It was magical, and it became a total environment. The festival had become the town, and the town had become the festival. I wasn't sure exactly what had worked, but from the time I saw the police putting flowers in their helmets, I knew that something had.

Lou Adler got his start in the music business producing records in a garage with his friend Herb Alpert. He has been involved with record production, music publishing and management for such artists as Johnny Rivers, Carole King, Jan and Dean, and Cheech and Chong, and he was one of the founders of Dunhill Records in 1964. Adler now heads Ode Records, and is directing his first film, The Adventures of Pedro and the Man.★

Opposite page, clockwise from top: Michael Bloomfield, David Crosby, Paul Butterfield and Elvin Bishop on stage at Monterey (Jann Wenner). Left: Adler in his festival director hat and Brian Jones (courtesy Lou Adler).

BILL GRAHAM
Guarding the Door at the Fillmore

The original Fillmore was at the corner of Geary and Fillmore streets here in San Francisco. It was up a flight of stairs, and there was a haberdashery and a doughnut shop on the street. The ballroom held around 2,000 people, and it looked like an old temple or meeting room with a high ceiling and chandeliers. Upstairs was a balcony, a large area where we had a restaurant. Pleasant but raunchy.

It was my first theater and my favorite, and one concert from those days sticks in my mind. The headliner was the Jefferson Airplane, who were already popular across the United States. In San Francisco, they were the gurus of fantasyland. The way they dressed was how other people dressed; and what they said was believed as gospel. There was nothing wrong with them, but their followers were wrong in assuming that everything they said was true.

The cashier's landing at the Fillmore Auditorium (Michelle Vignes).

I had a habit then, as I do now, of going around the building to get a feel of the line just before we opened the doors. On this night, they were lined up four abreast way down the street. The doors were already opened and I had gone around the block a few times and everything was going along fine. I was feeling very good.

The crowds started to come in through the big glass door at the bottom of the steps, and a young man approached me, wearing what I guess you'd call clean Goodwill. He was in his mid-twenties, and a little larger than I was. He said, "Are you Bill Graham?" And I said, "Yes, I am."

He spoke in the jargon of the day—"Dig it, like, this is where I'm coming from, I'd dig to see the show and get into the groove." Blah, blah, blah.

I pointed to the line and I said, "We're sold out. If you have a ticket, fine, there's the line."

He said, "Well, I don't have a ticket, but I'd really dig to get in. I couldn't buy a ticket anyway, 'cause I have no bread."

"Well," I told him, "then you can't come in."

He got into a whole lengthy dialogue: he was just there to share the vibes and he wasn't there for any riffs, and didn't want any problems.

"That's very nice," I said. "Neither do I, we just don't have any more tickets."

And he said, "Well, man, it's just me, why don't you just let me slip in?"

I had been in the business for only two years, but you get to be an expert on how to handle situations like this. You try to say, "No, no, no," in a very nice way, and over the remainder of our conversation, which lasted a good three or four minutes, I said a lot of no's. I was trying to be courteous, which was ironic because there are times when I'm not very courteous. I tried to explain to him: "I know it's just you, but do you know how many people come up to me and say 'Just me, just me, just me,' and I just *can't*?" And he said, "Of course you can, it's just me."

I told him, "If you came in regularly and you were out of bread one time, I could see it. If you were my cousin, if you were a good friend of mine, if we went to school together. But I don't know you. I have never seen you. You want to get good vibes—that's fine. So do these people on line, and I am sorry to put it this way, but it costs. I walk into a restaurant and I would love to eat for nothing, but I pay. That's the way it is—money is barter and I have to pay the groups on the stage."

"But, man, you can afford it," he said. "I mean, is one person going to kill you?"

This went on for a long, long time, and I finally cut it off. "Do me a favor and just leave." I started to walk back into the building.

A few minutes later I came back out and he was still there. It was like a splinter that kept going in deeper and I just couldn't get it out. The third time he saw me coming, and started saying things to that line that he wanted me to hear. "You are going into this capitalist pig's place, that mother-fucker ripoff bitch bastard. Music should be free, power to the people, the musicians want it to be free. It should be in the park, but people like Graham won't let them play in the park for free! He stole the music from us, made millions from us!"

He went on and on and never looked at me, but just stared out in space. Finally I caught his eye. I wanted to see if he would stay with those beliefs no matter what I did for him, because to me, one action doesn't show the character of a man. If I in fact *was* this person he thought I was, why did he want to come into this house of the devil to begin with?

I looked straight at him and with my head and my hand I gestured toward him. He stood ten feet away, and I gestured, nodded my head backward, as if to say, "Come in."

He looked at me and didn't believe what I was doing. I nodded my head again, as if to say, "Come on, it's okay, you can come in now." But before he came to me he veered toward the tenth or twelfth person in the line, and instead of coming right in the door, he pointed at me and said, "That cat is out of sight, I mean, he is really heavy duty. You know, he's a good dude. Man, he is for *us*, man, he's giving us the good music." When he got to the door, I grabbed him by his shirt. I picked him up and put him down again in front of me. He looked at me as though I was mad. He said, "What's the matter?" I looked straight at him and I *yelled* at the top of my voice—it was my guts, my stomach was speaking, it didn't even come from my head. The only thing I said to him was "I *give* you, you love me. I don't give you, you *hate* me! Get away from me! Just get away from me!"

*B*ill Graham produced his first concert on
November 6, 1965, as a benefit for the San Francisco
Mime Troupe. A month later he rented the Fillmore Auditorium
and was on his way to becoming America's foremost rock
concert promoter. In 1968, Graham opened another theater on
New York City's Lower East Side, calling it the Fillmore
East. He now heads a variety of companies in San Francisco
which deal with all facets of the entertainment business
—from local concert promotion and production to
national tours and artist management. ★

*A*bove, left: Graham in front
of the Fillmore East in New York
(© Gianfranco Mantegna/Photo Trends); and right:
at the door of the ballroom at Geary and Fillmore
in San Francisco (Michelle Vignes). Left: Graham
in the mid-Sixties (Michelle Vignes).

209

RALPH J. GLEASON

Ralph J. Gleason liked to joke that some vague imperative connected to the name of his high school alma mater—Horace Greeley—was what drove him, like many a young man, West. He forsook New York for the San Francisco Bay Area in the late 1940's and never looked back. Ralph began writing a jazz column for the *San Francisco Chronicle* in 1951, and it wasn't long before his unique perceptual abilities took the column well beyond the music itself. Ralph was a cultural observer and reporter as well as a music critic, and there was little that escaped his scrutiny.

He was the first nationally syndicated jazz columnist to recognize the artistic value and social importance of rock and roll, but that was just for openers. He homed in on the significant issues and lessons of the Free Speech Movement at the University of California at Berkeley in 1964 while his city-room colleagues were scrambling in confusion. He wrote intelligently of the Haight-Ashbury scene while the city's mayor was calling the district "Sodom and Gomorrah." He defended the blossoming dance concerts that came with the rise of the San Francisco rock bands while the police were trying to shut the ballrooms down.

In 1967, Ralph and Jann Wenner co-founded *Rolling Stone.* Ralph was its senior editor and essayist until his untimely death in June of 1975. He loved his column, "Perspectives." It was an ideal forum for his extraordinary range of ideas and insights.

Jane Wenner, who was also there at the beginning of *Rolling Stone*—and who later retired to marry its editor rather than work for him—picked the column Ralph wrote for the second issue of the magazine to reprint here. It concerns the complexities and ultimate tragedy of a marijuana bust. This was published in San Francisco, 1967, when the city was the fount of "hip" and "love," the proving ground of new (and often casually arrived at) values. Ralph took an unpopular position by explaining the difficult and unpleasant choices faced by any person boxed in a corner. He was well aware of the new standards being tested. He was also telling us to stay close to reality.

—Paul Scanlon, *Rolling Stone*

Victims and Villains

The biggest underground cancer in the rock scene this past year has been the Lovin' Spoonful situation.

As has been perfectly clear from the beginning, Steve Boone and Zal Yanovsky were busted in San Francisco over a year ago for pot. Testimony in court later revealed that they had made a deal with a San Francisco narcotics squad officer to "cooperate," and in the course of that cooperation, they had made a buy (according to narks' testimony) from a San Franciscan whom they did not know but who had been introduced to them by a mutual friend. The buy caused an arrest. Boone and Yanovsky left town free and the Spoonful was blacklisted by the underground for setting up a pot bust.

In subsequent developments, the Spoonful wouldn't appear in the San Francisco area because of fear of a court subpoena, and a mysterious package of $2,500 in cash was delivered to the San

Franciscan who got busted, for his defense.

He, in turn, xeroxed copies of the court testimony which disclosed the arrangements between the cops and the Spoonful and sent them to underground papers and other press ("I don't want to hurt anybody," he told me, "but . . . "), and eventually Steve Boone copped out to a Boston reporter that it had all been a terrible mistake, he had been pressured into it and both he and Zal had made affidavits which, it is hoped, will get the San Franciscan off the hook.

During the course of the miserable story, a full page in the *L.A. Free Press* was bought as an ad by somebody, urging people not to buy Spoonful records and not to attend their concerts and, to the girls, not to ball them. It didn't say anything about guys balling them.

Zal eventually quit the group, there were hard rumors of all sorts of tensions, and Steve Boone was obviously greatly upset.

At the Monterey Pop Festival, Cass Elliot commented that people had urged her not to talk to Zally. "He's one of my best friends," she yelled. "That's ridiculous."

The pressures were very strong and the issue was drawn with great poses of morality and righteousness.

There's a lot to be said about this. For one thing, if the reassessment of the entire social structure of the world which is implied in the whole rock generation means anything, it means that understanding and compassion are essential to life and that flat-out judgments are useless no matter who makes them.

Zal is a Canadian citizen. He could have been thrown out of the country if that bust had stuck. That's one thing. God knows what other pressures were brought to bear. And I do not condone fingering someone either. It was a terrible, tragic thing, and in some ways the ones hurt the most were Zal and Steve.

But if the Spoonful makes a new album, I will buy it and I will listen to their songs and I will go to see them and I will hope and do hope that their music grows and flourishes. It has been a very great thing and their contribution has been huge and the pleasure they have given has been immeasurable. Do you believe in magic? Really? Then it seems to me that the only thing to do is forgive and try to forget.

"Shove that hot lead up my ass and I'll name everybody," Lenny Bruce said once. That's reality. If they put *you* in a cell and belt your head around with saps and third degree you—psychologically or physically, it's the same thing—will *you* hold your mud?

When I heard the Spoonful news, I was shocked and saddened. When I saw what was going down, it became worse. There is no morality to it, in a righteous sense. It happened. It was bad. Nobody will defend it and nothing is either/or any more. Or is it?

We are all one. If what Zal and Steve did is a sin, then it is our sin, too. They are victims, just as the man who was fingered is a victim. Just as we are all victims.

Do we REALLY want to be selling postcards of the hanging?

R.J.G., 1967 (courtesy Jean Gleason).

VIVA
The Back Room at Max's

I first saw M. during the early days of my making movies with Andy Warhol at The Factory. The Factory was Andy's loft on East 47th Street, and every square millimeter was covered with silver foil, including the toilet seats. M. was from Brooklyn or the Bronx or something like that. She followed Andy with doglike devotion. Andy whispered to me to be nice to her, but we all thought she was crazy. I do remember being astounded that they were letting her hang around. She was so disruptive, so obsessed by something.

Then I saw her sitting alone at a small table in the front of Max's Kansas City. Just her, her dinner and a bottle of wine. I was still sitting with the artists (the Rauschenberg-Poons-Chamberlain "heavies") in the front room; I hadn't yet made the definitive transition to the Warhol-dominated glitter scene in the back. I watched her, and thought her really beautiful; she had a madonna quality about her: very white skin, very dark hair, like a Southern belle. But she was a Southern belle who belonged to the Boston "family" of Mel Lyman, a self-proclaimed messiah.

A beatific grin on her face, she came up to me and spoke in a slow Jackie Kennedy–type whisper. "I want to talk to you, because I love you, because you are beautiful." Then she told me about Mel Lyman: how beautiful he was. She talked about him as though he were God.

Weeks later, she was on her knees in the back room at Max's, which was dark and dreary and like a big empty beer hall that should have had piss on the floor. The only light came from a red neon sculpture in the corner that made everyone look vampirized. M. was begging Andy to marry her, telling him that she loved him and things like that. Andy just sat there silently in his leather jacket, cringing a little, his hands fluttering, occasionally asking her to get up or asking one of us to remove her. Someone finally got her on her feet and out of there. Andy left too, but two hours later, he called Max's from the house he shared with his mother, which was next to the New York fertility center on Lexington and 89th. He said, "You've got to come up here and get M. She's in my back garden praying and I don't want her to upset my mother."

I went uptown in a taxi with Danny Leatherpants. (We called him Leatherpants because no one knew his last name and he always wore leather pants.) When we arrived at Andy's, he came out of the house with a flashlight, led us around the corner and unlocked a door leading to the alley behind the townhouses. There was M., just as he'd reported, kneeling in the cement garden up against a wooden fence, saying the rosary with her beads in her hands.

Danny Leatherpants picked her up and slung her over his shoulder, and we put her in a taxi. We drove to Max's with her, but she wouldn't go inside. She said she had to see Bruce, a boy who wore a large-brimmed black hat and had long orange hair; he lived in the Albert Hotel, a seedy fleabag hangout a few blocks away. She said she was engaged to him. We took the elevator to the fifth floor of the Albert and walked through endless corridors, brilliantly lit like a hospital, until we got to Bruce's room. The walls seemed made of cardboard. M. insisted that Bruce was going to marry her. He was very kind to her but apparently refused to marry her, because she opened the window and said she was going to jump. We kept closing the window. She kept opening it. We called Bellevue.

While we waited for the ambulance, Danny Leatherpants hid in a room at the end of the hall. He was wanted by the police, for what I never knew. Two cops and three little men in white coats arrived with a stretcher. M., standing by the stove across from the bed, slid her left hand behind her back and turned on all

Above: Warhol and friends, circa 1965 (Nat Finkelstein/Black Star).

Opposite page: Viva (Jeffrey Blankfort). Overleaf: Warhol directs Edie Sedgwick in a love scene from the unreleased film "Beauties" (Bob Adelman).

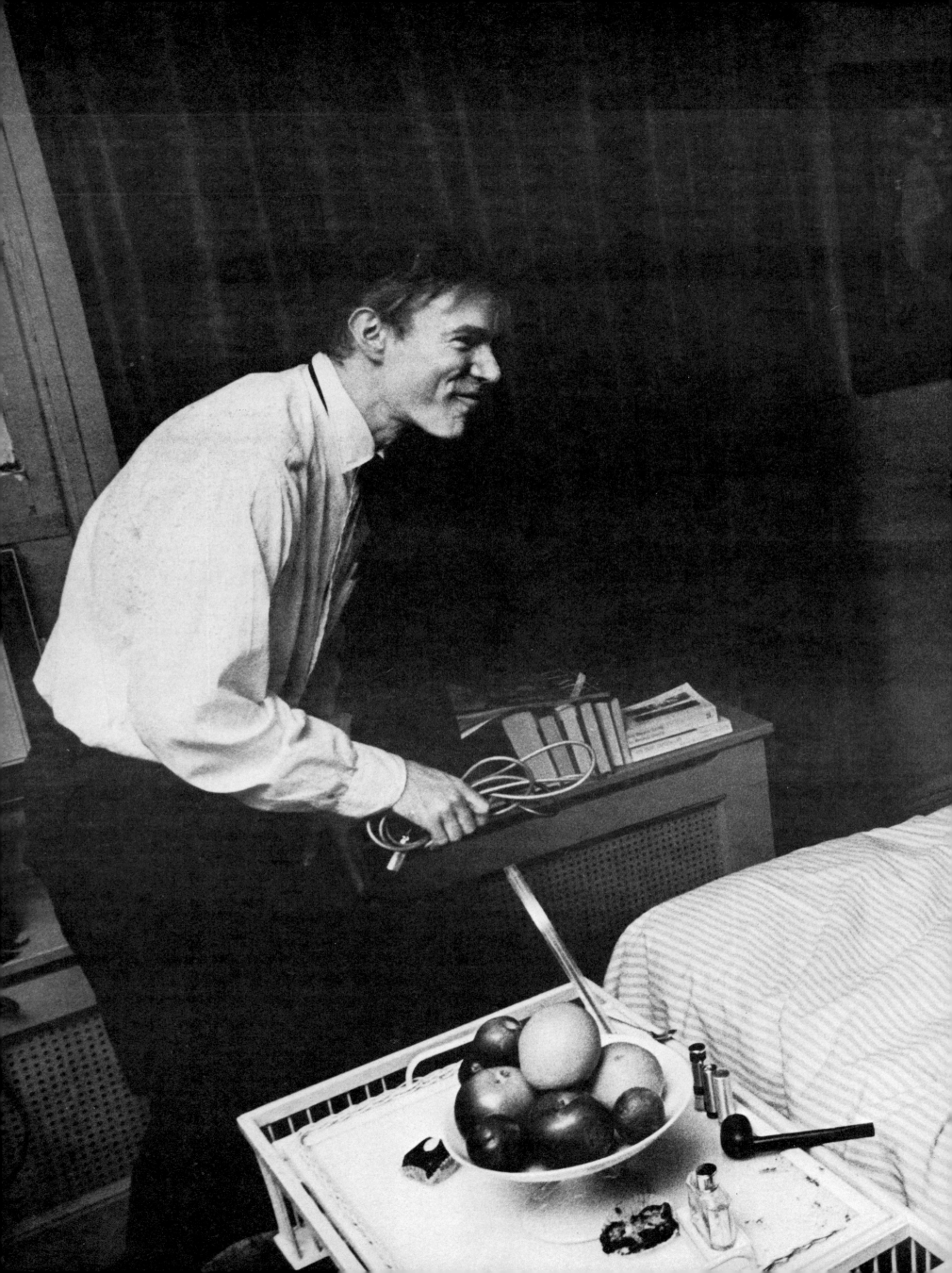

the gas jets. Then she extended the hand à la Greer Garson in a Forties movie and flashed the wedding ring on her finger. "How do you do?" she said. "I am Mrs. [whatever Bruce's last name was], and this is my husband Bruce." Then she pointed in my direction. "You don't want me! You want her!" I looked at the black velvet bathrobe I always wore and felt a little uncomfortable. At that moment we smelled gas, and Bruce screamed, "My God, she's trying to kill us all!" They just stood there staring at us closely. Finally one of them said, "Which one are we supposed to take?"

After they decided, Danny and I drove back to Max's and watched the outpatient show. M. called Andy from Bellevue and said she was getting a lot of sewing done. He stopped chewing gum for a moment and looked pleased.

Viva starred in a series of Warhol movies, including Lonesome Cowboys, Blue Movie *and* Nude Restaurant. *She is the author of two autobiographical novels,* Superstar *and* The Baby, *and has just finished a third,* Malibu.★

Two Warhol stars in front of Max's Kansas City. Jackie Curtis, left, and Andrea Feldman (Anton Perich).

RAECHEL DONAHUE
Underground Radio Surfaces

Tom Donahue and I were sitting around with some of our Telegraph Hill neighbors, smashed on his birthday, playing records for each other: The Doors, Judy Collins, all kinds of records that no one played on the radio. Tom said, "Do you realize that we sit here every night and smoke dope and play records for each other? I wonder why nobody's ever done this on radio." Tom did everything important on his birthday, so he started calling FM stations. He'd quit his job at KYA, a Top Forty station, because he had been forced to broadcast live from the Teenage Fair, and he couldn't stand being enclosed with kids pressing their noses against the glass and cursing him.

I don't know what made him think of calling FM stations, which at the time were inconsequential. I guess he figured that FM people were the only people desperate enough and dumb enough to do it. He called around until he found a station in San Francisco that had its phone disconnected, and that, my friends, was KMPX, formerly jazz station KHIP. He took a Preludin, which made his oratory particularly brilliant, went down to the station with a song and dance, and the owner bought it. Then we had to find a staff.

We got some of our neighbors together, pooled our records and put them all in one big box. We sprung a few people from jail and made one of them a salesman 'cause Tom always said that if you could sell dope,

Raechel and Tom Donahue square off (courtesy Raechel Donahue).

you could probably sell time.

Tom opened his new show the same way he'd opened his shows for twenty years: "My name's Tom Donahue and I play phonograph records." When we first started, we played a lot of things that people couldn't hear anywhere else. The average Joe could only afford two records a month, and KMPX became a fantastic musical education.

People started calling the station saying, "It's a dream. You're here!" We were monsters. We could have put almost anything on the radio—people were so thrilled not to have to listen to the same ten records over and over again.

The station itself was on Green and Battery, in an ancient warehouse. The studio looked like an enlarged bathroom with no toilet. Listeners came down in dribbles, then droves, to decorate it. The first people who came were very strange. Their names were Swan and JuJu, and they brought beads to hang over the windows, lots of Indian fringe and a Viet Cong banner.

We were definitely faking it, you know. We borrowed tape machines to run our spots. We were very frightening to look at for the people at the ad agencies. Our Leslie Salt commercial talked about Gandhi taking his people to the sea for salt. Thousands of people walked down and chanted *Aaagh-aah* in the background, and in a Maharishi Mahesh Yogi voice, Gandhi said that all they had to do was to go to the supermarket and look for the familiar red package.

When we finally hustled Pepsi-Cola, everybody who worked in the station said, "Shit, man, we are too hip for Pepsi. You really sold out. That clashes with how mellow we are." So we tried to get them to give us the R and B spot. They wouldn't. "I'm sorry, you're not black." We said, "That's all right, we like it better." No way. Finally we persuaded them to give us a very old Fifties spot they had almost thrown away.

All our sponsors were incredibly loyal. A local Saab dealer said to me, "I can't stand the music, and I can't stand the radio station, but I won't stop advertising on this station for *anything*. I've sold fifteen Saabs in the last four days." Hippies all over Berkeley were suddenly driving Saabs. Our record company sponsors, especially Elektra, were very loyal—as well they should have been. We were selling an amazing amount of records that had never received airplay. They were loyal when we needed them the most—for the strike.

In March of '68 we walked out on our jobs at KMPX and its sister station KPPC in Pasadena, in what was referred to as the Great Hippie Strike. We struck for freedom of dress, freedom of dope, freedom in general. We were also all working two jobs at the station, the top salary was maybe $125 a week, and our paychecks were bouncing. The owner of the station was a very weird person who used to sit alone in his office in the dark for hours. Just as we were becoming really successful, he started insisting on things like "wear a tie," "cut your hair." He started firing people he didn't like. We said, "Wait a second, we made this for you, you idiot, don't mess it up. Why are we being punished?" So we organized a strike, and all of the advertisers, every last one, pulled their spots off the air in support.

It was three o'clock in the morning when we announced that we were shutting down. Everybody in management was asleep. We walked out onto Green Street, a very broad avenue in the warehouse district, and thousands of people were there. The Grateful Dead came down and played. Stevie Winwood was in town and he came down and jammed with them. Everyone started playing and smoking dope and dancing.

Harry Bridges from the Longshoreman's Union offered to let us join. He said, "Hey, don't worry. If you join our union we'll take care of scabs." We thanked Harry and quietly formed our own union, the AAFIFMWW—the Amalgamated American Federation of International FM Workers of the World— printed stationery and got a great old mine-union lawyer.

For two weeks, we insulted anyone who tried to cross our twenty-four-hour picket line. A lot of people were tempted; it was their one chance to be on radio. But everyone rallied. People came down in the middle of the night with coffee and food. Squirkenworks donated several thousand dollars worth of roach clips that we could sell. Record companies donated thousands of dollars to our strike fund.

Our demands finally got a bit outrageous—such as time off for the summer solstice. And we eventually lost the strike. But we got another radio station, a new home, KSAN. So-called underground radio was alive and kicking.

Raechel Hamilton Donahue was an engineer and operations secretary at San Francisco's KMPX, the nation's first underground radio station, in 1967 and 1968. She went on to work part time at KSAN, where her husband Tom was program director and general manager, and in 1972 she became a full-time disc jockey. During 1975 and 1976, she could be heard on KMET in Los Angeles, where she now does free-lance radio production.★

The KMPX staff—post-success, pre-strike—with the Donahues seated at center (Baron Wolman).

RASHIED ALI
Trane's Last Stop

It was the last gig, but nobody knew it. It just seemed like another job, but it was a special occasion because Trane had only played two or three times in New York in two years. We hadn't been working much because Trane was complaining about being tired physically and tired of clubs, with the cash register ringing and the alcohol. He wanted to open his own place to play.

John Coltrane.

That last gig on April 23rd was a benefit for Olatunji's Center of African Culture in Harlem, a nice big room up above the street with a bandstand over in the right corner, five feet up from the floor, and all the energy of 125th Street going on right outside the window. As on all the jobs, the place wasn't big enough for all the listeners, musicians and writers who wanted to hear the band. Then again, in the last two years of his life when I played drums with him, no place we played—club or concert hall—had enough seats.

The music we were to play that afternoon and evening was probably shocking to many people, but that was part of why they came. Over the years, Trane had gotten people used to being shocked by what he was playing—shocked, surprised and challenged. That's why most of the musicians looked at him like he was a prophet. They looked at Trane's tenor genius the way he must have looked at Charlie Parker's alto genius during the bebop era of the mid-Forties and early Fifties. Parker, "Bird," had played the alto faster and more precisely than it had ever been played before, and had suddenly made everything seem antique. Trane was responsible for making the tenor dominant, playing it faster, higher and wilder than anybody imagined it could be played. He had musicians imitating him just like he'd imitated Bird's music and his dope habits. That killed Bird, but Trane pulled out just in the nick of time.

Playing there, covered with sweat, his horn never leaving his mouth, bearing down on the music—he made all kinds of weird stuff come out. Even musicians wondered what he was playing, with all those tones on top of tones. But he definitely knew what he was doing. It was everybody else that was slow. From the first time I heard him to the last, he played the same thing. The conception would just expand with different people. He was searching for a sound and he moved that sound on to different rhythms. It just so happened that by the time the audiences and the musicians were ready for one conception, Trane was *gone:* He had moved on to something else, new music and new personnel. He always wanted something to inspire him, not hold him back. That was why the younger musicians looked up to him: He had imagination, stamina and discipline, and wasn't afraid to change himself and everybody around him. After playing with Miles Davis and Thelonious Monk and exploring other things, he had both the masters of bebop and the young revolutionaries listening to him very closely.

When you were around him, you would see yourself change. When I joined his band, I was an arrogant black muthafucka, always ready to get on somebody's ass if they were saying the wrong shit. But Trane was such a kind man, and so open to other people, it would influence you. He gave people money, paid people's rent if they were serious about music. He always answered his phone, no matter what. He would get in his car and drive all the way from Long Island to New York City to help somebody who needed him.

Miles Davis.

When Trane got a gig he'd bring four or five drummers, ten or fifteen horns, and pay them out of his pocket so he could keep up with what was happening and provide a showcase for musicians who couldn't be heard in those clubs or concert halls any other way. If he heard somebody's baby was sick, he'd give them money to visit.

Opposite page: Trane in 1962 (Charles Stewart).

218

Nobody knew about it unless they were there when it happened. If he worked someplace, and the club owner fired us because Trane had gone beyond the repertoire which had made him famous and successful, he paid everybody what they were supposed to get for the *week,* gave them transportation money and said, "See you at the next job." That's the way he did things, and if you were around him, it was impossible not to be influenced.

He symbolized change for a lot of people. He had come through the whole dope/bebop Charlie Parker number and become very spiritual. He was always drinking juices, studying all kinds of religions and trying to lead an enlightened life based on love, compassion and kindness. And through it all, he held on to being a North Carolina, country-laughing person, who could wipe out a sweet potato pie by himself and loved collard greens and all of that heavy-duty Southern food.

Charlie "Bird" Parker at the Royal Roost in New York, 1948 (courtesy Charles Stewart).

He was studying Buddha sometime near the last gig and found that there was a chant where you could pound your chest and it would change the sound of your voice. He wanted to get that quiver on the horn, and when he couldn't get it, he'd put the horn down, beat on his chest and scream into the microphone. People really thought he'd lost his mind then. He wasn't even playing anything recognizable to them *with* the horn.

Near the end, he was in a big rush to get a lot of music out. We'd be in the studio recording at least once a week: duos, trios, stuff with two pianos and drums, with two basses and drums, all kinds of different recordings. We'd come in the studio, everybody talking, and Trane would start playing that tenor. We wouldn't know the tune, and when we'd stop him, he'd realize he hadn't written any parts for us. He was in such a hurry to finish that he didn't rehearse us. He'd just get the music together at home, pick up the phone to let us know what was happening and meet us at the studio.

At that last gig, with incense burning and the place packed, he did something I had never seen him do before—he sat down on the bandstand. I still didn't think he was sick, because when he put that horn in his mouth, there was no faltering; the fire was up at full blast. He'd say, "You don't know this, but listen and you'll hear it." Then he was gone and we were right there with him. That afternoon and evening he was sitting there sweating and playing his ass off, working just as hard as everybody else. Algie DeWitt was playing a big bata drum, which was strapped around his neck, and he came off the bandstand pissing blood—that's how hard he had to play to keep up with Trane! Algie damn near killed himself.

Trane was happy and optimistic. The band was the way he liked it. He had weaned it down from all those people he used to invite to play to a quintet. The music was where he wanted it to be. It didn't have to be read about, talked about. It was music that could speak to people on a private level, where a person could listen and find what he was looking for in whatever it was that he was playing. He wanted to touch people like that, to play music with no given tempo, key center or anything, just music. The audience was wild about it, too. He was beginning to communicate his conception, and the people were ready to hear what he had to say on his bandstand. He was very satisfied about that last performance. Not long after that, some cat came by and told me that Trane had died. He died from a liver ailment, maybe the result of some of the stuff he had been doing before he cleaned up. It was July 17th, 1967. Later, I was looking at some pictures—I had a lot of pictures from the last tour of Europe and Japan—and I noticed that we'd be looking at something in a music store, or Trane would be talking to some lady, and he'd have his hand on his liver. The man was in pain when we were on tour, and it was a mean tour, too. We played seventeen, eighteen concerts in fifteen days in twelve different cities, every night flying somewhere . . . no time for anything but the music.

Rashied Ali joined the John Coltrane Quartet in the latter part of 1965, and he performed with the band until Coltrane's death in 1967. He was one of the foremost avant-garde drummers of the time. Since then he has performed in various contexts from traditional to explorative, playing with Jackie McLean, Sonny Rollins and Eddie Jefferson, among others. At present he owns a club in New York's Soho district, Ali's Alley, and he has started his own record company, Survival Records.★ (Leni Sinclair)

1968

CALENDAR

January: 6 Magical Mystery Tour *and* Their Satanic Majesties Request *dominate chart;* **7** *Stamps go up to 6¢;* **8** *Debut of* The Undersea World of Jacques Cousteau; **22** Laugh-In *joins regular TV schedule;* **23** *North Korea seizes intelligence ship USS* Pueblo; *Release of* The Good, the Bad and the Ugly; **30** *Viet Cong launch surprise Tet offensive.*

February: 8 *Wallace makes third-party presidential bid;* **10** *Figure skater Peggy Fleming wins U.S.'s sole Olympic gold medal;* **12** *Publication of* Soul on Ice; **16** *Draft deferments abolished for most grad students;* **17** *Chambers Brothers enter LP chart with* The Time Has Come; **24** *Allies retake Hue from Viet Cong.*

March: 1 *New cars must have seatbelts;* **10** *Gallup poll finds 49% feel U.S. troops in Vietnam a mistake;* **12** *McCarthy nearly wins first primary;* **14** *U.S. combat deaths in Vietnam reach 19,670;* **15** *Barnard hassles Linda LeClair over coed living;* **16** *"The Dock of the Bay" reaches number one;* **17** *World gold crisis forces adoption of dual price system;* **31** *LBJ quits campaign.*

April: 3 *Film release of* 2001; **4-15** *Violence erupts across U.S. in wake of Martin Luther King's assassination, including Black Panther Bobby Hutton's death and Mayor Daley's orders for police to "shoot to kill arsonists";* **19** *Savings account interest rises to 6¼%;* **23-30** *Columbia student takeover;* **27** *National Mobe demonstrations in seventeen cities;* Traffic's Mr. Fantasy *enters LP charts;* **29** Airport *replaces* Myra Breckinridge *as best-selling novel;* Hair! *premieres on Broadway.*

May: 4 Days of Future Passed *on chart;* **6** *Mailer's* The Armies of the Night *is published;* **7** *Drug injection disqualifies Kentucky Derby winner;* **10-11** *Police brutality against Paris students sparks revolt paralyzing France;* **14** *Red Cross organizes relief for starving Biafrans;* **17** *Catonsville Nine, led by the Berrigans, burn draft files;* **30** *With military backing, De Gaulle recovers control in France.*

June: 6 *Robert Kennedy dies from assassin's bullet;* **12** *Film release of* Rosemary's Baby; **14** *Dr. Spock is convicted of conspiracy to counsel draft evaders;* **15** *Chart entry*

of Steve Miller's Children of the Future; **23** *Evictions close Resurrection City;* **26** *Chief Justice Warren resigns.*

July: 2 *Bill Cosby hosts Of Black America series;* **20** *Chart entry of* In-a-Gadda-Da-Vida; **29** *Best-selling nonfiction is* The Money Game.

August: 1 *U.S. troops in Vietnam total 541,000;* **8** *Nixon and Agnew are nominated amid Miami riots;* **10** Wheels of Fire *reaches top and the Band's* Music from Big Pink *enters LP chart;* **20** *Soviets invade Czechoslovakia;* **26** *FBI reports 61,843 state marijuana arrests, 98% jump over 1966;* **28** *Humphrey and Muskie are nominated while demonstrators clash with police in Chicago;* **31** Super Session *enters chart.*

September: 19 *Pitcher Denny McLain is first 31-game winner since 1931;* **24** *Sixty Minutes debuts;* **28** *"Hey Jude" tops singles chart.*

October: 2 *Fortas withdraws from Chief Justice consideration under fire for cronyism;* **8** *Zeffirelli's* Romeo and Juliet *premieres;* **12** Cheap Thrills *moves into LP lead;* **15** The Cancer Ward *is published one month after* The First Circle; **16** *DNA decoders win Nobel Prize;* **17** *Two U.S. runners are expelled from Olympics for their black power salutes;* **20** *Jackie Kennedy marries Aristotle Onassis; Reports link XYY chromosomes and criminal behavior.*

November: 1 *U.S. has dropped more bombs on Vietnam than in all of World War II; Film code ratings G, M, R and X in effect;* **5** *Nixon squeaks by Humphrey;* **13** Yellow Submarine *premieres;* **16** Electric Ladyland *captures top LP spot;* **17** Heidi *interrupts football telecast as Raiders come from behind to win;* **29** *LP* Astral Weeks *released.*

December: 2 *Nixon names Kissinger special assistant for national security; S. I. Hayakawa uses police to end San Francisco State strike;* **11** *Argument over shape of Paris conference table stalls four-way Vietnam peace talks;* **22** *Nixon-Eisenhower wedding; North Korea releases* Pueblo *crew after U.S. admits intrusion;* **25** *Apollo VIII crew sees far side of moon;* **28** *The Beatles'* "White Album" *leads LP chart,* Beggars Banquet *begins to climb.*

Top: Resurrection City—demonstrators camp on Washington's front lawn during the Poor People's Campaign (Bob Adelman). Center: Daniel, left, and Philip Berrigan on their way to court (UPI). Bottom: San Francisco police protect the S.F. State campus from the students (Alan Copeland). Opposite page: March 10, 1968—Cesar Chavez and Robert Kennedy at the Mass marking the end of Chavez's first fast (© William J. Warren).

RON KOVIC
On the Eve of the Tet Offensive

I really believed in what John Kennedy said about asking not what your country could do for you, but what you could do for your country. Like millions of Americans brought up in the Sixties, I believed that it was my duty to fight for my country, to go to Vietnam, to make the world safe for democracy. So when I came back from Vietnam the first time, I was enraged with the people who were demonstrating in the streets against the war. I felt they were traitors and that they were hurting the war effort. I volunteered to return to Vietnam, and did so in the fall of 1967. By that time I'd been promoted to Sergeant, U.S. Marine Corps.

I remember the day I arrived at the mouth of the Cuaviet River, just south of the demilitarized zone. I quickly began to realize that I was in a dangerous place. There were bunkers everywhere. Everybody was telling stories about the men who'd been killed and wounded by the rockets and artillery. I was excited and couldn't wait to get hit so I could see how brave I was. I wanted to be a man and feel like I was part of a war.

I got tired of sitting around, so I volunteered to take a patrol out one night. I set a perimeter on a hill above a village. To my left, I could hear the sound of the waves from the South China Sea; as I moved to my right, I could see the village. We were on a sand dune, surrounded by scrub pine trees, and I could see villagers walking around. There were very afraid of us. They always were.

It was beginning to get dark when we spotted what appeared to be a young man running across the open area. I told one of the men to go down and apprehend the suspect. He was brought back with his hands tied behind his back. We planned to bring him back to the battalion area for questioning. About that time, I realized that what had appeared to be a man was in fact a woman. We'd apprehended a woman.

After the men ate their C rations, we began to move down the sand dune toward the ocean. The woman was behind me, moaning and crying something in Vietnamese that I couldn't understand.

Then someone screamed. I looked behind me and saw fifteen or twenty dark figures running toward us from the village. Then rifles and flashes started going off. The Viet Cong were shooting at us! My men began shooting and running. I screamed at them to hold their ground and keep fighting, keep shooting.

Somewhere along the way, the woman was dropped and disappeared. I heard loud pops going off like firecrackers around my ears. I fired my rifle into the crowd of shadows in front of me and kept screaming for the men not to run. Now all the men were running in panic. They jumped into a ditch and so did I.

I looked toward the spot where the fire fight had begun, and saw a dark figure running toward me. His rifle was pointed directly at me. I remember feeling fear deep inside that this Viet Cong was about to kill me, and when he was almost on top of me, I raised my rifle, pointed it, and fired three times at his head and chest. The figure fell right in front of me.

Someone ran out and dragged the body back. He screamed, "Somebody has just shot Corporal ——" They said his name. I realized then that I had killed one of my own men.

I can't describe the pain. It was incredible, tragic. I felt like my whole being had been torn out. For those seconds, I felt like I was going to faint. My heart was racing. They were doing everything they could to save him. I couldn't look over to where they were talking and trying to bandage him.

Then somebody yelled over in my direction. "He's dead."

I rode back in the amtrack with him right by my foot, and he was dead.

It wasn't like a John Wayne movie at all; the good guys weren't supposed to kill the good guys. Each

Above: Marine outpost in the northern provinces (Tim Page).

Gatefold: South Vietnamese soldiers boarding choppers in enemy territory (James H. Karales). Page 225: Marines on patrol in Quang Ngai (Tim Page).

day I wondered whether I'd continue to live. One night in my tent I pointed my rifle at my head and tried to kill myself. I almost pulled the trigger.

I wrote home and told my parents that I wanted to become a priest.

But I stayed in Vietnam.

In October, I went out on a patrol. I'd killed the corporal and I had to make up for it. As we were crossing a rice dike, we were suddenly hit by a tremendous burst of automatic fire. It went on for an hour, and a strange feeling of relief and excitement—and victory—swept over me. But it turned out that we'd been attacked by the South Vietnamese, the ARVN. "They thought you were the Viet Cong," the major who told me this explained. And then he put me in for a medal.

I was very confused.

In December, we went out on another patrol and attacked a hut that supposedly contained a sapper team which had been planting explosives on our boats. When we ran into the hut it was covered with babies and children and men with their brains blown out—it was an unbelievable mess.

My men sat down and started crying. I started to shake and puke. Villagers screamed and shouted and cursed at us. I tried to patch the bodies together. I couldn't believe what had happened. A chopper came and picked up a boy and his foot fell off. I picked his foot up and bandaged it back on his leg and put him in the chopper.

A lieutenant came up and asked how many Viet Cong we'd killed. I told him we hadn't killed any.

When we walked back into the battalion area, I told the lieutenant that I didn't want to go out on any more patrols. He laughed at me: "You go to jail if you don't keep going out. You know that, Sergeant."

I said, "Well, I guess I'm going to keep going out, Lieutenant." And I did.

I kept going out on patrols, but I didn't care any more. I couldn't wait to get shot. I couldn't wait to step on a booby trap and get blown up so I could go back home. I just wanted to get the hell out of there, just wanted to leave that nightmare forever.

A Vietnam-style Marine (Tim Page).

On January 20th, I volunteered to lead the point with my squad into that same village where the hut had been. It was about a week before the Tet offensive began.

I took ten men across an open area. There was a bunch of South Vietnamese in a trench, and we had to walk over the top of it. I urged the South Vietnamese to come with me, but they wouldn't. I told them they were cowards, that they had no guts, that they were sitting out the war in a trench.

This was gonna be it. I was going to make up for everything now. I would go across that open area and take that village with my squad. I promised myself that when I started moving, I wouldn't stop moving until I'd gotten to the other side.

We made a direct assault, and all of a sudden the guys were getting hit by mortars. They were jumping like little toy soldiers off the tanks. The mortar sounded like cymbals crashing again and again in the sand.

The men began to run toward the tree line. I screamed at them to come back and keep attacking, advancing toward the village. Soon I realized that the only person out there was me. I kept moving toward the village and firing my automatic again and again, from the hip. I kept blasting everything I could into a pagoda, into the village. I wasn't going back. I was going forward. I wasn't going to quit. I was finally going to be a hero. Even if I had to be a dead hero.

Prisoner-of-war compound (Tim Page).

I kept firing my rifle until a crack went off at my foot. I felt my whole leg go numb. I was shot, and I felt so good inside, so good that I got shot. I was getting out of there. But I couldn't run back. I wanted to go home. I went down on my knees. I couldn't walk any more. I started shuddering and shuddering. A loud crack went off next to my ear, then through my lung, and I felt like a train had hit me. I thought I was dead. I couldn't breathe, my face was in the sand. *ALIVE!* I started to cry: "Someone please . . . I just . . . I just . . ." I tried to get up. I couldn't feel anything. I hoped my body was still there. I couldn't

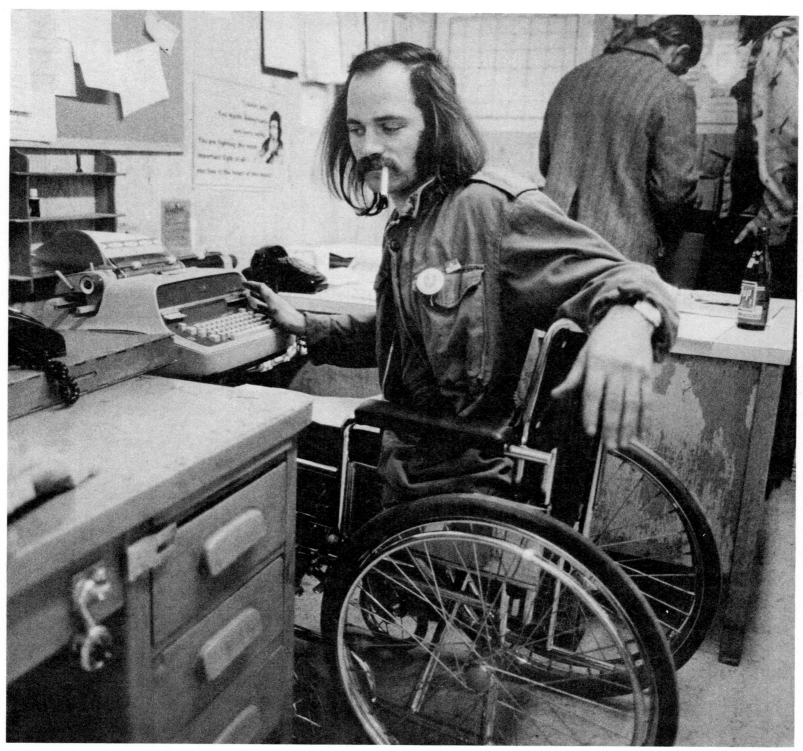

feel it—something was wrong. Then somebody came up from behind and yelled, "Sarge, Sarge, are you all right?" Then I heard another crack, and he fell down dead in back of me.

A black guy picked me up and finally dragged me out of there. He saved my life. Artillery was being dropped all around us. People were screaming and running. The Cong were blowing the shit out of us. Medics came and brought me back across the river, put me in a helicopter and sent me down to Da Nang, to the hospital. I had tubes stuck in my nose and I was placed in intensive care. I fought with everything I had to live. I made it out of there. I will be paralyzed for the rest of my life.

Two views of Kovic: above in Los Angeles circa 1973 (Annie Leibovitz); and left, nine years earlier at high school graduation (courtesy Ron Kovic).

Ron Kovic joined Vietnam Veterans Against the War in 1970. Arrested nine times during antiwar demonstrations, he was thrown out of the 1972 Republican Convention for attempting to shout down President Nixon as he began his acceptance speech. In 1976, Kovic addressed the Democratic Convention, nominating Fritz Efaw, a draft evader, for Vice President. He is the author of Born on the Fourth of July *and now works full time for unconditional amnesty for war resisters.★*

DORIS KEARNS GOODWIN
Back at the LBJ Ranch

By the time I joined the White House staff in the early spring, President Johnson was beginning to regain his spirits. The country had responded positively to his March 31st withdrawal from the Democratic presidential race. His public opinion polls had gone up, and for the first time in months, he was beginning to think that history might respond well to him. He thought, for a moment, that he could even bring about an end to the war in Vietnam.

Then Bobby Kennedy died, and the euphoria changed. Johnson began to wonder whether he couldn't have won after all. Hubert Humphrey wasn't doing very well; Southern senators were asking Johnson if he'd accept a draft. He waited nervously for the Democratic convention—and then it didn't want him.

I came away from the convention feeling depressed and guilty. All my friends there had worked for McCarthy; how had I ended up with Johnson? But when I walked into the Oval Office to discuss resignation, he began to talk to me in a very gentle tone about how hard the convention had been for him. He was sad that Daley had done what he did. But nothing made him sadder than to realize that the party he had been a member of for forty years had repudiated him so thoroughly at the convention. He couldn't even attend, and it was his birthday. He saw his party going up in flames and he knew that he was part of the cause. He felt that he had done everything he could have for the party and the country, and no one appreciated him any more—that everything had failed. I felt that my complaints were so minor that I didn't even think about finishing what I had come in to say.

Sometimes when I heard him speak like that he seemed deliberately self-pitying, but I began to realize at that moment that the feeling of being rejected hit something very deep in his person. He wasn't simply a politician who cared only about winning and losing. He felt emotionally tied to the things he was doing for the American people. This realization gave me a more personal sense of why he had chosen not to run.

The fear of losing the nomination to a Kennedy was an obvious factor. I think they represented something in his life that went far deeper than we all knew. It was not simply that John Kennedy had preceded him, and that John Kennedy was beloved, as Johnson had never been. It was that Kennedy represented a world that Johnson had always aspired to, and always felt rejected by: a world not just of beautiful people, but of artists, people from the media, and writers—people of words—a world that Johnson's mother, in my judgment, held up as an ideal from the time he was a child. He always feared that by choosing the manly world of the cowboys that his father represented—by becoming a practical, negotiating, hard-talking politician—he'd disappointed his mother and cut himself off from that ideal. Maybe that was part of the reason he tried to get through to me—because I was from Harvard, the Kennedys' school. I went to work for him at the Johnson ranch, after the election.

In those last couple of years he began talking to me about his childhood and his dreams. The situation is hard to describe without it sounding different than it actually was, but he simply couldn't sleep very well. He would wake up at five A.M. and not want to wake Lady Bird, who needed sleep in the morning. He needed somebody to talk to, so he would come into my room. I knew this as a pattern—just as I now wake up minutes before my baby in the morning, I would wake up right before I knew he was coming. I'd get dressed and sit in an easy chair by the window, and wait for him. He would come in, get into the bed that I had left, and pull the sheets up to his neck. Sometimes, while he talked, I would remember that he was the thirty-sixth President, and not just a person that I had gotten to know very well. Then I'd get scared because I'd realize that the notes I was taking were historically important, and I'd think, "Oh, my God, I've got to do this right.

Why am I not a psychiatrist or sixty years old and very wise?"

I always had to question how much of what Johnson told me was colorful and exaggerated, and how much was real. He described a nightmare he'd had in those last months in the White House, before he withdrew, and it was hard to know whether he had really dreamed it or whether he embellished a shadowy outline of a dream to make it more terrifying.

In the nightmare he appeared to be Lyndon Johnson lying in a bed, with his own head but with the body of Woodrow Wilson, who'd been partially paralyzed by a stroke in the last years of his Presidency. He was lying with his shriveled body in a bed, and in the next room his assistants debated about which parts of his powers they would divide among themselves. He couldn't reach them, he couldn't yell at them, and he couldn't talk to them. He was behind a screen and he couldn't move.

He said that the dream was so scary to him that he would get out of his bed with a flashlight and walk to the Red Room where Woodrow Wilson's portrait hung so he could assure himself that Wilson was dead and he was alive.

My first sense of the dream was that he had a terrible fear of losing control of events, at a time when he *was* very swiftly losing control of events. There was the war in Vietnam, there were racial riots, the economy seemed to be in a state of stampede. But in another sense the dream indicated a deep physiological fear. Johnson knew that his family had a history of early strokes, and he imagined that even if he was reelected something would happen to him physically between 1968 and 1972. The only thing worse than being at the ranch and out of power would have been being in power in the White House, but not in control of events. He was more fearful of paralytic stroke than of death. At the root of his decision to withdraw was a fear that he would be defying fate by trying for another four years.

Later, at the ranch, he went over again in his mind decisions he had made, wondering whether he had done the right thing. It was hard for him to justify the escalation of the war, because the war lost him so much. He had lost the Great Society, a fought-for place in the civil rights movement, and the love of the American people. Gradually he developed the idea that he had somehow prevented World War Three. He would say, "The war was horrible, I know that. We lost fifty thousand people. But if I hadn't entered the war, I would have lost World War Three, and everything would have been far worse than we could have imagined."

He was questioning the whole pattern of his life, wondering whether he mightn't have been happier after all as a family man. I remember him looking through biographies of Jackson and Lincoln. He said to me that, reading them, he couldn't conjure those Presidents to life in his mind—he couldn't make them walk in front of him. Then he wondered out loud: if he couldn't bring these Presidents to mind, how would anyone ever remember him?

In the spring of 1968, Doris Kearns, then a White House Fellow, was reassigned from her post in the Labor Department to a position on the White House staff at the request of President Johnson. After Johnson's term ended she continued to work for him, shuttling between Texas and Harvard University, where she was an associate professor. She married Richard Goodwin, political speech writer and author, in 1975. Ms. Goodwin is now a professor of government at Harvard. Her first book, Lyndon Johnson and the American Dream, was published in 1976, and her current project is a biography of John F. Kennedy.★
(Joan Bingham)

Opposite page: the Johnson family on Father's Day, 1968 (Wide World Photos); on the ranch, above and overleaf (Robert Lebeck/Black Star).

229

ANDREW YOUNG
Remembering Dr. King

I was surprised by his assassination. I didn't see the Poor People's Campaign as the threat to Washington and the establishment that I now see it was. We feared for Dr. King's life more in the early Sixties, through 1963, than we did by 1968. Up through 1965, there was a civil rights–related death every couple of months, though most of them didn't make headlines. By the end of '65, there was a lull in the killings, and I thought perhaps we were finally beyond all that.

In his last year, we worried about Dr. King's health. He was working eighteen to twenty hours a day. He would stay up all night reading, talking, clowning—whatever he felt like doing—and then wake up at five-thirty raring to go. His wife used to say that he had a war on sleep.

We would tell him that it looked like he was going to be around for a long time, and he couldn't possibly keep this pace up, because he was close to forty. But if you said anything, he'd brush you off. I could never argue with him anyway. He was a preacher. And whenever we argued, he'd get to preaching. You never won an argument because he would take off on flights of oratory, and you'd forget your point trying to listen to him.

The year he died was the year he felt he had to establish the agenda for America's future. For fifteen years he'd been struggling with the issues of racism, poverty and war. He refused to be just a civil rights leader. He was a sensitive lover of people who saw his primary responsibility in the black community. By 1968, though, it was clear to him that the black community could not concern itself with civil rights issues alone. The country was spending billions of dollars in Vietnam, and he saw racism and war becoming ever more tied up into one big problem for this country.

It was a time of increasing desperation for him. The SCLC had a fraction of the budget that it should have had, about $700,000, and a small staff of fifty people, trying to take on the problems of the urban North, as well as the South, which still had large pockets of resistance. Not only weren't we getting any aid from the federal government, but we had legions of FBI agents tracking us down, harassing us, trying to disrupt the work we were doing—work which I thought was the only thing that was giving America a fighting chance to survive.

James Earl Ray, convicted assassin of Martin Luther King, Jr.

The dangerous times when we were together were always the times he was most humorous. For years we couldn't go anywhere without FBI men following us around. Dr. King was philosophical about it and very friendly towards them. Every now and then, we would leave a meeting through another entrance—not to escape the car that trailed us, but to sneak up on them. King would say hello, introduce us and (we always gave them the benefit of the doubt) thank them for the "protection" they were giving us.

I think he would have been quite content to be pastor of the Riverside Church, maybe teach at a university or a seminary. He wanted to teach the philosophy of religion, which was the subject of his Ph.D. He turned down a chance for the presidency of the NAACP when he first came to Montgomery in 1954, because he wasn't sure he wanted to become that involved with the growing civil rights movement.

But when the bus boycott came in '55, he was pressed into action. He had to respond. He was just twenty-six, and he never had the time to be the fun-loving man that he really was. He made the cover of *Time* magazine only a couple years after he finished his degree, and then he was a celebrity.

From that time on he felt the burden of the country, his people and the world on his shoulders. He

Opposite page: Dr. King and Ralph Abernathy in a Florida jail after an attempted sit-in (UPI). Overleaf: Martin Luther King and Andrew Young at the Atlanta airport in July 1966 (Bob Fitch/Black Star).

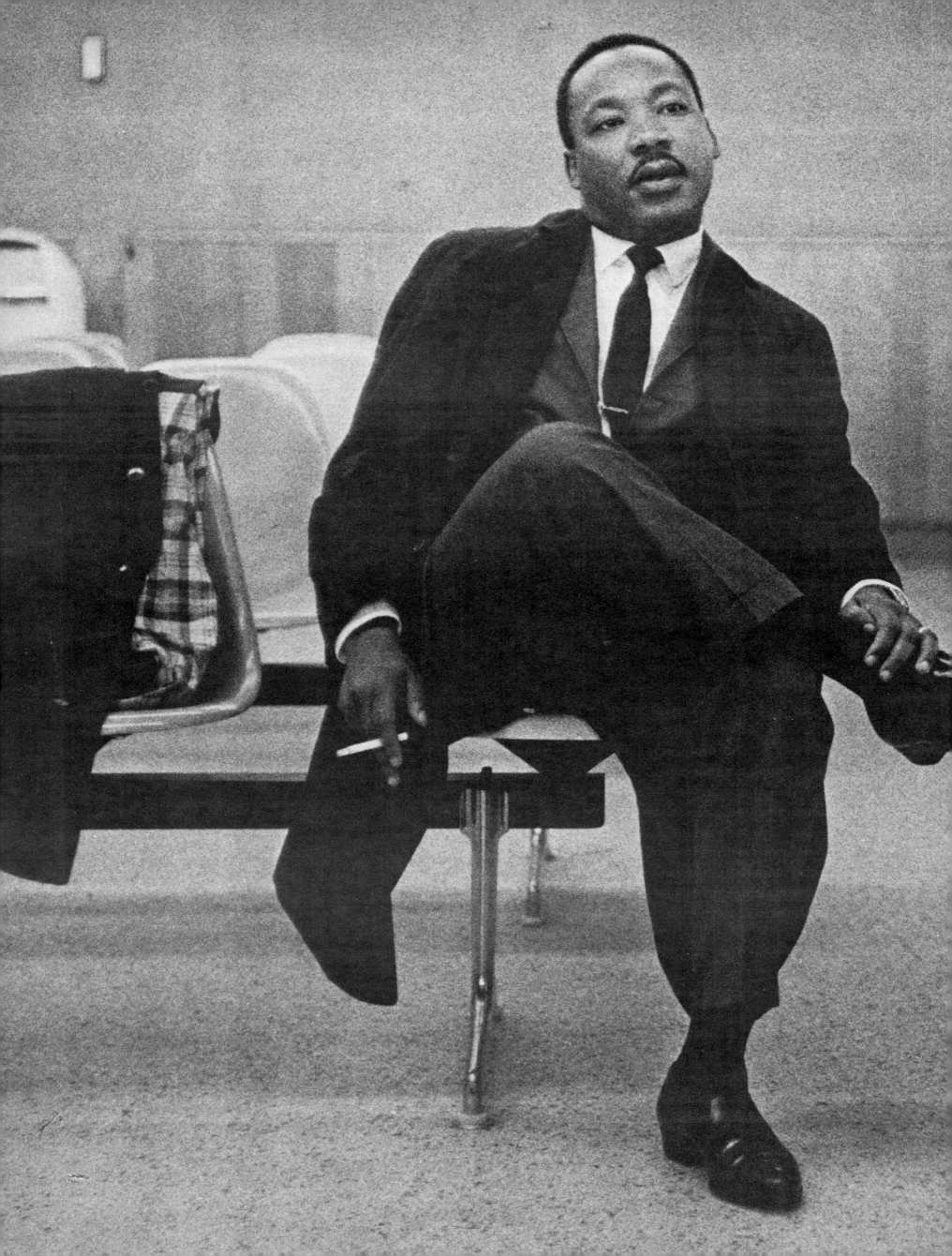

accepted it, but he always said he would have liked to do something else. He felt responsible for America's future and its survival because he said that nobody understands nonviolence except black Americans, and if America was going to learn to live with the rest of the world, we'd have to help her find a nonmilitary course. In his Nobel Peace Prize speech, in fact, Dr. King said that the choice was nonviolence or nonexistence.

I think back sometimes to what this country would have been like without Dr. King. The South was an armed camp in the Forties and the Fifties. The GI bill and better job opportunities had created the beginnings of a black middle class, and they were not going to tolerate oppression any further. The white forces of reaction were trying to resist the advance of this new black middle class.

Every black family in the South had a gun. My father was probably the least violent man I know, and yet there were at least four guns in our household. Had there been no Martin Luther King, Jr., the Southern part of the United States would have looked like Northern Ireland or Lebanon.

And yet Martin saw that blacks and whites did not hate each other. They were being forced down through history on a collision course. Martin Luther King straightened out that course. He made it possible for blacks and whites to move in a parallel course of development and work together by using the tactic and methodology of nonviolence. He did not blame the white man for the problems that blacks were having. He

saw blacks and whites caught up in a situation that they didn't create, that they inherited. He saw nonviolence as a means for bringing people to realize that they could work their way together out of the situation.

Dr. King never understood why Hoover couldn't comprehend what he was doing. If you read Hoover's FBI reports on the March on Washington speech, you realize that he never saw King's vision of a New America. He saw a powerful, radical political voice trying to destroy the nation.

I didn't know then, but I now think that there lies the indirect responsibility for his assassination. I don't know if it can ever be pinned down, but there were so many client groups that did dirty jobs around and for official people. I think now that Dr. King's assassination was directly related to the fear that officialdom had of his bringing large numbers of poor people to the nation's capital, setting up tents, demanding some response from them.

In 1960, Andrew Young began oranizing and teaching in the SCLC's program to prepare blacks for the literacy tests used historically in the South to keep them from voting. A former rural pastor in Georgia and Alabama, he became SCLC's executive director and an adviser to Martin Luther King. In 1972 he was elected to Congress, and in 1977, appointed by President Carter, he became the first black U.S. ambassador to the United Nations.★ (Bob Adelman)

This page, top: King and Abernathy arrested again, this time in Birmingham, Alabama (Wide World Photos); above: Martin Luther King's participation in the Montgomery, Alabama, bus boycott prompted his arrest, pictured here, and marked the beginning of his leadership in the civil rights movement in 1955 (Charles Moore/Black Star). Opposite page, clockwise from top left: King on his way to court (Wide World Photos); Members of the American Nazi Party with a message for Dr. King (UPI); funeral marchers follow King's casket through Atlanta (Wide World Photos).

JAMES S. KUNEN
The Student Strike at Columbia

In the days that led up to the spring explosion, Columbia was not a happy place. People were always morose at Columbia, and added to that was the fact that the war was going on. Students were unhappy with the school's affiliation with the Institute for Defense Analyses, a war research organization. Also, Columbia was a white enclave in a decaying urban neighborhood—Harlem formed its border. Columbia kept expanding into the black neighborhood, buying up buildings and throwing people out. The students felt lousy and miserable anyway, which was bad enough, but they also felt guilty because who were they to feel lousy and miserable? And now Columbia was building a new gym in Morningside Park—with separate facilities for Columbia's black neighbors.

On April 22, Mark Rudd, the chairman of SDS, and five others were placed on disciplinary probation for demonstrating inside a university building against regulations. Rudd was never particularly revered on campus. He didn't have much charisma, to put it mildly, and other radicals had more genius. He was just a guy who was around all the time. Nevertheless, the action against him provoked another demonstration, at the Sundial. A rally at the Sundial was quite theatrical, a central event on campus. I was an SDS person to the extent that I was on their mailing and phone lists, a body they could count on at rallies. So when they called

for a sympathy rally, I came.

The rally convened the next day. The speeches were suitably impassioned, but neither they nor any plan caused what followed. After a few false starts, the rally moved en masse to Hamilton Hall in order to show solidarity with Rudd and the others by demonstrating inside a building, and then the crowd simply stayed there. We were still there the next morning when the *New York Times* came out—and we were on the front page. It was a shock—society was paying attention to us! The strike was on its way.

* * * *

April 24th, six A.M. We had been sitting in Hamilton Hall all night, but now the black students wanted the white students out. Black feeling was very separatist at Columbia. We had our full share of white guilt, so we left—and headed for Low Library, the university administration building. Someone, maybe more than one, smashed the glass in the door, opened it, and we ran straight for President Grayson Kirk's office.

I was excited and nervous. The classroom building, Hamilton, was ours in a way, but the president's office was the inner sanctum—beautiful carpets as far as the eye could see, a $450,000 Rembrandt on the wall—and Kirk was extremely remote. If you saw him three times in four years it was truly amazing, and then he was either getting into or out of a limousine.

We stayed until nearly eight A.M., then someone said the police were coming. All but twenty-seven of us jumped out the window and ran away. I stayed. I was reading *Lord Jim* in English class, and the guy in the book jumped off a boat he thought was sinking—only it didn't sink. As a result, he lost his integrity and looked like an asshole. I wasn't running anywhere.

The police stuck their heads in and said hello. They were quite affable—then. People gathered outside Low in the rain in support of the people inside, and eventually they started coming back inside through the windows. Everyone who climbed back in was wet, which distinguished them from everyone who had remained inside. I felt quite superior to the people who were wet and contemptuous of them. I resented their presence, because as they dried out, it took away my identity as a nonjumper. Pretty soon Low was filled with a lot of people again.

Low Library before the bust, above, and
after, opposite page (Bonnie Freer/Photo Trends).

238

Early the next morning two more buildings were taken. In the middle of that night, I went with a group of students to take Mathematics Hall, because Low was getting too crowded. We tried hard to be nice to the janitors and cleaning ladies, but we immediately barricaded the door behind us by stacking up furniture. Later, that became an issue. It seemed silly to talk about scratching furniture when American planes were bombing Vietnam. But when you were destructive to furniture in college, you were not considered destructive to furniture, you were destructive to the entire tradition of humanistic education.

Counter-demonstrators in front of the library (Bonnie Freer/Photo Trends).

The most fervent radicals were in Mathematics Hall. We had a "be true to your school" kind of feeling. We were the hard core, we wore red armbands and flew a red flag. Tom Hayden was there, too. I knew that he had had something to do with the Port Huron Statement, and he'd been organizing in Newark. That meant he'd been out among the people, from whom, seemingly, I was so hopelessly shut off. SDS insisted on participatory democracy, and Hayden led the discussions—he was in control: he called the votes, he chose who would speak and for how long. Someone had to in order to get anything done at all those endlessly long mass meetings.

We had to decide who should be on the food committee, the blanket committee, the press committee, the strike coordinating committee. Every detail of living had to be discussed and voted upon. The meetings went on until speakers weren't making sense any more. They were too tired and dirty. Tempers ran short. Egos tripped. I gave myself the job of keeping the lid on the mayonnaise jar because I'd read somewhere that mayonnaise was a breeding ground for poisonous bacteria.

After a week in the buildings the bust finally came. Information filtered in via walkie-talkie and runner—descriptions of people being dragged by their hair down stairs, clubbings, blood being spilled. The cops took one building after another by force. The blacks, however, walked quietly out of Hamilton. We were the last building to be emptied.

We were prepared to resist. We coated the steps with green liquid soap so the cops would slip. We stacked more furniture against doors. Suddenly I could see five helmets bobbing outside. They were swearing and grunting, working at cutting the hoses and ropes around the door, pulling the furniture down piece by piece. I thought when they got to me, they'd kill me. People up and down the stairwell were beating a rhythm on overturned wastepaper baskets. The whole thing had everyone's blood racing.

The police grabbed me and broke through our linked arms. Then, holding on to my feet and arms, they threw me under a tree.

The paddy wagons were at the Sundial, the whole place was floodlit and illuminated. Even at a night baseball game, when the night is suddenly turned to day, an exhilarating feeling overcomes me: "This is history." An enormous crowd, densely packed, shouted: "Strike! Strike! Strike!" with their hands in Vs waving back and forth in the air.

After that, the police were called in again, to break up two more demonstrations that sprang from reaction to the first bust. That first bust had completely swung all the "undecideds" over to us, and had formed a mass base for protest. The second was kind of dull and got poor reviews on campus. The last was the most violent and terrifying of the three, but like the whole experience, it was unsatisfying—we didn't end the war, and it seemed we succeeded in changing Columbia's policies only in a cosmetic way.

Sometime before the last busts we went on a march into Harlem. We walked down 125th Street and I held a sign that read, "Columbia, get out of Harlem." But *we* were Columbia and we were *in* Harlem.

James S. Kunen was nineteen and a sophomore at Columbia University when New York magazine bought an article he had written on his experiences as a student radical. That article led to contracts for a book and a movie about the Columbia strike. In 1969, The Strawberry Statement: Notes of a College Revolutionary was published, and a year later a movie based on the book was released. Kunen is currently a columnist for New Times magazine and a law student at New York University. ★ (courtesy James S. Kunen)

Opposite page: still protesting Columbia's role as a slum landlord, Mark Rudd, with hands raised, speaks at a demonstration in Harlem two and a half weeks after the "occupation" of the university ended (Bonnie Freer/Photo Trends).

Side Trips

*Above, clockwise from top: Swami Satchidananda arrives at Woodstock
(© Jim Marshall); Jesus freaks, late Sixties (Annie Leibovitz);
Harvard professor Richard Alpert, before meeting his
guru, left, and after, right, renamed Baba Ram
Dass (both Gloria Stavers). Opposite
page: Tim Leary at Millbrook
(© Don R. Snyder).*

*On the following pages: Swami Bhaktivedanta and devotees in
San Francisco (© Gerhard E. Gscheidle); at a New Mexico
commune (Timothy Carlson); mediating at the
Lama Foundation (Bonnie Freer/Photo
Trends); a late Sixties New
York City crash pad
(Charles Gatewood).*

MYRA FRIEDMAN
Taking Care of Janis

Janis was not what most men thought. It's not fair to generalize, but more men than women took the surface for granted and accepted her as this big "Red Hot Mama" type who "lived life to the fullest"—which is a lot of bunk. But then most of the men she knew weren't exactly flowing over with sensitivity either. You could tell a lot about Janis by her style of speech. Around women, she would drop her Mae West number, and become much less strident and crude. She was terribly afraid of men, and women just made her less anxious. Sometimes she'd call in the middle of the night. "I can't sleep," she'd say. "I wake up terrified that people are going to find out." She meant find out what *she* thought was true: that she couldn't sing, that she

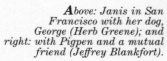

Above: Janis in San Francisco with her dog, George (Herb Greene); and right: with Pigpen and a mutual friend (Jeffrey Blankfort).

was a fraud. Janis didn't know who she was.

Early in December 1968, the morning before her last East Coast concert with Big Brother, she called me around seven A.M., which was not exactly my waking hour. "Can I come to your apartment and sleep there while you go to work?" she said. "I can't sleep here at the Chelsea. It's too noisy."

She arrived about eight-thirty, tremendously overwrought, going a mile a minute, with that infernal bottle of Southern Comfort in her hand. She wanted me to get her some Seconal from my doctor, but I refused—not with all that booze.

Finally I agreed to call him because she'd been awake all night and had to perform that evening. "How am I ever going to go on if I can't sleep?" she kept saying.

My doctor was adamant when I explained the problem. "I will prescribe two Seconal. Period. Exactly two."

When I ran down to the drugstore to get the pills, I also took Janis's bottle. She was still wound up when I got back. She dropped her first excuse, that it had been so noisy at the hotel, and told me the truth, that she'd taken some speed. Someone had laced her drink, she said, which I didn't believe. I left her with the two pills and headed off to work at the office of her manager, Albert Grossman. The bottle of Southern Comfort was in my handbag.

At four that afternoon, I got another frantic call from Janis. Her voice was so hoarse I could scarcely hear her. "I can't talk," she gasped. "I'm really in bad shape. There's no way I can carry the show alone."

No other act had been booked to open. It was strictly to be an hour and a half of Big Brother. "Will you tell Albert he's got to get another act to go on first!"

I nearly dropped dead. If you know Albert, you know it's sometimes impossible to get through to him, and right then he was in a meeting. It was horrible, because at the same time I had to find her a throat specialist. Finally I located a doctor who specialized in treating singers. "Listen," I told him. "I've got this woman singer here, and she can't sing."

Meanwhile Albert was floating around the office, totally oblivious to anything being wrong. Every time I'd try to see him, his secretary would say, "Sorry, he's in a meeting." I was carrying on something terrible. Finally he came to get a drink of water outside my office. "Albert!" I yelled. "I've got to talk to you." He answered with a toss of his long gray hair and a curt "Sorry, in a meeting. Busy now." He walked back into his office, all smiles, and closed the door.

In concert, 1968 (Jeffrey Blankfort).

I had told Janis to grab a cab and pick me up in front of the office. The doctor's appointment was for five-thirty. Everything was completely crazy. Finally I told Albert's secretary that she had to get through to him, that Janis couldn't sing, that I was taking her to a throat doctor, and that he should get another act on the show. I was praying he'd hear all of this in time. Albert could easily continue his meeting until five of eight and arrive at the concert just in time to discover that there was no show.

Janis came by around five-fifteen and we shot on up to the doctor's. *She* was relaxed, maybe from the Seconal. I was a nervous wreck. We convinced the cabdriver to wait while the doctor checked her out, and then Albert actually called. This was about six, so he had barely enough time to find another act.

When Janis emerged, we had the cabdriver breaking the speed limit to get to my apartment to change, because she hadn't even tried on the outfit she was going to wear—a handmade crushed-velvet dress that had never been pressed.

As we rushed downtown, she started to cackle, but kind of softly.

"So what's wrong with your throat?"

"Nothing."

"*Nothing!*" I was pretty sure she hadn't told the doctor about the alcohol or anything else she'd been taking.

"He says I should speak up." She laughed. "I should talk louder. I talk too soft. That's what he said."

I thought for a bit about the loudness that was part of her public style. The doctor was right about her speech, because when Janis was being herself, she had this tiny little voice—wispy, really.

At 14th Street and Sixth Avenue, we got out of the cab and started walking toward my apartment. I looked around, and suddenly, no Janis. Good God, I thought, where the hell has she gone now! I was standing on the street looking around when I spotted her coming out of this 14th Street bargain department store.

"I wanted new panties," she said, showing me the purple bikinis she'd bought.

"Now!" I said. "You had to get panties now!" I didn't know how we were ever going to get up to Hunter College in time. I had to change; she had to change.

Once inside, she washed her hair. I went to take a shower, leaving her drying her hair over my radiator. When I came out of the bathroom, she was gone—*again*. In a minute she was back. It was freezing outside, and with wet hair, laryngitis, and all, she'd gone downstairs to the cleaners to get that dress pressed. The cleaners was closed. We ironed the dress together, slipshod, and made a mad dash to Hunter College for the concert. Somehow or other, Albert had taken care of things and had booked James Cotton to open. I was drained.

Janis in the country (©Lisa Law).

There was a lot of tension between the band and Janis that night because she was leaving them. Dave Getz kicked over one of his drums; Janis thought he had done it on purpose, which may or may not have been so.

Janis's feelings were hurt, but she also had a lot of guilt. No one would ever have known. Her performance was marvelous, one of the greatest I can remember. Just incredible.

Time and again, her speaking voice would tell what was really going on. In the 1968 recordings on *Joplin in Concert,* she talked naturally, very quietly between songs. Two years later, her voice was blunt and tough, which had a lot to do with the increase in her drinking. The way she treated herself—that kind of studied self-execution—started to show badly. She talked more and more about quitting, about playing

Overleaf: Big Brother and the Holding Company in 1966, left to right: Janis Joplin, James Gurley, Peter Albin, David Getz and Sam Andrew (© Lisa Law).

251

smaller halls so it could be "like it used to be." She talked about getting old—she was twenty-seven—and about getting married. She became more self-involved. There was a time when Janis was always interested in what was going on with other people—that changed. She would call and say, "Hi, I . . . " It was the junk.

The last time I saw her, she was talking about a fellow she'd met in Brazil. He was a schoolteacher, and, I don't know, less fly-by-night than her other boyfriends. At one point she popped up and said, "Can you see me married to a schoolteacher?"

I said, "Yeah."
She didn't laugh.

Myra Friedman worked as Janis Joplin's publicist from January 1968 until Joplin's death on October 5, 1970. She wrote Buried Alive: The Biography of Janis Joplin, *which was nominated for a National Book Award and received the ASCAP-Deems Taylor Award in 1974. She is currently a free-lance writer living in New York City.★ (Toshi)*

JULES WITCOVER
The Last Day of the RFK Campaign

The night of the Oregon primary, Kennedy had a fair idea that he was in trouble. I remember him coming into the Benson Hotel in Portland with his pregnant wife, through a big crush and up to a suite. He had never lost an election. But there was something about that night that was kind of ominous; it wasn't going to work. I had been with McCarthy in downtown Portland that day, and for the first time he was getting the kind of reaction the winner gets; he was being mobbed on the streets.

But when Kennedy actually did lose, it was a shock to everybody. No Kennedy had ever lost before. At what was supposed to be a victory celebration, he came down and spoke. It was a very teary kind of scene, with a lot of young people crying. He made a very gracious speech in which he thanked the people of Oregon for being so courteous to him. He was in some ways more gracious in defeat than he'd been in victory; he used to be kind of flip and a little smart-alecky when things were going well.

Later in the evening it was very somber in the suite. There were a lot of the familiar Kennedy people hanging around, moping, all kind of jolted by the whole thing. Bobby was there, sitting on the armchair in shirt-sleeves with a watered-down drink in his hand. People came over and said things to console him because he was very down, and he in turn would try to get *their* spirits up. I particularly remember a few other reporters and myself started asking at one point about what happened. He said he'd realized he was in trouble, that he'd gone to a plant someplace in the state a week or two earlier and had gotten a very flat reaction. He realized that this was a state that didn't have the kind of coalition that he had used effectively in other primaries, the blue-collar and black vote. Beyond that, McCarthy had been in Oregon early, and the antiwar movement there was strong.

I stayed for a while, and I said to him, "Why do you put up with these questions at a difficult time like this?" And he reached over and put his arm around me and said, "Because I like you." It was a kind of experience that you could only have with Robert Kennedy—here was a guy who had everything; he had money and fame, everything that anybody would want—and there was still something very vulnerable about him that made people feel sorry for him. It was a kind of hold he had on people, and I know that some of us were concerned that we were going to get too close to him and would not be able to be objective. In fact, a reporter said to me the following week that he was going to ask to be taken off the Kennedy campaign after California, because he felt that he couldn't be objective any more.

Opposite page: Robert Kennedy in Buffalo, New York, 1964 (Cornell Capa/Magnum).

On the flight to California, Ethel Kennedy came through the plane, not quite able to understand that her husband had actually lost. She was trying to convince herself or us that it was only one state, that it didn't really matter. We landed in Los Angeles for a ticker-tape parade through downtown, and no one was prepared for the response. It was an incredible turnout—just overwhelming. The atmosphere was noisy and full of confetti and stuff thrown out of windows—like the greeting of a hero after a war. It buoyed Bobby up again. That whole week in California it was the same; wherever he went the campaigning was very high intensity—particularly in the black neighborhoods. At one point the motorcade organizers were concerned over the possibility of backlash among white voters. They detoured a couple of times around black neighborhoods, because every time he would go through a black neighborhood it would just explode.

I remember the final day, the day before the primary, he hit all the major media markets in California. During lunchtime in San Francisco we were motoring through Chinatown and somebody set off a string of firecrackers. It sounded just like shots. For a moment everyone was petrified, and Bobby reacted nervously. Then it seemed all right. But it was a tense moment. That night we wound up in San Diego, and he was so exhausted that he broke down on the platform and couldn't continue. He finished speaking, then he went and sat down on the edge of the platform and doubled over. Then he went into the men's room and got violently sick. He persevered through that night.

Later a bunch of reporters and staff members sat up at the Ambassador drinking and partying. I remember John Hart doing imitations of Billy Graham and other people; it was a typical night on the campaign trail. We got so loud the manager came up and asked us to leave. So we went to Bobby's suite and cavorted around there for another couple of hours. I remember we left some kind of note pinned to his bed, to thank him for the use of the hall.

The next day, Election Day, he stayed at a friend's house on the beach. I was told that it was a relaxing day; he bounced around in the water with his kids—in fact one of his kids got pulled out by a wave and Bobby saved him.

At the Ambassador that night he proceeded to hold court in his suite. I was in and out of the room—Bobby was in the bedroom making phone calls to various people because it looked like he was going to win. There was a lot of pressure on him to go down and talk to the crowd, but he insisted on holding off to get more returns.

He eventually decided to come downstairs. I was standing in the kitchen with Bob Healy of the *Boston Globe* when he came down a back elevator, through the kitchen and into the pantry area. He had always been criticized as being ruthless and I remember remarking that I thought he'd been very "ruthful" in his interview with Roger Mudd. Bobby had been very benign, and now he laughed about it. He said, "Well, I'm getting better all the time." I think it was the last thing he ever said to any member of the press, other than the speech he made.

During the speech I saw Fred Dutton, who mentioned that Bobby was sorry he had missed all the fun in his suite the night before. It was a festive atmosphere. When his speech was over he was supposed to go to a press conference, in the room at the far end of the pantry area. I ducked through, walking about twenty feet ahead of him. I was almost out of the pantry and into the press room when I heard the shots.

Washington Star *political writer Jules Witcover covered Robert Kennedy's 1968 presidential primary campaign for the Newhouse newspaper chain. His books include* Eighty-five Days, *an account of Kennedy's campaign;* A Heartbeat Away: The Investigation and Resignation of Spiro Agnew; *and* The Resurrection of Richard Nixon. *His latest book,* Marathon, *is about the 1976 election.* ★

Opposite page: RFK at a Los Angeles campaign appearance (© William J. Warren). This page: Kennedy, his wife Ethel, bodyguard Roosevelt Grier and supporters walk from the Ambassador Hotel victory rally, top, into the hotel kitchen, above, movements before Kennedy's assassination (Photo Trends). Left: Witcover on the 1972 campaign trail (Annie Leibovitz). Gatefold: Kennedy rides through Los Angeles (Liaison).

EUGENE McCARTHY
Kennedy's Betrayal

*RFK vs. McCarthy
(Jim Foote/Liaison).*

The turning point in the quest for the 1968 Democratic nomination was the day before St. Patrick's Day, when Bobby Kennedy came into the race. The turning point in our campaign against the war was June 5th, the day he was assassinated. By the time we arrived in Chicago, we knew we couldn't win the nomination. The only controversy left was how the people who controlled the convention would deal with the issue of the war, and with the half of the party who opposed it.

When we started, nobody thought we had a chance. Neither did we. We were raising an issue, the war. Kennedy had stated publicly that he wasn't going to run, and he repeated the same reasoning to me in private. Perhaps if he had said he was undecided before the New Hampshire primary, we might have conducted our campaign differently. We might have run anyway, but his prior assurance influenced the way we did run.

After we demonstrated in New Hampshire that Johnson was vulnerable on the issue of the war, my daughter Ellen called and told me the rumor that Kennedy was going to "reassess his position." I don't know whether I was surprised or not. You wonder about it when someone tells you he is not going to do something, you shake hands on it, and a few months later he changes his mind.

I knew instantly that we would have to alter our tactics. We were going to have to fight Bobby Kennedy, and we were no longer sure that the campaign would be focused on the issue of the war. The issue was all but wiped out. It was now a matter of fighting over the remains of Lyndon Johnson—not the idealistic commitment to end the war. It was suddenly an altogether different campaign.

I might have felt close to winning right after the Wisconsin primary, where I'd won 57 percent of the vote. But by this time Kennedy was in the race, and the point at which we might have had any real chance for the Presidency had passed. Anybody who had any political sense knew that the combination of Bobby Kennedy and the situation of the party meant that I wasn't going to get nominated..

With Kennedy gone, we learned that, except for the California delegation, two-thirds of his people were not really interested in making a fight on the issue of the war. They were interested in power. One group would have been for Bobby had he favored the invasion of China. The other consisted of political hangers-on who'd been left out of the Humphrey-Johnson organization. With his death, it became clear that both groups would support the party position.

Nevertheless, I spent the whole summer working for their support. I went to state conventions, party meetings and the rest; I worked hard in those states Kennedy had won, and in those where he and I together had pulled a substantial majority of the vote. Indiana was a prime case of what happened. Between us, Kennedy and I had 70 percent of the primary vote. Yet, at the convention, McGovern got a few votes, I got a few votes. The other 80 percent of Indiana went to Humphrey.

The choice was between pragmatics—elect a party Democrat—and having some integrity with respect to what had happened in the primaries. We filed protests against twenty delegations before the credentials and rules committees, on the grounds that our support was unrepresented. We fought every way that we could, all through the summer and at the convention. We didn't go to Chicago with great anticipation. In fact, I gave an interview saying that I didn't think we had the votes. People said that I was giving it all away by saying that I couldn't win. That was ridiculous. Anyone could see that we didn't have the votes.

When Kennedy entered the race, certain people in my campaign backed out. But, as I said when Arthur

*Opposite page: Senator Eugene McCarthy,
the peace candidate, 1968 (Jeffrey Blankfort).*

Schlesinger left, it looked a little like mistletoe blowing out of a beech tree. I confess that mistletoe is one of the worst parasites, and I really hadn't intended the image to be carried so far. I just wanted to say that Arthur was not a vital part of our operation, and that he could blow out of the beech tree without hurting our operation very much. But I do think that if people like Schlesinger had said that they were not going to go with Bobby—John Galbraith and Dick Goodwin for example—then we might have won in California. If we had won in California, and if Bobby hadn't been shot—if you start to speculate on that, you are off into another world.

Certainly we could have carried the convention in opposition to the war, and whoever was nominated would have taken that issue to the country. Had it not been for the assassination of Robert Kennedy, and for the rules of the Democratic party in 1968, the war in Vietnam might have ended three years earlier.

Eugene McCarthy campaigned for the 1968 presidential nomination and lost. He was Minnesota's representative in the House from 1949 to 1959 and in the Senate from 1958 to 1970, where he sat on the Foreign Relations Committee. In 1976 he ran as an independent candidate for the Presidency.★ (M. Biber/Photo Trends)

ABE PECK
The Other Convention in Chicago

We were the alternate delegates to the 1968 Democratic Convention, and our forum was the street. Our plenary session convened along Michigan Avenue, across from the Conrad Hilton Hotel. The police challenged our right to assemble, but we stood firm, literally bloodied but righteously unbowed, and told the TV cameras that "the whole world was watching." Our nominating dues were everywhere, from the overturned chairs near the Grant Park band shell to the windowless façade of the Hilton's Haymarket Lounge, where the glass had given way before the weight of our helpless rank and file.

I participated in the Grant Park protests, but never felt quite at home in that wide-open space east of Michigan Avenue and the downtown Loop. As a North Side Chicago hippie, my neighborhood turf was Lincoln Park, close by the Old Town youth ghetto, and the *Seed* was my neighborhood paper. When the police bowed to merchant pressure and swept Wells Street, (our Haight Street) in the spring of '68, the *Seed* organized a Bust-In that regained the hippie right to creative loitering. And when the warmer weather came along, concerned citizens with names like Walrus and Treeman, Blind Al and The Mole, joined the *Seed* in suing for permits to hold a series of be-ins in the park.

Spring had also brought us Jerry Rubin, who supplied us with visions of a countercultural Festival of Life that would transcend politics and complement San Francisco's tribal gathering of the year before. It sounded good, and we became Yippies!

Our first public meeting to plan the Festival was raided. We were followed by casually clad men who drove ominous brown Chevrolets. We were first humored, then threatened, and finally ignored by city officials when we asked for park permits. Police officials told us that they would not hesitate to clear thousands of people from the park if they saw a single marijuana cigarette being smoked. The New York Yippies and the people from the antiwar movement were militant in their resolve to come to Chicago. Finally I wrote in the *Seed* that the gentle people should stay away. Furious arguments between the "spaced-out hippies" and the "politicos" ensued. Then the convention put an end to the debate. Nightsticks forged a unity ticket.

It was the first night of the convention, and the Lincoln Park caucus of our alternate delegation was meeting on the grassy rise at the southwest corner of the park. Nobody wore suits; we were more inclined to

Above, the alternate delegates caucus at Lincoln Park (Jeffrey Blankfort) and at the Grant Park statue of Civil War Major General John Logan, opposite page (© Howard Harrison). Overleaf: the Grant Park band-shell battle in progress (Jeffrey Blankfort).

be Loose for Leary than Clean for Gene. Drummers called the roll with tattoos beaten on overturned picnic tables and dented trash cans. Allen Ginsberg led a group of chanters in Ommming a benediction.

On the other side of the park, along Lake Shore Drive, the police formed a skirmish line. Bullhorns blared that the curfew of the Chicago Parks District would be strictly enforced. Bonfires declared our defiance. When eleven o'clock came and went, I hoped that the endless round of permit negotiations had finally struck home. The crackle of the police radios hinted otherwise.

There was no reason to be surprised. Hadn't I seen Tom Hayden dragged from Lincoln Park after he supposedly let the air out of a police car's tire? Wouldn't well-dressed suburban ladies be trampled when the police cleared the Grant Park band-shell area? Wouldn't Jerry Rubin's bodyguard turn out to be a policeman who'd finger him and many of the bikers who'd come to our weekly be-ins? Even our new brothers, the Black Panthers, were in from California to talk about how today's pig was tomorrow's bacon. Violence was inevitable. The spirit of tear gas was in the air.

The police moved just after midnight. A squad car buzzed our line, speeding away from a few haphazardly tossed rocks. A second car probed, and some, but not all, of our people cheered as a window disintegrated.

Then they charged.

The helmeted wave flowed across the park, lofting tear gas and smoke bombs and waving nightsticks over their heads. They tromped on the spot where the hippies had danced. They had no use for the "peacecreep dope-smoking faggots," and they told us so with a scream that said it all.

"Kill! Kill! Kill!"

When they were about twenty-five yards away, most of us took the hint.

Some of us didn't take it fast enough.

"Walk! Walk!" said the ever-concerned clergy in our midst before they were smashed to the ground.

"Help! Help!" screamed a girl as the police tossed her into the park lagoon.

"Oh, my God!" moaned a boy as a gas-station attendant, frenzied by the herd stampeding past him, broke his arm with a baseball bat.

Allen Ginsberg stood across the street from the carnage, still trying to center the crowd with a series of desperately bellowed OMMMMMMs. Around him, the flowers were dying everywhere.

Above: Tom Hayden, Rennie Davis and Jerry Rubin conspire in Grant Park (Jeffrey Blankfort). Opposite page: a member of the alternate delegation to the 1968 Democratic Convention in Chicago (Mark Godfrey/Magnum).

Some, though, were sprouting thorns. Abbie Hoffman had said that Yippies were hippies who'd been hit over the head, and the affinity groups that coalesced out of the chaos took him at his word. I watched a hulking *Seed* streetseller, who could have played the biggest droog in *A Clockwork Orange*, hurl a trash can through the window of an occupied police car. I was amazed by his boldness. I was depressed by the end of a dream. I understood as the peace signs turned to fists.

The battling swirled into the streets of Old Town. Passers-by were clubbed as they opened the doors to their own homes. Vicious alley games were played with bottles and truncheons. Pistols were fired—only into the air, by the grace of God.

The spirit of tear gas spread from the parks into the city itself. Abbie Hoffman was threatened by a man with a gun. Hugh Hefner went for a walk and was hit on the ass. Fifth-columnists inside the Hilton blinked their lights in a show of solidarity when our delegates spoke from across Michigan Avenue; later a few were arrested in their rooms. At the amphitheater, Senator Ribicoff denounced the violence and was in turn denounced as a "Jew son of a bitch and a lousy motherfucker" for his troubles. Only the black people of Chicago, who'd fought with death and torches after their dream had been killed on a Memphis balcony a few months before, remained aloof.

Originally, the *Seed* had called for celebration; now it became a movement center. We manned the phones, raised bail money and tried to write copy for the next issue. Two of us were in the *Seed*'s storefront office on the last night of the convention when a crack rang out and the front plate-glass window dissolved. Like fools, Walrus and I ran to the door. The street, a broad boulevard, was empty . . . except for a blue-and-white squad car, cruising slowly north.

Abe Peck was the editor of the Seed, *Chicago's underground newspaper, during the 1968 Democratic Convention. He had the mixed blessing of negotiating with city officials for permits for the ill-fated Festival of Life. He is currently a feature writer for the* Chicago Daily News *and a contributing editor at* Rolling Stone *magazine.*

Above: Chicago's finest protect Major General Logan (Jeffrey Blankfort). Opposite page, top left: police clear the Grant Park band-shell area (Dennis Brack/Black Star); top right: the National Guard halts a march on the International Amphitheater, where the convention was held; center: a demonstrator confronts the police at the Logan statue; bottom: band-shell rally participants William Burroughs, left, and Allen Ginsberg and Jean Genet, right (all Jeffrey Blankfort). Left: Abe Peck, who no longer looks like this (courtesy Abe Peck).

266

JULIE NIXON EISENHOWER
My College Diary

I was a nineteen-year-old sophomore at Smith College when the campaign of '68 began. In January, the month my father declared his candidacy, I started keeping a diary. Throughout the campaign, I led an almost double life—on campus I could not escape sensing the hostility felt towards my father and his campaign, yet, while campaigning, the enthusiasm and excitement were overwhelming.

I traveled to thirty-three states, and I'll never forget some of the receptions where my family stood in line for four hours at a time to shake hands with all the people who came to see my father—with two three-minute breaks at most. Nor will I ever forget the mood of ugliness and desperation that gripped the country through that tumultuous spring, summer and fall.

I kept the diary as a kind of companion through everything, a place in which I could express feelings both of joy and despair—feelings that were difficult to share with the people I knew at Smith. Looking back, I realize how important the diary was to me, and how faithfully I recorded my real emotions concerning the events swirling around me and my family. A typical entry dated April 17, 1968, reads:

It seems as if it takes something special to make me sit down and write. I have so many thoughts now—how hard it is to commit them to paper, how inactive I feel. I want to help more with the campaign. There are many girls on this campus who are doing more work for McCarthy than I'm doing for my father. And I keep thinking how much I dislike being here at Smith.

I am very emotional tonight. It's been a strange day—a day when I thought I was on top of the world, planning my life. I planned all of my courses for the rest of the semester at Smith, and talked to my advisor about honoring in History. Then came a disturbing dinner with my proseminar teacher and the class. I have always felt uneasy about him, tonight was no exception. He makes me feel like Julie *NIXON*. He'll be talking, and then he'll throw in the wrench. I asked him if he didn't think writing a book was hard work. His reply: "Why don't you ask your father."

I saw David for a few minutes before he had to go to Zumbyes [his college singing group]. Then I foolishly decided to go to the government department's mock Republican Convention. It was hell on earth for me. My friend Marsha Cohen was asked to give RN's speech, because there were no volunteers. As she spoke the word "selflessly," it came out "selfishly worked for his party." The audience loved it. And then another laugh when she praised Daddy. I just couldn't bear it. I was sitting in the back of the room, and walked out.

I tried to rationalize on the way back to the dorm. I realize that the whole mock convention is a joke; I realize that this is a McCarthy campus—and yet—*that's my father* they are reacting to and judging. I know why I went—it wasn't for self-torture; it was because I had a secret hope that perhaps there would be a genuine response for my father.

I am so pessimistic about this election. It is so difficult for me to believe that there is a deep and sincere feeling for my father outside of Smith-Amherst. I am always surprised by the reception he receives [on the campaign]. I can't help it. The world I live in dominates my outlook.

Marsha Cohen called me an hour after I left [the mock convention]. She heard from someone that I had walked out. Marsha is very liberal, yet she has always been one of the nicest girls in the dorm to me. Around her, I feel completely natural. She said something very beautiful on the phone. She said that

Opposite: in David's room at Amherst College (Arthur Schatz/Life, © *Time Inc.).*

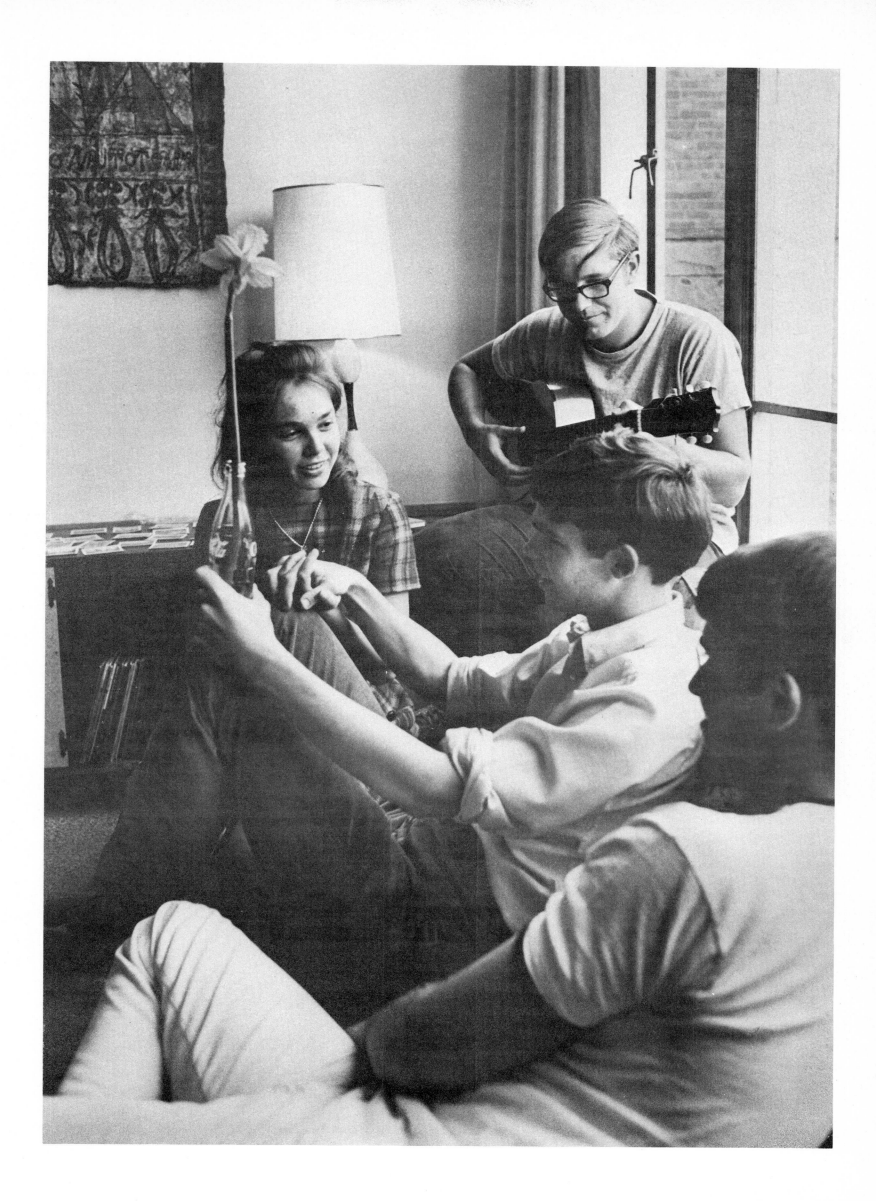

people often accuse politicans of being selfish, and they do not realize how much they have to give of themselves; they do not realize that politicians have feelings too.

This mock convention episode isn't such a crisis in itself. It's just that it confirms what I have believed about Smith, and more importantly, it is the culmination of a lot of things I have been experiencing lately. Like yesterday at lunch, when the Curriculum Committee Representative asked for a girl to serve as Young Republican Representative for Baldwin [my dorm]. When there was no response, she said, "Aren't there any staunch Republicans?" Still no response, and no representative.

I hate being a celebrity—and I use that word hesitantly. I am a "celebrity" only in that I am stared at when I walk on campus, eyes and heads turn. Sometimes, when I am speaking, I feel as if people were taking mental notes. And sometimes I feel so disgusted later when I *have* put on a show.

I am wondering, and doubting—whether another school, a Republican school, is the answer. I realize that it's not. I also realize that most of the girls in Baldwin House have problems comparable in degree to mine. If it weren't the problem of politics for me, it would be another. And yet, sometimes it's so difficult. And I feel sorry for myself. And then hate myself for this feeling of self-pity.

Julie Nixon Eisenhower graduated from Smith College in 1970. She has edited seven books, and authored one, Special People, *a collection of six portraits of public figures.*

Julie Nixon with fiancé David Eisenhower (Dwight D. Eisenhower Library).

1969

CALENDAR

January: 12 *Joe Namath's Jets stun NFL Colts in Super Bowl III;* **18** *Presidential salary is doubled to $200,000;* **19–20** *Counter-inauguration greets Nixon;* **31** *First oil spill in Santa Barbara Channel.*

February: 8 *The Saturday Evening Post ceases regular publication;* **12** *National Guard moves onto University of Wisconsin campus after black studies protest;* **15** *"Everyday People" takes over singles lead, with "Proud Mary" second.*

March: 1 *New Orleans jury acquits Clay Shaw in JFK conspiracy case;* **6** *Viet Cong push threatens Saigon;* **10** *I Am Curious (Yellow) premieres; West Virginia miners win "black lung" compensation;* **12** *Beatle Paul weds Linda Eastman; Levi Strauss markets bell-bottom jeans;* **20** *Ono-Lennon marriage;* **24** *Portnoy's Complaint tops fiction list;* **29** *Blood, Sweat and Tears is the number one LP;* **31** *Publication of Slaughterhouse Five.*

April: 3 *U.S. combat toll in Vietnam surpasses Korean toll at 33,641;* **4** *CBS cancels The Smothers Brothers Show after ongoing censorship battles;* **11** *Harvard students call strike to back black studies and end-to-ROTC demands;* **12** *"Aquarius/Let the Sunshine In" rides top of singles chart;* **14** *Oliver! takes best-picture Oscar;* **16** *Michigan is first state to ban DDT;* **18** *Bernadette Devlin's election gives Ulster Catholics a voice in Parliament;* **19** *Blacks carry guns on Cornell campus;* **20** *Princeton to go coed in fall;* **28** *DeGaulle resigns in France.*

May: 5 *Nabokov's Ada is published;* **9** *Pope cuts 200 saints from church calendar, including St. Christopher and St. Patrick;* **11–19** *Rockefeller faces riots on first Latin American tour;* **15** *Justice Abe Fortas resigns under pressure; Berkeley police use shotguns in battle for "People's Park," fatally wounding James Rector;* **17** *Chicago Transit Authority enters LP chart;* **25** *Midnight Cowboy premieres.*

June: 7 *The Who's rock opera Tommy hits chart;* **20–21** *Weatherman faction forces SDS split at national convention;* **22** *Judy Garland dies of drug overdose;* **25** *Release of The Wild Bunch;* **28** *Chart entry of Crosby, Stills and Nash.*

Top to bottom: students occupy the faculty room in Harvard's University Hall (Timothy Carlson); People's Park (Stan Creighton, reprinted by permission of the San Francisco Chronicle); members of the Rainbow Alliance in Chicago (Joseph Stevens/Photo Trends); Professor Angela Davis (Michelle Vignes); an Alcatraz heir (© Beth Sunflower). Opposite page: My Lai—a Vietnamese man just before American soldiers killed him (Ronald Haeberle/Time-Life Picture Agency).

July: 8 *First reduction of troops in Vietnam;* **14** *Premiere of Easy Rider;* **18** *Mary Jo Kopechne drowns at Chappaquiddick;* **20** *Neil Armstrong is first man on the moon.*

August: 3 *Publication of sex spoof, Naked Came the Stranger;* **6** *Senate fight to halt ABM fails;* **9** *Five die in Tate murders;* **12–16** *British troops are called in to quell Belfast rioting;* **15–17** *Woodstock Festival;* **23** *Johnny Cash at San Quentin is top LP;* **24** *First sit-down strike of combat troops in Vietnam; Movie release of Alice's Restaurant;* **25** *The Godfather and The Peter Principle head book lists.*

September: 3 *Ho Chi Minh dies;* **10** *Sale of oil leases on Alaska's North Slope;* **13** *Santana enters chart;* **19** *UCLA fires Angela Davis;* **23** *TV debut of Marcus Welby, M.D.;* **20** *"Sugar, Sugar" and Blind Faith top charts;* **24** *Trial of Chicago Eight begins; Butch Cassidy and the Sundance Kid premieres.*

October: 6 *Cinderella Mets take World Series from Orioles;* **8–11** *Weatherman "Days of Rage";* **15** *Candlelight march past White House marks first Moratorium;* **18** *HEW bans cyclamates by 1970;* **22** *Is Paul Dead?* **24** *U.S. loses 6,000th plane over Vietnam.*

November: 1 *"Okie from Muskogee" moves on to pop chart; Abbey Road takes LP lead;* **3** *Nixon calls on "silent majority";* **9** *Chicago street gangs form Rainbow Alliance;* **10** *Sesame Street comes to TV;* **12** *Lt. Calley is charged with My Lai murders;* **13** *Agnew attacks TV for biased news coverage;* **13–15** *Second Moratorium;* **14** *Dow Chemical gives up its napalm contract;* **20** *Native Americans seize Alcatraz;* **22** *Joe Cocker enters chart;* **24** *Hershey discontinues its 5¢ chocolate bar.*

December: 1 *First draft lottery;* **2** *747's inaugural flight;* **4** *Police kill Black Panthers Hampton and Clark;* **5** *Venceremos Brigade harvests Cuban sugar;* **8** *Charles Manson and four followers are indicted for Tate-LaBianca murders; Film premiere of Z;* **15** *The Selling of the President, 1968 is nonfiction leader; Church amendment bars U.S. ground troops in Laos and Thailand;* **27** *Led Zepplin II is top LP, with Let It Bleed a new entry.*

WAVY GRAVY
Hog Farming at Woodstock

We never knew we were going to Woodstock. The Hog Farm commune had formed in New Mexico, though all the Woodstock talk began when most of us were living in New York City, trying to figure a way to get out. A guy who looked like Allen Ginsberg on a Dick Gregory diet kept popping up, saying, "How'd you like to do this music festival?" And we said we would like to do this music festival, but we were going to be in New Mexico. He felt saying, "Oh, well, we'll fly you there when it's time."

We said, "Sure, have another toke," but he kept showing up. When we got to New Mexico, he showed up again, and then left the next day in a plane. We began to think that maybe there was something to this. We quickly sent out a feeler through the communes—New Buffalo, Arroyo Seco, Canyoncito, the Juke Savages, and some amazing people who were just communes unto themselves. We pulled in eighty-five of the best people, those who were the central fulcrum in commune after commune, and formed a collective.

The day came and there were eighty-five of us and fifteen Indians on an American Airlines Astrojet. We were very shy, embarrassed and blown away in this airplane, there was nobody in it, it was our airplane. We didn't quite know how to handle it.

When we got off the plane in New York City to go to Woodstock, we found a lot of reporters who asked, "What are you going to do for security?" And we suddenly realized that we weren't there just for cutting the trails. I said, "Do you feel secure?" A reporter said, "Yeah," so I said, "It seems to be working." He said, "Well, what are you going to use?" And I said, "Custard pies and seltzer bottles. And a bear suit." I wanted a bear suit and a rubber shovel, so I could say, "Remember, folks . . ."

When the festival began I worked at the freak-out tent, which was a hospital called Big Pink. Abbie Hoffman separated the doctors from the patients. There were a bunch of straight doctors and me standing around, waiting for the first freak-out. I had on a cowboy hat that once belonged to Tom Mix, with a yarmulke inside that Lenny Bruce gave me, so I could say, "Howdy, goyim." It had a squeaky rubber pig that crawled out of the top.

I had no teeth, and *I* was supposed to tell these doctors what to do about crazy people. A guy came staggering into the joint, looned out, yelling, "Miami Beach! 1944 . . . Joyce, Joyce . . . Miami Beach!" A big Australian doctor said, "Body contact, he needs body contact," and started laying down on the kid. Another doctor kept saying, "Think of your third eye, man." I said, "Can I try something?" It was time for me to make my move. The guy was still yelling, "Miami Beach!" and I asked, "What's your name?" He said, "Joyce," and I said, "No, what's your name, your given name, your name, your name."

"My name is Bob." His name was Bob, and he really liked it. So I said, "Your name is Bob" a number of times, and then "Bob what?"

"Bob Brown."

I said, "Your name is Bob Brown. You took a little acid, a little LSD, and guess what—it's going to wear off."

That was all he wanted to know—no third eye, just that whatever it is, is, and soon it's not going to be there any more, so hang in.

When he was normal, ready to go out and boogie and join the scene, I said, "Hey, man, hold it a minute. You see that guy coming through the door right now with his toes in his nose? That was you four hours ago. Now you're the doctor. Take over."

The Woodstock security force, above, prior to departure from Albuquerque; and opposite page, arriving in New York led by Wavy Gravy in white jump suit and hat (© Lisa Law).

All those people, later on, stoned in the mud. Maybe they'd have one biscuit, but they'd take that biscuit, break it up and give it to the person to the left of them and the person to the right. They got the picture of what sharing is about. I think it began with the very early arrivals, those who joined us and had fun helping each other out: setting up the cities, passing out the plastic when the rain came, getting people settled. A lot of excitement goes into putting together an instant city in which half a million people can live in a very high way. That's what people came to the festivals for. The music became a sound track for that incredible rush of sharing.

My moment of truth was when I announced breakfast in bed for 400,000. I don't know where I got that one from, except somebody grabbed my left nostril with a little of the thinking man's Dristan, and there it was. The cuisine was the first hippie granola. The oats were raw and it was a struggle to get them down, but if you did it was good for you. We fed thousands of people a day. It was interesting that by the time *Life* magazine photographed the Hog Farm kitchen, there wasn't a single Hog Farmer there, because each job had regenerated itself—like that first freak-out, Miami Beach and Joyce.

On the plane ride back we were ready and prepared, and also ripped out of our collective consciousness, thanks to a friend with six hundred tabs of green acid. The stewardesses made an agreement with us to lock themselves in a little room if we would give them the plane back fifteen minutes before Albuquerque. Meanwhile it was *ours*.

People just freaked out all over the place. A bunch of men and women wore stewardess uniforms and cooked omelettes. There was music and a lot of dope being smoked and I lay on the floor speaking over the microphone, reading a Mr. Natural comic over the plane PA. Some guy came up to me and said "Hey, man, the pilot says he wants the sitar player in the cockpit because he's bored." Somebody'd dosed the pilot, I thought. I staggered to my feet and made my way up to the front of the plane, and there was this guy, he looked like a pilot. I looked right into his pupils; I don't know what he thought. I was just kind of hovering over him, and I spoke to him right from the hip. I said, "Can I steer?" And this guy was so cool, he was so far out, he said, "Fly any way you want, as long as you Fly American."

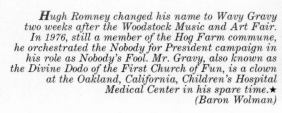

Hugh Romney changed his name to Wavy Gravy two weeks after the Woodstock Music and Art Fair. In 1976, still a member of the Hog Farm commune, he orchestrated the Nobody for President campaign in his role as Nobody's Fool. Mr. Gravy, also known as the Divine Dodo of the First Church of Fun, is a clown at the Oakland, California, Children's Hospital Medical Center in his spare time.★ (Baron Wolman)

This page, top: volunteers dispense granola and other goodies from the Hog Farm kitchen; above: the instant city at Yasgur's farm (Baron Wolman). Opposite page: a Woodstock couple (Charles Gatewood). Overleaf: backstage at the Woodstock Music and Art Fair (Baron Wolman).

276

BUZZ ALDRIN
On the Moon

Our back-up crew strapped us into our suits and hooked up our oxygen supply hoses. Neil Armstrong and Mike Collins went up to the spacecraft first; I remained at the bottom of the elevator, three-quarters of the way up the umbilical tower, awaiting my turn. That gave me about fifteen minutes to myself, though with the heavy portable air-conditioning unit I was carrying it seemed like a half-hour.

The sun was just coming up, and the morning clouds were dissipating. I looked at the big Saturn-5 rocket in front of me. I could see hundreds of people watching us, and I could see the waves coming in over and over again on the shore of Cape Kennedy. I knew that everyone within a hundred miles of us was aware of what was going on, and this feeling came over me: "I want to save this moment."

Until now, our mission hadn't seemed real. For a month before the flight, we'd worked twelve hours a day on a simulated lunar surface, tromping around in a fifty-by-fifty-foot litterbox filled with sand, with heavy equipment on our backs and a bunch of guys popping flashbulbs at us. My kids couldn't assimilate what was happening, my wife could only stand by. Now, at least, it was finally happening.

I stood by the tower, all by myself, reflecting on what it was all about: that nature went on anyway, with and without man. Then I thought, Man is about to do these things, and I'm a participant.

At 9:32 A.M. Eastern Daylight Time we lifted off on schedule. But we didn't sense the movement of the lift-off until it was announced a second or so later by the voice of launch control.

For the millions who watched on television, our lift-off was ear-shattering. For us there was a slight increase in the amount of background noise—not unlike taking off in a commercial airliner—and in less than a minute we were traveling ahead faster than the speed of sound.

The first twelve seconds of any flight are the most dangerous as the rocket rises alongside the launch tower. If anything should go wrong with the automatic guidance system and the rocket collides with the tower, the entire Saturn-5, loaded with highly explosive propellants, could turn into a gigantic fireball. When launch control announced, "Tower clear," there was a sense of relief stretching from Cape Kennedy to Houston to us as Houston assumed our control.

After the first couple of busy hours, we had nothing to do for long periods of time. We looked out the windows, but didn't talk or reflect too much. There were moments of levity—we had to keep our balance and perspective—but mostly we were concerned with what we had to do next.

Astronaut Aldrin on the moon (NASA).

We weren't afraid. Fear is of the unknown, and all our training had been geared to eliminating the unknown as much as possible. As test pilots, we'd learned to cope or get out. You can't live with fear; it's too disabling. We maintained a kind of gun-barrel vision, looking straight ahead.

From orbit, the moon looked as we expected it would, but once we'd landed, it was like nothing I'd ever seen before. Mike Collins remained in the spacecraft Columbia while Neil and I explored. We were farther away from our homes now than any men had ever been before, yet we had more people thinking about us than any men ever had before.

Nothing prepared me for the starkness of the terrain. It was barren and rolling. The earth was almost straight up, and it was hard to look at because of the strain of our suits. The weight on our backs caused us to lean forward a certain number of degrees, and forced us to concentrate on where we were walking. I felt the moon rocks crunch beneath my feet, pliant somehow. It is easy to understand why for centuries the earth was

Opposite page: three astronauts in zero gravity. Left to right: Theodore Freeman, Buzz Aldrin, Charles Bassett (Ralph Morse/Life, © Time Inc.).

thought to be flat, but my outstanding impression on the moon was that we were indeed on a ball, on the knoll of a hill that extended a mile and a half or so and was clearly rounded.

I felt a twinge of stage fright. I think we all did. The immense feeling of aloneness probably hampered our operations slightly, but it also gave us the adrenaline to keep functioning.

I couldn't look directly at the sun, nor could I during orbit. It was too brilliant—almost like a floodlight of not orange, but pure white light. The amount of ambient light it reflected off the lunar surface was so high, that, as if I were walking in sun-illuminated snow, it contracted my pupils, and I had to look downward. I could see no planets or stars, only blackness.

The color of the moon depended on the angle of the sun. It could be shades of gray or it could be quite bright if the sun was at my back. If I looked into my shadow, it gave off a whitish color. But if I looked toward the sun, it took on a darker charcoal color. The rocks themselves actually had no color until you studied the crystals themselves. Everything was covered with a very light powder.

I was just fascinated with kicking up the moon dust. I didn't expect it to fall as it did—if you kick sand on a beach or any dusty surface, clouds build up as it begins to fall. The moon dust did not cloud at all. Instead of being disturbed by the air and falling at varying distances from where it was kicked, it uniformly fell four or five inches away in a sort of ring.

Another unanticipated factor of the low gravity was the difficulty we had in determining whether or not we were on level ground, which was vital for the experiments. One of them was extremely simple—an array of one hundred reflectors, a foot and a half square, pointing roughly at the earth. Little glass prisms about an inch in diameter were very precisely aligned so that laser beams from the earth could be reflected back, and the result would be extremely precise measurements of the motions between the earth and the moon. This has since enabled us to determine the drift between the continents on earth, but it had to be level to be any use at all.

The manufacturer had chosen a BB as the leveling indicator on the passive seismometer, but it simply wouldn't stay put. Because of the extremely low gravity, it just whirred around in a circle. I didn't know what to do, but Neil said, "Just leave it alone for a while," and sure enough in a few more minutes the BB was right in the center where it belonged.

We left the passive seismometer there, powered by solar panels to determine quake movements. We also left a patriotic patch commemorating the three American astronauts who had gone up in flames in their spacecraft during the simulation of an Apollo flight—Virgil Grissom, Edward White and Roger Chaffee—two medals in memory of the Russian cosmonauts who had also died, and a disk containing messages from the heads of state of seventy-two countries. And we left a plaque proclaiming that "We came in Peace for all mankind." To me the most important symbol from our flight was the gold olive branch we thought long and hard to come up with. I had four made up—gold pins. We left one on the moon and took back the remaining three for our wives. I thought it would convey a lot more of the significance of our first flight—that it was more than just the culmination of our long national effort to reach the moon by the end of the decade. There was greater meaning to our mission than that.

On July 20, 1969, Dr. Edwin E. "Buzz" Aldrin, Jr., became the second man to walk on the moon in his capacity as lunar module pilot of the Apollo 11 mission. His MIT doctoral dissertation on space rendezvous provided a model for all U.S. rendezvous missions, including the recent joint U.S.- Soviet mission. As a result of personal disclosures in his autobiography Return to Earth, *Buzz became a member of the Board of Directors of the Mental Health Association and was voted national chairman in 1974. He is now working with groups concerned with the impact of alcoholism on young people.★ (NASA)*

Opposite page: the launch of Freedom 7 *and America's first man in space, Alan B. Shepard (NASA).*

GLORIA STEINEM
Up from Powerlessness

In February, the New York state legislature in Albany held hearings on abortion—this was before the liberalization of the law—and fourteen men and one nun were invited to testify. A group of feminists decided that made no sense at all, and soon after, decided to hold their own hearings in a church basement downtown in the Village. I had a regular political column then for *New York* magazine, and so went down to cover their hearings.

I'm not sure what attracted me to that story. I had read a little feminist literature, but I was still too much of a journalist to get personally involved or identified with an organization. It's true that I had always felt an emotional tie to "out" groups and causes, and that was regarded as a bit odd. After all, I was white, middle-class and college-educated, so no one—including me—understood why I identified with black or Chicano groups, or why sitting in a room with rich white men with vests on made my palms sweat. I certainly didn't understand that women were an "out" group too, and I would even insist that I wasn't discriminated against as a woman. As a writer, I took pride in not writing about "women's subjects," and I thought that my chance to do good work lay in being a professional journalist—which meant that I was often the only woman in a group of men. People would say to me, "You write like a man." And I would say, "Thank you."

But when I listened to those women at the hearing, I knew something very deep had started to change in them—and in me. It was one of the most incredible meetings I've ever seen. Women stood up and told the truth about their lives. They weren't talking about statistics, or a war thousands of miles away, or fighting imperialism from the top down. They were telling the truth about what it was like to have an abortion.

You could see that most of the women had never talked about this in public before. Some of the stories were tragic, some were funny. Most of them were about risky and humiliating experiences. One very shy young woman wearing a dress with a white collar got up. She said that she had been pregnant when she was seventeen or eighteen. Her parents were poor, and she hadn't known where to go for help. She went to hospitals and was made to stand up before examining boards and explain how she'd gotten pregnant, where she'd been, how many times she'd had intercourse. At least one hospital agreed to perform an abortion only if she would be sterilized.

Other women talked about entering the criminal underground to find an abortionist—the shame of it, and the danger. One woman told us that her boyfriend had convinced her that she couldn't get pregnant after the second or third orgasm. The audience broke up in laughter. It was like the early civil rights meetings; women were moved to stand up and testify. They were telling the truth about something they had been forced to conceal all their lives.

I'd also had an abortion. I had never told anyone except the doctor. Not a friend, not the man involved. No one. I didn't stand up and say it at the meeting, but afterward, I felt free to talk about it for the first time. I began to read more feminist literature; it made sense to me intellectually *and* emotionally. My other political understandings seemed intellectual and learned, but this was organic. The column I wrote for *New York* magazine was called "After Black Power, Women's Liberation?" I was too insecure to use a period, so I used a question mark.

It's very hard to describe a personal transformation, because it always sounds corny. There are really no words for it. All of a sudden, I started to listen to and read other women, and it made sense of my life. It made me understand why I had felt angry and humiliated and hadn't admitted it. I just didn't want to face how bad things really were. It made me realize that all the time I was insisting that women were not discriminated against, I had been unable to get an apartment because, the reasoning was, a single woman wasn't financially responsible—and if she *was* responsible, she was probably a prostitute. I also saw political events differently. I had raised money and written speeches for McGovern's '68 presidential campaign, for instance, and yet when Abraham Ribicoff held a meeting to discuss McGovern's plans for 1972, I was crossed off the list of participants. I heard that Ribicoff saw the list and said, "No broads." McGovern protested. Ribicoff said, "No broads," and McGovern accepted it—though he never would have accepted "No blacks" or "No Jews."

Feminism changed everything for me. I began to realize that all my professional dreams had come before adolescence. I was going to be a poet, a horse trainer, lots of things—then came adolescence and I became convinced I couldn't *be* something, I had to marry it. Feminism also made me see that in a patriarchy, women as a group were always going to be powerless and humiliated. I began to understand that the sexual caste system was political in the deepest sense, perhaps the model on which other oppressions of race and class—which I'd identified with without knowing why—were based.

The article in *New York* was my "coming out" as a feminist. Male journalists who had been my friends for years took me aside very kindly and said, "Look, you've worked very hard to be taken seriously as a journalist. If you identify yourself with all these crazy feminists, you'll ruin yourself." When I kept at it, they encouraged antifeminist women in *New York* to write counterarticles.

The next year, the piece that my male colleagues hated so much won a journalism prize as a first above-ground report on this wave of feminism, on women's liberation. But still they took me aside and told me that I'd destroy myself, and that I could never be taken seriously again. After all, it was a prize for writing on women, so it didn't count.

I wanted to write about women in a new, serious, political way—and nobody was interested. Either they said I was a woman and couldn't be objective, or they said, "We published our feminist article last year." After a few months, I gave up and started to lecture.

This in itself was revolutionary for me. I was very nervous. I had a major terror of public speaking and yet I cared so much about explaining what feminism really was (as opposed to bra-burning, as the press was saying) that I forced myself to speak. I spoke in tandem with black feminist friends—first Dorothy Pitman Hughes, then Flo Kennedy or Margaret Sloan. We did this consciously in order to say that feminism meant *all* women, not just the integration of a few privileged women into patriarchal systems.

We were often ridiculed. Men would come up with a big smile and say, "I'm a male chauvinist." A man stopped me in the street and said, "I have ten women employees and I pay them a third of what I pay men, and if I had to pay them more, I'd fire them. What do you think of *that?*" It was as if they could get rid of the whole contagious idea by getting rid of a few troublemakers.

Feminism is an enormous gift. It has given me life. It's given me the courage to stop imitating and be an individual. It's true, though, that I started having a dream in the Sixties, and it's never stopped. In the dream, I'm fighting with someone; I'm punching and kicking as hard as I can because they're trying to kill me or to kill someone I love. I'm fighting with all my strength—but I just can't hurt them. No matter what I do, I can't hurt them. They just smile. It must be a classic dream of rage and powerlessness.

I've often found myself in another can't-win dilemma. If you are conventionally attractive, you do well in the world; people say that you got there through men. If you're not pretty, they say that you're doing it because you couldn't get a man. If you really stand up for yourself and for other women, they say you're a lesbian. That's the worst dilemma—lesbians are twice discriminated against, so you feel disloyal if you are not a lesbian. Should you tell the truth about your private life?

The best retort I ever heard was at a feminist lecture down South. A hostile man stood up in the back and directed the question at Flo. "Are you a lesbian?" She said, "Are you my alternative?" He sat back down.

Gloria Steinem is an editor and cofounder of Ms. *magazine. She is a member of the National Organization of Women and a founding member of the National Women's Political Caucus and the Women's Action Alliance.★ (Nick DeSciose/Globe Photos)*

Opposite page, left to right: Amanda Burden, Senator George McGovern and Steinem at a Farmworkers' benefit, 1968 (Joseph Abeles Studio). Above: Steinem at New York magazine's founding party with Milton Glaser, left, Tom Wolfe and Gabe Pressman, right (© 1977, Jill Krementz).

DAVID DELLINGER
The Gagging of Bobby Seale

Bobby Seale is the perfect example of how the defendants in the Chicago conspiracy trial were selected; it was not on the basis of anything they had done in Chicago, but because of their prominence in the various constituencies of the antiwar movement or other movements which the government wanted to intimidate. And his gagging, more than any other event connected with the trial, was the perfect example of the breakdown of justice in the country at that time.

The government knew that Bobby had not been involved in the organization or planning of the convention protests. On a few hours' notice, he had come to speak in Lincoln Park as a replacement for Eldridge Cleaver. He stayed in Chicago for less than a day, made two speeches and left. When he was indicted seven months later, it was clearly because the Civil Rights Division of the Justice Department wished to destroy the Black Panther Party.

Bobby was brought to Chicago from California illegally and in chains to face a possible ten-year sentence with a group of white strangers—Jerry Rubin was the only one of his codefendants he'd met before the arraignment in April of 1969. He was also denied the attorney of his choice when Judge Hoffman refused to grant a postponement to enable his lawyer, Charles Garry, to recuperate from an emergency gall-bladder operation. This became the issue that led to Bobby's gagging.

While Bobby was in jail, William Kunstler filed papers as legal counsel so that Bobby would not be in total isolation. Kunstler in no way intended to represent Bobby during the trial, and we were all stunned when the judge insisted that Kunstler proceed as the attorney of record.

Contrary to the picture that many people had, Bobby was mild-mannered during the opening days of the trial. He spoke softly, and only when somebody testified against or about him. Then he'd stand and object, saying that his lawyer wasn't present and that he wanted to defend himself.

When Judge Hoffman turned down his first motion to defend himself, Bobby said, "If I am consistently denied this right of legal defense counsel of my choice, then I can only see the judge as a blatant racist of the United States Court." Reporters rushed into the hallways of the Federal building to call in stories about Bobby's "name-calling." Just as Judge Hoffman's personality, not his rulings, became an issue, so "name-calling," not the denial of rights, became the news.

One day the delegation of Black Panthers who'd come to support Seale filled the gallery, and the atmosphere was tense. Marshals brought Bobby in to sit at the defendants' table. He turned to face the Panthers and said that they should not take action even if they saw him abused. He said that they had the right to self-defense, but he told them to be cool. "If they make us leave, then we just leave," he said.

The judge wasn't in the courtroom yet, but when he came in, one of the prosecuting attorneys, Richard Schultz, told him that Bobby had urged the Panthers to attack the court. It was such an outrageous lie you could hear gasps from all over the courtroom. Schultz was shouting, and Bobby screamed for the first time in the course of the trial. He screamed and banged his fists on the defense table. It was the only way he could be heard.

Judge Hoffman's response was to note in the record that "the tone of Mr. Seale's voice was one of shrieking and pounding on the tables and shouting." Bobby was shocked. He asked Schultz to tell the court what he really said. Schultz hemmed and hawed but never fully retracted.

During that long morning, the marshals threw Bobby into his chair whenever he tried to rise to speak. I was sitting next to Bobby after he protested Schultz's lies, and saw the pain in his face as one marshal got him in a hammer lock and another jabbed him in the groin. The next two times he was attacked, I wedged myself between the marshals and Bobby to deflect the blows and call attention to their sneak punches. Later this action earned me a month's contempt sentence. After the second incident, Bobby looked at me and said, "I know what you are doing and I love you for it, but don't give them any excuses to say that you are being violent and revoke your bail."

Bobby was right on the mark. Just before lunch the judge ordered the defendants to tell him by the beginning of the afternoon session whether or not we would continue to support Bobby "in what he is doing." If we did, he would take that to mean that we preferred to sleep in jail from then on.

When we returned to the courtroom Kunstler made a long statement for all of us in support of Bobby's rights. Then Bobby asked for, and was denied, permission to speak for himself. After a few sharp exchanges and attacks by the marshals, Judge Hoffman declared a recess. Everyone knew what was going to happen; the day before the judge had threatened to gag Seale because of his interruptions. Now he told the marshals, "Take that defendant into a room and deal with him as he should be dealt with."

As we filed out of the courtroom our spontaneous reaction was anger and a decision not to return. In our packed conference room, Rennie Davis, Jerry Rubin, Abbie Hoffman and I argued that we could not go back if Bobby was gagged. Then Tom Hayden made an impassioned statement that the government had acted against Bobby as a ploy to jail us all and put an end to our organizing for the forthcoming Mobilization march on Washington against the Vietnam War.

"In a situation like this," Tom said, "we have to become like the Vietnamese. We have to keep on doing what has to be done as if we feel no pain. I don't know what it will be like in that courtroom. I may vomit. But we can't let the government maneuver us into jail, where we would be useless."

I tried to lay out the opposing argument. It was time for solidarity, I said, and for resistance. The act of refusal would say more from jail than the speeches we could make or the organizing we could do on the outside. If we didn't resist, then how could we ever say, "Now is the time to resist."

The defendants wavered. The marshals kept banging on the door, warning that the judge was waiting for us. Finally somebody suggested that we didn't have to decide immediately. The afternoon was half over. Why not feel it out, and take the night to decide? That way we could even meet with Bobby after court. He was the one who was being gagged, and maybe he wouldn't want us to risk our bail.

With a sinking feeling in our hearts, we went back into the courtroom. There was Bobby, bound and gagged. It was an awful sight, and in my mind the failure of the defendants to act decisively was a fundamental error. True, Bobby agreed with Tom's argument when he met with us after the session, and true, it "made sense" for me, the only pacifist and the only member of my generation among the defendants, to go along with the others and accept the "realistic" over the "moral" argument. Still, I feel now that I should have followed my own course, even though it would have broken the united front.

*D*avid Dellinger, a revolutionary pacifist since the 1940's, became increasingly well known in the Sixties due to his leadership in the antiwar movement. A defendant in the Chicago 8 trial, he and four of his six codefendants (Bobby Seale's case was severed from that of the others) were found guilty of inciting riots at the 1968 Chicago Democratic Convention, a conviction that was later voided. Dellinger helped found the Liberation Press, and edited and published Liberation magazine. He is now a lecturer and a writer, and an editor at Seven Days magazine.★ (Michael Abramson/Photo Trends)

*A*bove, left: Bobby Seale in 1969 (© 1969 Stephen Shames); right: the Chicago 8 minus one, left to right, lawyer Leonard Weinglass, Rennie Davis, Abbie Hoffman, Lee Weiner, David Dellinger, John Froines, Jerry Rubin, Tom Hayden and lawyer William Kunstler (David Fenton). Overleaf: for the benefit of the press, Jerry, left, and Abbie reenact the gagging and binding of Bobby Seale (Photo Trends).

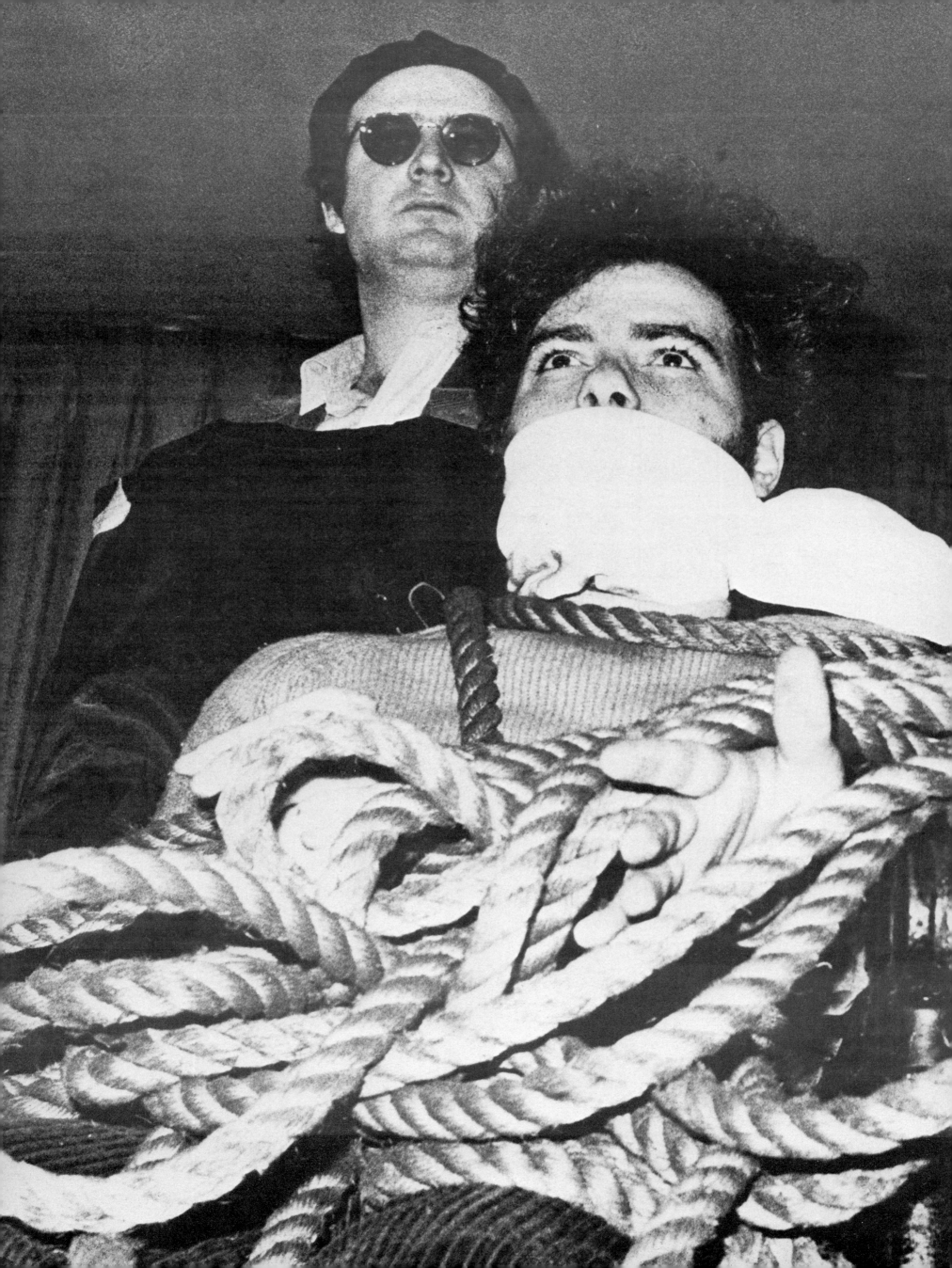

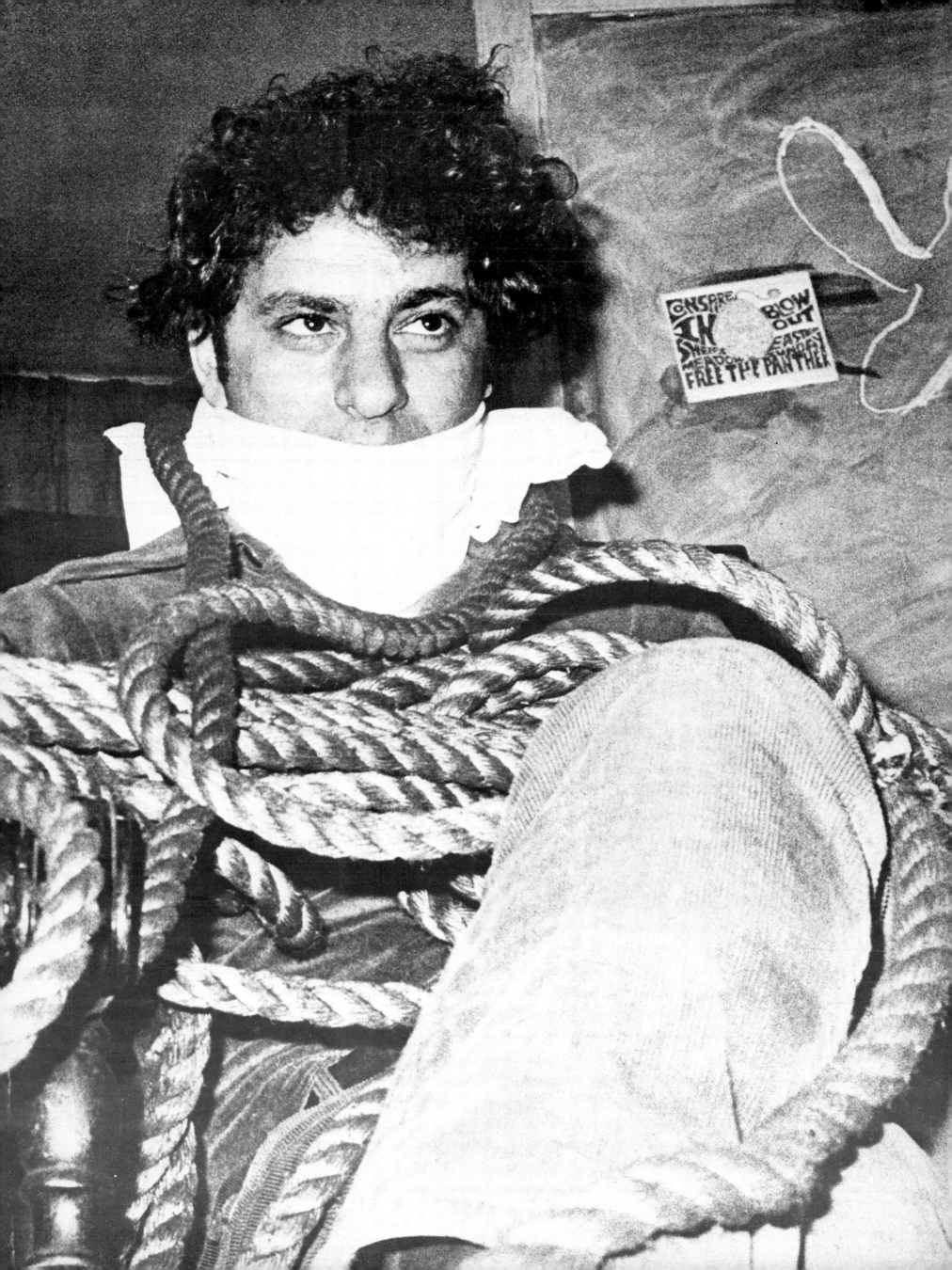

JOHN DEAN
On the Other Side of the Demonstrations

Richard Kleindienst pulled up in a car at the corner of 17th and Constitution. "What do you think?" I asked. "Goddamn, these kids are really having fun," the deputy attorney general answered. He had a big grin on his face, and his eyes were beaming. "If I were a kid I'd be out there myself." We could smell the grass and see the movement inside the sleeping bags. "I know what the hell is happening," Kleindienst added with a smile.

I'd taken Kleindienst to the October Moratorium march in Washington, D.C., because he'd appointed me to negotiate with the demonstration leaders for their permits at an unusual meeting at the Justice Department a few weeks before. I was associate deputy attorney general, and I'd received a call to hustle up to Kleindienst's office. When I arrived there, I looked around and thought it was a pretty awesome group: a military–police–Justice Department axis. I quickly sat down and listened.

Kleindienst said, "John, this group has a new job for you." They wanted me to find out what the demonstration leaders wanted, and report back. They figured that because I was young, I might have rapport with these guys.

We were able to work out the details for the October march easily because, contrary to the repressive image everyone had of the administration, both the Moratorium leaders and the government feared violence and wanted to avoid trouble. The march ended without incident in a candlelight procession around the White House.

But there was another march scheduled for November 15th and we were receiving information that indicated it might be quite different. Large numbers of people were expected, and there were reports that some Weathermen might try to take advantage of the situation. In addition, the leaders of the second march were old-timers, heavyweights. They had been around in the labor movement and the socialist movement, and some of them had been to international conferences where they had actually met with people from North Vietnam. I remember Bob Mardian (later assistant attorney general of the Internal Security Division) offering me a big stack of papers after one meeting on the situation. He said, "John, I think you ought to read these. They're the FBI background reports on these dudes you're dealing with." He thought they were a pretty tough group.

I never accepted Mardian's offer, thinking it would be better for me to deal with them at face value, on neutral territory. I ended up negotiating with Phil Hirschkop, an able lawyer-at-large for the demonstrators, in the cocktail lounge of the Watergate, a rather prophetic place for me to have discussions.

I also went to an intelligence evaluation committee meeting held in the office of Deke DeLoach, who was then an assistant director of the FBI. It was the goddamndest meeting I've ever been in; they didn't know anything about what was happening, all they really knew was numbers—buses, trains and cars bringing demonstrators to Washington. The big issue had become whether or not the demonstrators could march down Pennsylvania Avenue. People were saying, "Goddamn, we're going to tell these people where they're going to march. They're not going to tell us!"

I wasn't high up enough to know if the directives were coming from the Oval Office. I knew that Kleindienst never made a move without checking with Mitchell, and I assumed that Mitchell never made a move without checking with the White House, presumably with Ehrlichman, who in turn probably talked with the President.

Above: Senator George McGovern, right, with Coretta King and Senator Charles Goodell at the November Moratorium in Washington (Wide World Photos). Opposite page: two years before the first Moratorium, troops move on antiwar demonstrators surrounding the Pentagon, October 1967 (Wide World Photos).

Mitchell's attitude, though, was kind of blasé: "What a nuisance this all is." He'd attend the meetings at Justice sometimes, and sit there puffing away at his pipe, annoyed by the whole thing.

Bud Krogh, who worked for Ehrlichman at the White House, and I argued that the administration should give in on Pennsylvania Avenue. Otherwise we'd give the demonstrators millions of dollars' worth of free publicity, and actually draw more people to the march. We even worked on a plan behind the backs of our superiors to get Walter Washington, the mayor of Washington, D.C., to paint a disastrous picture of what would happen if access was denied.

Nevertheless, Kleindienst held a press conference to announce the denial of permission to march down Pennsylvania Avenue. He decided to stick me in front of the cameras, because he wanted a non-hard-line face out there. When the reporters started to pump me with questions, though, Kleindienst, knowing my sympathies on this point, suddenly pulled me away and started answering the questions himself.

The day finally came when the decision had to be made as to how to keep these people from coming down Pennsylvania Avenue. They'd announced they were coming—come what may. Kleindienst asked a general, "How can you stop them?" The general said, "There's only one way. Concertina wire, several rolls of it." Kleindienst said, "I can't really imagine Coretta King walking through that. That does it for me." His own kids had long hair and were antiwar participants themselves, so he could picture them coming down there and getting hurt. He called Mitchell and said, "Listen, this is absurd. We've got to let these people go down Pennsylvania Avenue."

During the demonstration, the Washington police and the Secret Service decided to protect the White House by circling it with D.C. Transit buses. The buses formed an enormous circle around Lafayette Park and then all the way back down the South Lawn of the White House. It was the weirdest feeling to come up through all the marchers and walk inside the circle of buses. Inside the circle, there was a strange calm. It was almost like being in an amusement park after it had closed.

I saw a guy heave a Coke bottle over a bus and hit a policeman right in the forehead, splitting his skull. About a half-hour later, with the police enraged, a demonstrator tried to wiggle his way under a bus. He was sprayed in the face with mace. I thought, My God, and remembered, for a second, a march I'd joined four years before while a student at Georgetown Law School. Johnson had just escalated the troops in Vietnam, and I was returning from lunch at the National Gallery when I saw the demonstration. I joined it. I was a potential draftee in those days, too.

But now I was on the other side.

Former presidential counsel John Dean's testimony before the Senate Watergate Committee in 1973 led to the unraveling of the Nixon Administration's cover-up of the Watergate break-in. Dean served four months in prison for his part in the cover-up and wrote the book Blind Ambition, *about his experiences in the Nixon White House.★ (Wide World Photos)*

Above: one day into the Moratorium weekend, police and demonstrators of the Weatherpeople persuasion clash near the South Vietnamese embassy (Jay Cassidy). Opposite page, top: protesters on their way to the March Against Death, which began November 13th and lasted about 40 hours— the marchers carry crosses with the names of soldiers killed in Vietnam to deposit in coffins set up at the Capitol (© Charles Gatewood); bottom: the weekend culminates in a rally at the Washington Monument, November 15th (David Fenton).

SEYMOUR M. HERSH
The My Lai Massacre Uncovered

The first story I wrote about My Lai came out two days before the burst of the November 15th Vietnam moratorium. It had almost zero impact, but I remember being very excited when I marched in the Washington antiwar demonstration and saw a sign reading REMEMBER THE PINKVILLE 109.

The essence of that first story was simple. There was a young man named William L. Calley, Jr., a meek, mild-mannered agricultural-school-graduate type of guy. Army investigators said he'd murdered 109 people. That's where I began.

It was a smash story, all over the newspapers. But even so, one story doesn't make a real impact. I was appalled that it didn't open up right away. Nobody wanted to read that kind of story; it was too much for the American people.

That weekend I saw a couple of paragraphs in the *Washington Star*—Ronald Ridenhour, an ex-GI, was claiming credit for initiating the Army's investigation. He had written letters to the Pentagon, to members of Congress, and to others describing what he'd heard about the massacre at My Lai.

I had to see the guy. I dashed out to California, found Ridenhour and interviewed him. He was relieved to see me; he wanted the story to be kept alive. I got the names of some of his sources and I flew from Ridenhour's place to Utah.

In Utah, I interviewed Michael Terry, a Mormon, who gave me a wonderful line. "It was a Nazi-type thing," he said. The American troops just shoved the Vietnamese into ditches and killed them.

From Utah, I went to see a guy named Michael Bernhardt, who was at Fort Dix in New Jersey. He turned out to be the most articulate of the sources. He said that the operation was supposed to be a combat assault in an area where there were allegedly 250 Viet Cong, but instead, there were only women and children and old men.

Bernhardt told me that he had gone over a hill and looked down into the village, where he had heard a lot of shooting and saw GIs running around murdering people. "For a second," he went on, "I said to myself, maybe I screwed up in basic training, missed a couple of days, and maybe this is what war is all about."

He had never really seen combat before, and it certainly didn't look like they were doing anything more than murdering people.

I put the Bernhardt and Terry interviews together with another I had done by phone with Gregory Olsen, a GI who was stationed at Fort Lewis in Washington. I filed the story on Wednesday and it ran in Thursday's papers, November 20th. By this time it was a big issue in London, but in the United States there were just little vague stories, vague Army denials. I kept on working, kept on flying.

I went back to the West Coast. Just before the weekend I saw Olsen at Fort Lewis. He told me about a fellow who had been more than just an observer—he'd been a participant. His name was Paul Meadlo, and he lived in a little farm town west of Indianapolis, near Terre Haute, called New Goshen, Indiana.

All my sources agreed that I should find Paul Meadlo—he had done most of the shooting. There were rumors that he had been very upset about it. GIs saw him as a big, dumb farm kid, one of the few Calley could push around.

The day after the My Lai massacre, the company continued search-and-destroy operations, as though they'd had a great success. They knew what they had done, but they pretended otherwise. Meadlo stepped on

a land mine, and it flipped his foot and bone away. Every GI I talked with—and I think I talked with sixty in the company—recalled Meadlo waiting to be helicoptered out, his foot blown off, and screaming at Calley that God had rewarded him for what he had done, and God would punish Calley too.

I found Meadlo through telephone Information. I spoke to his mother. She said that he didn't want to talk. I answered, "Well, let me try. He's got to talk; I know the story anyway."

You can't yell at people, but you can cajole them. What I said was "Look, I know what he did. I'm writing the story, and I'm going to mention his name in the next article. It seems to me that it would make more sense to find out from him what happened."

I flew to Indiana on Friday, November 21st. I sat in Meadlo's house and talked with his mother for a long time. She said a terribly pointed thing: "I gave them a good boy, and they made him a murderer." Meadlo had been back twenty months and she was suffering with this.

Finally she said she thought he ought to tell me the story. When I saw him, I immediately sensed that he had no idea why he had done what he did. If I had to write the story again, I'd come to the conclusion that people like him were as much victims as the people they murdered.

I'll never forget this. He came in and I shook his hand. His mother and wife were there. I said, "Let me see your ankle, see what they did." He took off his shoe and showed me his artificial foot. He said that it was all right, although it sometimes hurt and he was having trouble getting benefits. We talked about that for a while. Then I said, "Tell me what happened."

We talked five or ten minutes, and I showed him that I had no qualms. It was going pretty nicely. He said, "We got into the village on a search-and-destroy mission and we shot up everything outside the village." I remember this literally. He talked in a straight, calm, unaffected voice—very toned down, with every word and syllable equally enunciated, very flat and nasal.

"We were choppered into the landing zone and got out, expecting it to be hot; filled with the enemy. Nobody was there. We started moving in. Somebody saw an old man by a well and shot him. Calley came up to me at one point and said, 'Round everybody up.' I rounded 'em up and he said, 'Take care of 'em.' So I watched them, and when he came back, he said, 'Hey, Meadlo, I said take care of 'em.' So then I just started shooting."

I remember saying—this got to be a little cold-blooded, although I didn't feel that way—"Paul, how many do you think you killed in that first batch?"

He said, "Oh, about ten or fifteen, I guess."

I asked him what happened then. He was beginning to get a little edgy. His mother said, "Oh Lord." And his wife said nothing while I wrote away. He continued, "Later we had a bunch more, and Calley told me to push them in a ditch, and he named two or three other guys, and then we just shot them in the ditch." Absolutely deadpan.

I remember calling David Obst, who had been releasing the My Lai stories through his Dispatch News Service. My Lai still wasn't a big issue. David and I discussed our options and agreed that writing another story wasn't enough. By this time, CBS, ABC and NBC were after us. We wanted the story on TV, particularly if TV would pay us.

CBS agreed to pay if Meadlo would appear. He was worried about the legal implications. Our lawyers talked. We all said, "Look, we can't guarantee you anything."

I said, "It's unlikely that your going on TV will increase the risk because I'm writing a first-person interview now." We talked the whole night, and I took notes like crazy.

I flew to New York Saturday afternoon for negotiations with our lawyers about the CBS offer. I returned to Indianapolis on Sunday, and took the Meadlos out to lunch. I told them exactly what was going to happen. Meadlo wanted to do it. Everybody wanted to. People ask why anyone talked. They talked because they were asked to. In his case, expiation was very important.

I went over the story with him very carefully. It was the third or fourth time I had gone over it, and I wrote it that afternoon in my motel for the Dispatch News Service to release simultaneously with the CBS interview.

I spent the night on a couch in Paul's house. He tossed and turned and moaned—obviously I had stirred up an awful lot of things. In the middle of the night, his wife came out to talk. They had a young baby, born while Paul was in Vietnam. It was clear that the baby brought back memories he wanted to expunge. But he didn't talk much about his experiences there. Who could he have told it to?

At five A.M., we all got up and caught an early morning plane to New York for the Mike Wallace interview.

Wallace started the interview saying, "Well, tell me about it." Meadlo began exactly as he had with me: "We landed and we began shooting." That was the inteview. That did it. It was on the CBS News that night, in fifty papers—the story broke wide open. My Lai was the issue.

Seymour M. Hersh has received the Pulitzer Prize for International Reporting, the George Polk Memorial Award, the Worth Bingham Prize and the Sigma Delta Chi Distinguished Service Award for his reporting of the My Lai massacre in 1969. A reporter for the New York Times *since 1972, he has written prize-winning stories on the bombing of Cambodia, and domestic spying by the CIA. Mr. Hersh's latest book is* Cover-Up: The Army's Secret Investigation of the Massacre at My Lai 4.★ *(Annie Leibovitz)*

BO BURLINGHAM
Bringing the War Back Home

In the summer of 1969, I visited Cuba as part of a delegation led by Bernardine Dohrn. Our group met with representatives of the Vietnamese liberation forces, who made a profound impression on me. They were humane and seasoned veterans of a struggle that most of them had been waging all their lives, and they exuded a mellow fortitude that provided me and my friends with a model. But what was noble courage in Cuba became desperate courage in America. When I returned, I was ready for well-nigh total commitment to the revolution, prepared to risk all for all. For the next six months, I ran with the Weathermen.

Most of our bad-ass reputation originated from a four-day rampage through Chicago which became known as the Days of Rage. Against all reason and good sense, some four hundred of us donned hard hats, padding, and work gloves, picked up chains and rocks, and went wild in the streets—before the astonished eyes of America's roughest, toughest police force.

Preparing for the Days of Rage (Timothy Carlson).

At first, I was every bit as astonished myself. Our contingent from Ohio arrived late on the afternoon of October 8th and proceeded to a church, where we dressed for the action. Toward evening we drove to Lincoln Park, which we circled several times before spotting a bonfire. We parked and walked toward the light. I could make out the silhouettes of solitary figures against the fire. We had expected thousands of people to turn out. As I approached, it dawned on me just how few of us there were. This realization aroused such a tumult in my stomach that I had to force myself to think of other things. I remember what followed as a dream.

A chant went up from the crowd, and the shock troops raced out of the park, the rest of us in tow. Scarcely had we hit the street than I heard the crisp tinkle of breaking glass, followed by utter silence—or so it seemed. Then chaos. People yelled and began attacking parked cars, lamp posts, storefronts, apartment-house entryways. I felt a kind of nauseated high—terror and exhilaration in the same short breath. We charged ahead, not a cop in sight, until we came to an intersection blocked by police cars. Suddenly lights

Opposite page: two of the 123 Weatherpeople arrested on Saturday, October 11th, the last day of the National Action in Chicago (Timothy Carlson).

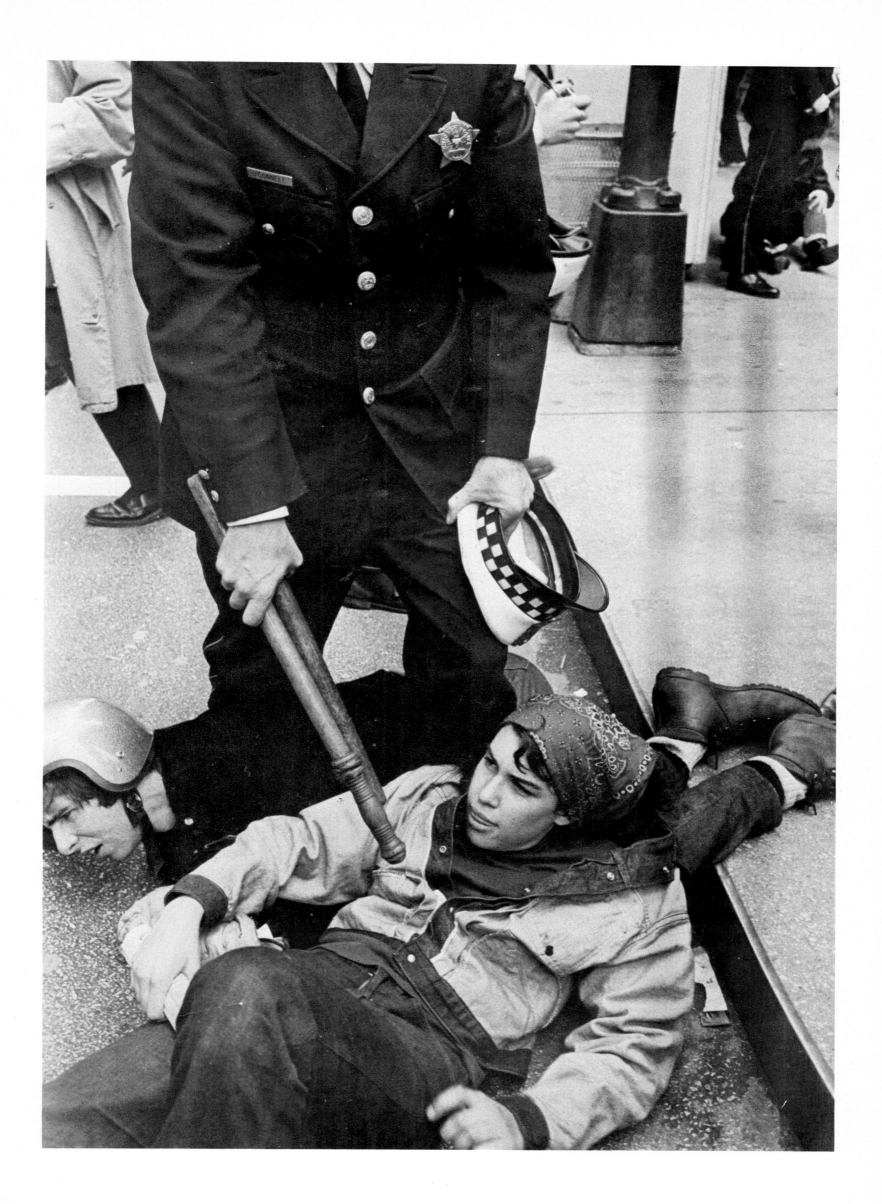

flashed and I heard what sounded like a string of firecrackers; someone said it was gunfire. A few of us were shot that evening. I remember running, running, running until my sides and throat ached. I wanted to sleep. I felt like vomiting. But I just followed the people in front of me wherever they ran.

A friend came up alongside me. She said a police agent was leading the crowd into a trap. She and I ducked into a yard. A moment later a plainclothesman followed us, his gun drawn. I tried to leap the fence but couldn't. My friend opened the gate and we made our getaway, winding up in a blind alley where we hid for an hour before catching a taxicab back to the church.

The next two days were devoted to newspaper reading, wound licking, courage bolstering and criticism/self-criticism. Having worn out our welcome in Chicago, we repaired to some churches in neighboring Evanston, from which we conducted minor forays into the Windy City. I myself participated in one commando raid on the home of a Chicago city official of Polish ancestry whose name I could not pronounce. In the dead of night, we spray-painted a slogan on the side of his house: So-and-so "is a racist pig" or some such profundity. Unfortunately, the person who did the spraying—a Radcliffe alumna—was weak on spelling, and so it came out "rasist." I don't suppose the official in question really cared.

It was clear from the newspaper accounts that our behavior had taken the city fathers by surprise. "We never expected this kind of violent demonstration," one of them said after the first night's action. "There's always been a big difference between what they say and what they do." But they soon recognized the name of the game, and when we gathered in Haymarket Square for the final march, the law-enforcement authorities of that part of the country—uniformed police, detectives, FBI agents, the National Guard, state police, sheriff's deputies, and vigilantes—were out in force, and we knew it. I have yet to encounter a single participant in that day's action who did not believe he or she was going to die on October 11, 1969, in the City of Chicago, County of Cook, State of Illinois, at the hands of the police. Terrified though we were, we screwed up our courage and put on a defiant face.

The march lasted all of about twenty-five minutes. We trooped out of the Square, and then suddenly I heard a shout and everyone in front of me began running east on Madison Street, toward the downtown Loop. Instantly the entire area seemed to fill with cops—from cars, buses, stores, side alleys, and even from our midst. There was bedlam for maybe ten minutes. Etched in my memory is an image of a Chicago riot policeman standing in a crouched position in the middle of the street. Two Weatherpeople charged him at top speed. At the last moment he dodged to avoid the full force of their momentum, but even so was spun around 360 degrees, his helmet flying. As he came up, I glimpsed a look of utter terror in his face. His right hand held a pistol which he waved wildly about. I lit out.

When it was all over, more than one hundred people were under arrest on charges ranging from disorderly conduct to attempted murder. Some of us were injured, as were some of the police. But I think I was not alone in feeling a relief bordering on euphoria to find myself alive and in one piece in the Cook County Jail.

Why did we do it? The status quo meant to us war, poverty, inequality, ignorance, famine and disease in most of the world. To accept it was to condone and help perpetuate it. We felt like miners trapped in a terrible poisonous shaft with no light to guide us out. We resolved to destroy the tunnel even if we risked destroying ourselves in the process.

It all seemed simple and frightening. We organized into tight, closed collectives, which enabled us to sustain our courage and commitment, but which shut us off from the world outside. In our Weather enclaves, we wrestled with fear and despair, criticizing each other mercilessly for any flagging of the faith. To what actual purpose? Most of us didn't think the question through dispassionately. If we did, we hoped that the

Above: Saturday's march begins in Haymarket Square (Timothy Carlson). Opposite page, clockwise from top: out-of-uniform police arrest a disguised Mark Rudd on October 11th (David Fenton); a Weatherwoman (© Paul Sequeira); Saturday's busts: en masse (David Fenton); and in twos (© Paul Sequeira); Weathermen march through the streets of Chicago, October 8th, 1969 (© Paul Sequeira).

crazed violence of outraged youth would at least bring indirect pressure on the Nixon Administration to moderate its course. At most, we felt we were the wave of the future.

Bo Burlingham was placed on probation for five years as a result of his participation in the Days of Rage. He ended his association with the Weathermen early in 1970, and two years later became the managing editor of Ramparts *magazine. Now a free-lance journalist whose work has appeared in* Harper's, New Times, *and* Esquire, *he is writing a book on cancer. (courtesy Bo Burlingham)*

GREIL MARCUS
The Apocalypse at Altamont

Hell's Angels wielding pool cues (Bill Owens).

I had seen the naked woman perhaps a dozen times during the day. Repeatedly she would choose a male, run toward him, throw her arms around his neck, and rub her body up and down his. The comeback was predictable: "Hey, baby, wanna fuck?" At this, the woman would commence a series of psychotic screams and run blindly into the crowd. After a few minutes she would calm down sufficiently to begin the game all over again. Eventually people began to keep their distance.

But now, in the dark, behind the stage, with only a little yellow light filtering through to where I was standing, waiting for the Stones to begin their first tune, the woman looked different. As she passed by, her head on her chest, I realized her body was covered with dried blood. Her face was almost black with it. Someone had given her a blanket to cover herself with—it was very cold by now—but she didn't wear it. She held on to a corner, as if she'd simply forgotten to throw it away, and it trailed behind her as she walked.

Then I saw the fat man. Hours before—it seemed like days—he had leaped to his feet to dance naked to Santana as they kicked off the day. All good times, let it loose, don't hang me up, uh-huh. The huge man seemed full of the Woodstock spirit, but those sitting near the stage, as I was, noticed that in fact he used the excuse of his dance to stomp and trample the people around him, particularly several young blacks. After a short time the Hell's Angels, who had been placed in charge of crowd and stage "security," got sick of the sight of him; they came off the stage swinging weighted pool cues and beat the fat man to the ground. He didn't seem to understand what was happening; again and again, he got up and continued his dance-stomp. Ultimately the Angels got him out of the area and took him behind the stage, where they could continue their work with greater efficiency.

Like the naked woman, the fat man was now brown with blood. His teeth had been knocked out, and his mouth still bled. He wandered across the enclosure, waiting, like me, for the music.

As the Stones began, the mood tensed and the gloomy light took on a lurid cast. The stage was jammed with sound people, Angels, writers, hangers-on. There wasn't an extra square foot. Kids began to climb the enormous sound trucks that ringed the back of the stage, and men threw them off. Some fell ten and fifteen feet to the ground; others landed on other trucks. I climbed to the top of a VW bus, where I had a slight view of the band. Several other people clambered up with me, waving tape recorder mikes in the hopes of capturing the sound. Every few minutes, it seemed, the music was broken up by waves of terrified screams from the crowd: wild ululations that went on for thirty, forty seconds at a time. We couldn't see the screamers, but with their sound, the packed mass on the stage would cringe backward, shoving the last line of people off the stage and onto the ground. As the fallen climbed back, small fights would break out.

By this time it was impossible even to guess what the screams meant. All day long people had speculated on who would be killed, on when the killing would take place. There were few doubts that the Angels would do the job. A certain inevitability had settled over the event. The crowd had been ugly, selfish, territorialist, throughout the day. People held their space. They made no room for anyone. Periodically the Angels had attacked the crowd or the musicians. It was a gray day, and the California hills were bare, cold and dead. A full beer bottle had been thrown into the crowd, striking a woman on the head, nearly killing her. Fantasies of the 300,000 turning back toward Berkeley to take People's Park back from the fence that surrounded it shifted by midafternoon to fantasies of the War Machine eliminating 300,000 enemies with nerve gas as they

sat immobilized by the prospect of the Rolling Stones.

Behind the stage I could hear Keith Richard cut off the music and berate the Angels. I heard an Angel seize the mike from Keith. The screams were almost constant by this time. People on the stage were rushing forward now, then scurrying back. Two more kids made it onto the top of the VW, and it collapsed. They went right through the roof. Some of those who fell off proceeded to punch out the windows.

With all this, the music somehow picked up force. It was very strong. I turned my back on the stage and began to walk the half-mile or so to my car. Heading up the hill in the darkness, I tripped and fell head-first into the dirt, and for some reason I felt no need to get up. I lay there, intrigued by the blackness and by the sound of feet passing by me on either side and by the sound the Stones were making. I began to abstract the music from the events that surrounded it, that were by now part of it. The Stones were playing "Gimme Shelter." I tried to remember when I'd heard anything so powerful. I reveled in the song, and when it was over, I got up and went on to my car to wait for the friends from whom I'd been separated hours before, when the Angels first jumped off the stage and into our laps.

* * *

I didn't suffer at Altamont; like a lot of other people, I had a particularly bad time, but once home I was ready and eager to forget all about it. The murder of Meredith Hunter made that impossible; at the same time, the murder crystallized the event. A young black man murdered in the midst of a white crowd by white thugs as white men played their version of black music—it was too much to kiss off as a mere unpleasantness. For the year that followed, not a day passed when I didn't think about Altamont. I stopped listening to rock and roll and bought a lot of country blues records. Somehow Robert Johnson's songs contained Altamont; those of the Stones deflected it, just as they had done in the moments before I finally left the place. Johnson's music was calming and ominous at the same time, and that was just what I wanted: a mood to get myself out of the past and into a future to which I was hardly looking forward.

In the middle of the day at Altamont, as a refugee from the front ranks of the crowd, I met Marvin Garson, the founder of San Francisco's finest underground newspaper, the *Express Times,* called by then the *Good Times,* reflecting a shift from politics to vibe-ism. Marvin had transformed himself into a Ranter some months previously (the Ranters were a loosely organized group of Antinomians who emerged in the middle of the seventeenth century in England, resurfacing 150 years later as a body of Primitive Methodists; their basic tactic consisted of shouting down priests and other pillars of the established order). Marvin was very good at Ranting, and this day, he was crowing: "What an ending! What an ending!" "To what?" I asked. "The Sixties?" "No, no!" he cried. *"To my book!"*

In terms of cause and effect there was little more to Altamont than that. It did not in and of itself "end" anything. Rather, as Robert Christgau has said, it provided an extraordinarily complex and visceral metaphor for the *way* things of the Sixties ended. All the symbols were marshaled, and the crowd turned out, less to have a good time than to help make counterculture history. The result was that the counterculture, in the form of rock and roll, Hell's Angels ("our outlaw brothers," as many liked to call them), and thousands of

The concert in the afternoon, top
(John Burks) and later that night as
Jagger watches a fight, bottom (©Beth Sunflower).

On the following pages: one of the many
freedom-seekers at Altamont (Michelle Vignes);
the fat man and the Angels (© Beth Sunflower).

politicized and unaffiliated young people, turned back upon itself. No one knew how to deal with a spectacle that from the moment it began contradicted every assumption on which it had been based, producing violence instead of fraternity, selfishness instead of generosity, ugliness instead of beauty, a bad trip instead of a high. Only the music kept its shape—in fact, driven on by the fear and danger of the day and the moment, the music, as the Stones played it, achieved a shape more perfect than it had ever taken on before. Take that for

what it's worth.

Greil Marcus has been writing about music since 1968 for publications like the San Francisco Express Times, *the* Village Voice, *the* New York Times *and* Creem. *He is a contributing editor to* Rolling Stone, *where his book column appears regularly, and is the author of* Mystery Train: Images of America in Rock 'n' Roll Music.

Marcus and his daughter, Emily (Dennis Galloway).

LANCE FAIRWEATHER
Manson

There have been many dancers in this world that I have seen, but no one ever danced like Charlie. When Charlie danced, everyone else left the floor. He was like fire, a raw explosion, a mechanical toy that suddenly went crazy.

Charlie was certainly a fascinating cat. He represented a freedom that everybody liked to see. That is why we wanted to document him. He really was an active revolutionary of the time in that area. Like Castro in the hills before he overthrew the government. Charlie advocated the overthrow of the government and the police force and everything. He thought it was all wrong—it was as simple as that. He wanted to do more than talk about it, but like so many revolutionaries, he really had no solution. And he didn't have the patience to really wait. Had he waited, he could have had so much more effect with his music. I would say to him, "Charlie, you can do so much more with your music and with film than you can ever do running around in a bus with your girls and preaching the stuff."

Then in January or February of 1969, eight or nine months after I met him, we started recording him. Charlie was living at the ranch at that time, and Dennis Wilson and I fooled around recording him over at Brian Wilson's house—Brian has this studio in his house. But Charlie couldn't make it with those people. They're too stiff for him.

Charlie used to say to me, "I don't care what you do with the music. Just don't let anybody change any of the lyrics." That was one of his big beefs with Dennis. Dennis had taken some of his songs and changed the lyrics around, which really infuriated him. Charlie had a big thing about the meaning of words that came out of your mouth. To him all that a man is, is what he says he is; so those words better be true. If Charlie said he would be someplace at four o'clock, he would be, even if he had to walk. And it used to infuriate him that Dennis would immediately forget what he promised. Charlie and Dennis never got along that well.

One day Charlie gave me a .44 slug to give to Dennis, saying, "Tell Dennis I got one more for him." Charlie was really bugged because Dennis ran off at the mouth so much.

I wanted Terry Melcher to meet Charlie and make a film of him. If we could sell the man, his music would emerge, so I wanted some backing for the film. I used to think of Charlie almost as a missionary who would take his people and start communities.

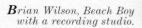

In fact, one thing that locked me into Charlie and made me think he was really a humanitarian was his great compassion for young girls on their way to San Francisco and the Haight. He wanted to stop them because he knew what the Haight had turned into and that these naive, dumb, wide-eyed girls would be hopelessly lost in

Brian Wilson, Beach Boy with a recording studio.

that jungle. He said they would be beaten up by niggers, they'd be raped, they'd go onto speed and so on. And he wanted to put a song out, telling them, "Don't go to the Haight, come to me." And that made sense to me.

Terry was impressed the first time he went to the ranch. But the second time he was a little leery of Charlie and didn't want to follow up the idea any more. Maybe it was the Randy Starr thing that scared him.

The second time at the ranch Terry and Charlie and I were sitting down by the stream, and Charlie was singing. And Randy Starr, this old Hollywood stunt man, was drunk and goofing off and waving his gun around. And Charlie yelled, "Don't draw on me, motherfucker!" and went over and beat the shit out of him right in front of us.

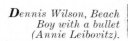

Dennis Wilson, Beach Boy with a bullet (Annie Leibovitz).

But it was in the spring of 1969 that Charlie really changed radically from what he had been the former year. He started collecting material things, accumulating motorcycles and desert vehicles and even weapons. He kept saying, "I got some great guns," and I'd say, "What is this shit? I don't even want to hear about it." He used to say he needed money to go to the desert, he needed supplies, he wanted ropes to go down into those holes in the desert. He really believed there was an underground people living out there. That was Charlie's dream—to go underground, really live underground, to wait for the revolution.

He believed there would be an open revolution in the streets, the black man against the white man. He said the only people who survive will be the ones who go into the desert. He said the black man doesn't want to go out in the desert in the hot sun; that's where he's been all of his life. He wants to be in the shade, in the city. He believed he would be continuing the race out there, because most of the race would die, as in Revelation 9.

And he believed that the Beatles were the spokesmen: "Helter Skelter" became a symbol. He believed they were singing about the same thing he already knew about. He believed they were all tuned in together. He thought he would meet the Beatles; he even sent some telegrams. This philosophy developed in the last year.

The last few times I saw Charlie, he was like a wild animal. I wasn't frightened, but I could just see it. It was like walking alongside a wild animal, his eyes . . . He wasn't handling the city at all. He said to me, "I gotta get out of here." And I said, "Go to the desert, man. That's where you belong."

After the Tate thing, he came to my house in the middle of the night a few times. The police were looking for him. Also, he supposedly shot a spade in the stomach in Topanga. A friend called me up and said, "You know that crazy guy Charlie? He shot some spade in the stomach, then took his jacket, bent over, kissed his feet and said, 'I love you, brother.' " And I said, "That sounds like Charlie, all right." The spade lived, incidentally. This was early in the summer of '69, when Charlie was collecting weapons and hanging out with the motorcycle people.

Charlie had a big Negro thing. His philosophy was that the black was the last race to evolve and was going to take whitey's place. And whitey was going to move up to a more spiritual level. The black man was here mainly to take care of the white man—the police department, the President would be a Negro, everything down to the waiters. Charlie said this is because they are stronger physically and more clever than we are, and they even have more love.

But he's completely against intermarriage. His philosophy here was a mindblower, too. In fact, when I heard it, I broke out laughing. Charlie said you have to be very careful about selecting your mate, because you'd be making love to yourself. And then he jumped to a reincarnation level where you'd be making love to your own children. He believed in a master-race philosophy, that you have to improve the race.

I don't think he's sane. He's a danger to society. He represents a danger to life. Charlie himself has no fear of death.

He used to love to get me into the car and drive a hundred miles an hour on Sunset in Dennis' Ferrari or in his dune buggy. And I'd just sit there. And finally he'd get the idea that I wasn't digging it but would put up with it, so he'd slow down and drive very slowly, ten miles an hour.

I think like most schizoids or insane people he walks a very thin line, and when he does walk over the

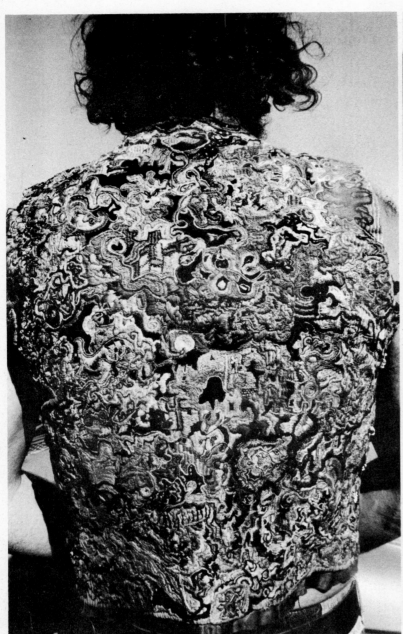

line, he explodes momentarily and then comes back.

Charlie used to say, "What would you do if I put a gun to your head and made you come and live in the desert with me?" And I'd say, "If you put a gun to my head, the worst you could do would be to kill me; and I'd just go with you till I could escape."

I'm sure that if that thing hadn't happened that August, maybe in a year or two we would have heard about a whole town, like Lone Pine, being taken over by a tribe of people. Because he wasn't kidding. He had machine guns and walkie-talkies and dugouts. He really wanted to build a fortress up there.

I asked myself many times, "What made Charlie change? What was the main cause?" And one thought kept recurring: If *Abbey Road* had come out sooner, maybe there wouldn't have been a murder.

That's far out, I know. But *Sgt. Pepper* was such a happy album, such a happy acid trip, and it made Charlie very happy. And then the white double album was such a down album. I know it affected Charlie deeply. And I just can't help thinking: If *Abbey Road,* another happy album, had come out sooner, maybe Sharon Tate would be alive today.

Lance Fairweather is the pseudonym of a talent scout and producer of sorts—a friend of Beach Boy Dennis Wilson, producer Terry Melcher and Charles Manson. Fairweather met Manson early in 1968, and a year later, impressed with Manson's message and his music, introduced him to Melcher as a prospective recording artist and subject for a documentary. In 1970 Fairweather described Manson's philosophy to Vincent Bugliosi, the prosecuting attorney in the Tate-LaBianca murder case, providing Bugliosi with much of the information he used to establish Manson's motive for those killings. ★

Above, left: a vest for Manson, embroidered by the Family women; right: Randy Starr, a stunt man who specialized in being hanged, hanging out at the ranch. Opposite page, top: Charles Manson —winter 1969 to spring 1971 (Wide World Photos). Center: Family members at Spahn Ranch in the early months of 1970. Bottom, clockwise from top right: another view of the ranch; Susan Atkins, one of the convicted Tate-LaBianca murderers (Wide World Photos); Lynette Fromme and Sandra Good—though neither were implicated in the murder case, both are now in prison for crimes indirectly related to their continuing support of Manson; an album of Manson's songs released after his indictment.

ANTHONY FAWCETT
The Beatles in Four Part Disharmony

Apple was a very grand Georgian townhouse on a snobby conservative street named Savile Row. It was painted white and had a flagpole outside and a brass plaque on the front door. Inside everything was white, with elegant Italian furniture and ornately carved fireplaces. The first day I came to work with John and Yoko they had just returned from their bed-in for peace, held during their honeymoon in Amsterdam. They were planning myriad projects, including sending acorns to all the world leaders, and I was soon immersed day and night helping them to arrange all of this.

The strange thing about what was going on in 1969 was the incredible overlay and interweaving of all the different things happening in John's life—all going on at the same time. Besides the daily flux of John and Yoko's projects (films, art events, recording new music), there were also business affairs, which were usually chaotic. For instance, every other day there would be some sort of meeting between bankers and stock-brokers, what I called "monopoly at Apple." All that was going on on one level, and then there were the problems between the Beatles themselves.

I noticed right from the beginning that John had almost no contact with Paul. Paul never came by our office, as George and Ringo did. And in the middle of the year, right around the time I started working with him, John made a conscious decision that if the Beatles really couldn't progress musically in the recording studio, if they couldn't go in and do what they really wanted to do—then that was it, he was ready to give up and do things on his own. When they were recording *Abbey Road,* things were very strained in the studio. I had expected to see John and Paul working together, but they seemed to be completely isolated from each other. John was very quiet, with Yoko standing or sitting right next to him, and he'd cut himself off from whatever was going on to talk to her. She and John were so much in love that they never wanted to be apart.

John and Yoko in bed at the Queen Elizabeth Hotel during the Montreal bed-in.

Few people, except for specialists in the art world, understood Yoko's work. John, however, was becoming very influenced by Yoko's ideas and the whole avant-garde scene, which she turned him on to. She had worked with John Cage and was interested in using her voice in an experimental way—John Lennon was already moving in that direction with his music. In his country house he had worked up in his attic on ten or twelve tape recorders all hooked up with one another. He used to bring home new Beatle songs and play them backwards, looping parts of them together and getting into all sorts of new sounds.

From the time of *Sgt. Pepper* on, John was feeling very dissatisfied with what the Beatles were doing—he really felt that it was more or less a dead end. One of the crucial things that was happening with the group right up until the end, and I think one of the things that really caused the breakup, was that there just wasn't room for John, Paul *and* George to record all the songs that they each wanted to have on one album. Paul had become the dominant one in the studio and John found himself having to fight to get his songs included; often he just gave up. On both the "White Album" and *Abbey Road* the close collaboration of the past was gone, and the sessions had turned into Paul with a backing group, John with a backing group, or George with a backing group—there was so much uncertainty and the spirit was broken within the group.

John didn't like songs like "Maxwell's Silver Hammer" or "Ob-la-di, Ob-la-da"—he thought that a lot of Paul's songs were mediocre, much too middle of the road. He'd say to Paul: "Why can't we give songs like these to other Apple artists who need them?" When John was excited about a new song he had written, "Cold Turkey," Paul wasn't even interested. It was a heavy song about pain and heroin, but Paul didn't think it was right for the Beatles. John was upset; he said, "Fuck it, I'll do this on my own. I'll get my own band

312

together!" Which is exactly what he proceeded to do in the guise of the Plastic Ono Band.

In September 1969, John decided on a whim to play live with Eric Clapton and some other friends, who became the Plastic Ono Band, at a Toronto rock 'n' roll revival. In the meantime Paul was planning a TV special—he thought that the Beatles should do something to appease the fans, to keep the whole thing going.

John returned from the success of the Toronto festival feeling very confident—he'd played as John Lennon, not as one-quarter of the Beatles. Almost immediately after he returned, there was a confrontation with Paul. Upstairs at Apple they were in a meeting with "financial adviser" Allen Klein. Suddenly John came rushing down and stormed into the office. He was red in the face and extremely angry. He explained that Paul had been pressuring him about the TV show even though he knew that John didn't want to do it. John had given in in the past: for instance, Paul had persuaded him to do *Let It Be* against his better judgment. And now at this meeting Paul just wouldn't give up pushing and goading John. Finally John just exploded and shouted at Paul: "That's it—it's over! I'm leaving the group!"

*A*llen Klein, Beatles'
financial adviser and, in
John's phrase, a Mississippi
gambler (Photo Trends).

The craziest thing is that they decided not to make it public. Klein argued that it wasn't time to announce publicly that the Beatles were finished; it would only devastate Apple and its other business concerns. John was convinced by Klein's persuasive argument, and Paul was very relieved. Paul said, "Well, if you're not going to announce it, then it's not really over." So he just carried on as if the Beatles were still the Beatles.

One of the last times that they ever really talked to each other as a group was to decide what to do with Apple—whether or not to sell it. It was a business meeting at the end of '69. They were sitting at a round table, continually drinking cups of tea, trying to get down to the nitty-gritty of the group's problems. They all freely admitted that there wasn't enough time on an album for all of them to get their songs on. Paul took the "military approach" as he called it—divide the time up into four tracks for John, four for Paul, four for George and one for Ringo. John said, "What if I've got more! What if George has more?"

*T*he Fab Four
in the Apple days.

There was a lot of tension, especially between Paul and George. Suddenly Paul, sitting right across from George but not looking at him, said to John, "George's music hasn't been as good as ours up to now."

George was taken aback. He said the songs of his that they were recording now were written a year or two ago. "Maybe now I just don't care whether you're going to like them or not, I just do 'em," he said. "Before, if I didn't get a break, I wouldn't push it, I'd just forget about it. For the last two years I've pushed it a bit more."

There was a long pause as each Beatle seemed lost in contemplation. Not wanting to admit that they were becoming individual musicians, Paul spoke slowly, "When we get in a studio, even on the worst day, I'm still playing bass, Ringo's still drumming, and we're still there, you know."

Then George said that for a lot of his songs he didn't even have the Beatles backing him. That hurt John. "Oh, c'mon, George!" he shouted. "We put a lot of work into your songs, but in the last two years there was a period when you went Indian and we weren't needed!"

George sat back and said nothing. He was feeling a little hurt. They were all feeling a little hurt. And it was all over.

*A*nthony Fawcett was an art critic in
London when he first met and began helping
John Lennon and Yoko Ono with their various art
projects. In April 1969 he began directing
their office at Apple Corps Ltd. and assisting
in many of their peace ventures. After Apple,
Fawcett worked as Stephen Stills' European
representative and began a consulting/managing
business, A.P.T. Enterprises. His first book,
John Lennon—One Day at a Time: A Personal
Biography of the Seventies, was published in 1976.★
(Christine Birrer)

Fear and Loathing at the Inauguration

The Inauguration weekend was a king-hell bummer in almost every way. The sight of Nixon taking the oath, the doomed and vicious tone of the protest, constant rain, rivers of mud, an army of rich swineherds jamming the hotel bars, old ladies with blue hair clogging the restaurants . . . a horrow-show, for sure. Very late one night, listening to the radio in my room I heard a song by the Byrds, with a refrain that went: "Nobody knows . . . what kind of trouble they're in; Nobody thinks . . . it all might happen again." It echoed in my head all weekend, like a theme song for a bad movie . . . the Nixon movie.

—Hunter S. Thompson

Above: the counter-inauguration—protesters greet the new President (© Alan Copeland).

Opposite page: Richard M. Nixon, 1969 (© William J. Warren).

Lynda Rosen Obst, now a senior editor of *The New York Times Magazine,* is a graduate of Pomona College in Claremont, California. She studied philosophy at Columbia University until she began studying the Sixties. She was editorial consultant on the national stage production *Beatlemania,* and resides in Manhattan with her husband, publisher David Obst.

Robert Kingsbury, a graduate of the University of Michigan and the Swedish State School of Art, has been art director of *Rolling Stone* magazine, where he now handles special projects. He has taught at the University of California and has exhibited as a sculptor at several museums, including the Pasadena Art Museum and the Museum of Contemporary Crafts in Manhattan. He was the designer of *The Rolling Stone Illustrated History of Rock and Roll.*